Getting Started

Y0-CDH-272

CFA®

Level III CFA® Exam

Welcome

As the VP of Advanced Designations at Kaplan Schweser, I am pleased to have the opportunity to help you prepare for the CFA® exam. Getting an early start on your study program is important for you to sufficiently **prepare**, **practice**, and **perform** on exam day. Proper planning will allow you to set aside enough time to master the Learning Outcome Statements (LOS) in the Level III curriculum.

Now that you've received your SchweserNotes™, here's how to get started:

Step 1: Access Your Online Tools
Visit **www.schweser.com** and log in to your online account using the button located in the top navigation bar. After logging in, select the appropriate level and proceed to the dashboard where you can access your online products.

Step 2: Create a Study Plan
Create a study plan with the **Study Calendar** (located on the Schweser dashboard) and familiarize yourself with your financial calculator. Check out our calculator videos in the **Candidate Resource Library** (also found on the dashboard).

Step 3: Prepare and Practice
Read your SchweserNotes™ Volumes 1–5
At the end of each reading, you can answer the Concept Checker questions for better understanding of the curriculum.

Attend a Weekly Class
Attend live classes online or take part in our live classroom courses in select cities around the world. Our expert faculty will guide you through the curriculum with a structured approach to help you prepare for the CFA® exam. The Schweser **On-Demand Video Lectures**, in combination with the **Weekly Class**, offer a blended learning approach that covers every LOS in the CFA curriculum.

Practice with SchweserPro™ QBank
Maximize your retention of important concepts by answering questions in the **SchweserPro™ QBank** and taking several **Practice Exams**. Use **Schweser's QuickSheet** for continuous review on the go. (Visit **www.schweser.com/cfa** to order.)

Step 4: Attend a 3-Day, 5-Day, or WindsorWeek™ Review Workshop
Schweser's late-season review workshops are designed to drive home the CFA® material, which is critical for CFA exam success. Review key concepts in every topic, **perform** by working through demonstration problems, and **practice** your exam techniques.

Step 5: Perform
Take a **Live** or **Live Online Schweser Mock Exam** to ensure you are ready to **perform** on the actual CFA® exam. Put your skills and knowledge to the test and gain confidence before the exam.

Again, thank you for trusting Kaplan Schweser with your CFA exam preparation!

Sincerely,

Derek Burkett, CFA, FRM, CAIA
VP, Advanced Designations, Kaplan Schweser

The Kaplan Way

Prepare
Acquire new knowledge through demonstration and examples.

Practice
Apply new knowledge through simulation and practice.

Perform
Evaluate mastery of new knowledge and identify achieved outcomes.

Visit our website,
www.schweser.com/cfa-free-resources,
to view all the free materials we have to help you prepare.

 Question of the Day

 Kaplan Schweser Adaptive CFA® Review Mobile App

How to Pass Videos

Contact us for questions about your study package, upgrading your package, purchasing additional study materials, or for additional information:

888.325.5072 (U.S.) | +1 608.779.8327 (Int'l).
staff@schweser.com | www.schweser.com/cfa

BOOK 4 – EQUITY PORTFOLIO MANAGEMENT, ALTERNATIVE INVESTMENTS, RISK MANAGEMENT, AND DERIVATIVES

Readings and Learning Outcome Statements v

Study Session 12 – Equity Portfolio Management 1

Self-Test – Equity Portfolio Management 50

Study Session 13 – Alternative Investments Portfolio Management 53

Self-Test – Alternative Investments Portfolio Management................................ 94

Study Session 14 – Risk Management.. 97

Self-Test – Risk Management 135

Study Session 15 – Risk Management Applications of Derivatives 138

Self-Test – Risk Management Applications of Derivatives 238

Formulas.. 241

Cumulative Z-Table 243

Index 244

SCHWESERNOTES™ 2018 LEVEL III CFA® BOOK 4: EQUITY PORTFOLIO MANAGEMENT, ALTERNATIVE INVESTMENTS, RISK MANAGEMENT, AND DERIVATIVES

©2017 Kaplan, Inc. All rights reserved.

Published in 2017 by Kaplan, Inc.

Printed in the United States of America.

ISBN: 978-1-4754-6040-7

If this book does not have the hologram with the Kaplan Schweser logo on the back cover, it was distributed without permission of Kaplan Schweser, a Division of Kaplan, Inc., and is in direct violation of global copyright laws. Your assistance in pursuing potential violators of this law is greatly appreciated.

Required CFA Institute disclaimer: "CFA Institute does not endorse, promote, or warrant the accuracy or quality of the products or services offered by Kaplan Schweser. CFA® and Chartered Financial Analyst® are trademarks owned by CFA Institute."

Certain materials contained within this text are the copyrighted property of CFA Institute. The following is the copyright disclosure for these materials: "Copyright, 2017, CFA Institute. Reproduced and republished from 2018 Learning Outcome Statements, Level I, II, and III questions from CFA® Program Materials, CFA Institute Standards of Professional Conduct, and CFA Institute's Global Investment Performance Standards with permission from CFA Institute. All Rights Reserved."

These materials may not be copied without written permission from the author. The unauthorized duplication of these notes is a violation of global copyright laws and the CFA Institute Code of Ethics. Your assistance in pursuing potential violators of this law is greatly appreciated.

Disclaimer: The Schweser Notes should be used in conjunction with the original readings as set forth by CFA Institute in their 2018 Level III CFA Study Guide. The information contained in these Notes covers topics contained in the readings referenced by CFA Institute and is believed to be accurate. However, their accuracy cannot be guaranteed nor is any warranty conveyed as to your ultimate exam success. The authors of the referenced readings have not endorsed or sponsored these Notes.

Readings and Learning Outcome Statements

Readings

The following material is a review of the Equity Portfolio Management, Alternative Investments, Risk Management, and Derivatives principles designed to address the learning outcome statements set forth by CFA Institute.

Study Session 12

Reading Assignments
Equity Portfolio Management, CFA Program 2018 Curriculum, Volume 4, Level III
    25. Equity Portfolio Management   page 1

Study Session 13

Reading Assignments
Alternative Investments for Portfolio Management, CFA Program 2018 Curriculum, Volume 5, Level III
    26. Alternative Investments Portfolio Management   page 53

Study Session 14

Reading Assignments
Risk Management, CFA Program 2018 Curriculum, Volume 5, Level III
    27. Risk Management   page 97

Study Session 15

Reading Assignments
Risk Management Applications of Derivatives, CFA Program 2018 Curriculum, Volume 5, Level III
    28. Risk Management Applications of Forward and Futures Strategies   page 138
    29. Risk Management Applications of Option Strategies   page 164
    30. Risk Management Applications of Swap Strategies   page 214

LEARNING OUTCOME STATEMENTS (LOS)

The CFA Institute learning outcome statements are listed in the following. These are repeated in each topic review. However, the order may have been changed in order to get a better fit with the flow of the review.

STUDY SESSION 12

The topical coverage corresponds with the following CFA Institute assigned reading:

25. Equity Portfolio Management

The candidate should be able to:

a. discuss the role of equities in the overall portfolio. (page 1)

b. discuss the rationales for passive, active, and semi-active (enhanced index) equity investment approaches and distinguish among those approaches with respect to expected active return and tracking risk. (page 2)

c. recommend an equity investment approach when given an investor's investment policy statement and beliefs concerning market efficiency. (page 3)

d. distinguish among the predominant weighting schemes used in the construction of major equity market indexes and evaluate the biases of each. (page 4)

e. compare alternative methods for establishing passive exposure to an equity market, including indexed separate or pooled accounts, index mutual funds, exchange-traded funds, equity index futures, and equity total return swaps. (page 6)

f. compare full replication, stratified sampling, and optimization as approaches to constructing an indexed portfolio and recommend an approach when given a description of the investment vehicle and the index to be tracked. (page 8)

g. explain and justify the use of equity investment-style classifications and discuss the difficulties in applying style definitions consistently. (page 10)

h. explain the rationales and primary concerns of value investors and growth investors and discuss the key risks of each investment style. (page 10)

i. compare techniques for identifying investment styles and characterize the style of an investor when given a description of the investor's security selection method, details on the investor's security holdings, or the results of a returns-based style analysis. (page 12)

j. compare the methodologies used to construct equity style indexes. (page 18)

k. interpret the results of an equity style box analysis and discuss the consequences of style drift. (page 19)

l. distinguish between positive and negative screens involving socially responsible investing criteria and discuss their potential effects on a portfolio's style characteristics. (page 20)

m. compare long–short and long-only investment strategies, including their risks and potential alphas, and explain why greater pricing inefficiency may exist on the short side of the market. (page 21)

n. explain how a market-neutral portfolio can be "equitized" to gain equity market exposure and compare equitized market-neutral and short-extension portfolios. (page 22)

o. compare the sell disciplines of active investors. (page 25)

p. contrast derivatives-based and stock-based enhanced indexing strategies and justify enhanced indexing on the basis of risk control and the information ratio. (page 26)

©2017 Kaplan, Inc.

q. recommend and justify, in a risk-return framework, the optimal portfolio allocations to a group of investment managers. (page 28)

r. explain the core-satellite approach to portfolio construction and discuss the advantages and disadvantages of adding a completeness fund to control overall risk exposures. (page 29)

s. distinguish among the components of total active return ("true" active return and "misfit" active return) and their associated risk measures and explain their relevance for evaluating a portfolio of managers. (page 32)

t. explain alpha and beta separation as an approach to active management and demonstrate the use of portable alpha. (page 34)

u. describe the process of identifying, selecting, and contracting with equity managers. (page 35)

v. contrast the top-down and bottom-up approaches to equity research. (page 37)

STUDY SESSION 13

The topical coverage corresponds with the following CFA Institute assigned reading:
26. Alternative Investments Portfolio Management
The candidate should be able to:

a. describe common features of alternative investments and their markets and how alternative investments may be grouped by the role they typically play in a portfolio. (page 53)

b. explain and justify the major due diligence checkpoints involved in selecting active managers of alternative investments. (page 54)

c. explain distinctive issues that alternative investments raise for investment advisers of private wealth clients. (page 55)

d. distinguish among types of alternative investments. (page 56)

e. discuss the construction and interpretation of benchmarks and the problem of benchmark bias in alternative investment groups. (page 61)

f. evaluate the return enhancement and/or risk diversification effects of adding an alternative investment to a reference portfolio (for example, a portfolio invested solely in common equity and bonds). (page 65)

g. describe advantages and disadvantages of direct equity investments in real estate. (page 71)

h. discuss the major issuers and suppliers of venture capital, the stages through which private companies pass (seed stage through exit), the characteristic sources of financing at each stage, and the purpose of such financing. (page 71)

i. compare venture capital funds and buyout funds. (page 72)

j. discuss the use of convertible preferred stock in direct venture capital investment. (page 72)

k. explain the typical structure of a private equity fund, including the compensation to the fund's sponsor (general partner) and typical timelines. (page 73)

l. discuss issues that must be addressed in formulating a private equity investment strategy. (page 74)

m. compare indirect and direct commodity investment. (page 74)

n. describe the principal roles suggested for commodities in a portfolio and explain why some commodity classes may provide a better hedge against inflation than others. (page 75)

o. identify and explain the style classification of a hedge fund, given a description of its investment strategy. (page 75)

p. discuss the typical structure of a hedge fund, including the fee structure, and explain the rationale for high-water mark provisions. (page 77)

q. describe the purpose and characteristics of fund-of-funds hedge funds. (page 78)

r. discuss concerns involved in hedge fund performance evaluation. (page 78)

s. describe trading strategies of managed futures programs and the role of managed futures in a portfolio. (page 80)

t. describe strategies and risks associated with investing in distressed securities. (page 81)

u. explain event risk, market liquidity risk, market risk, and "J-factor risk" in relation to investing in distressed securities. (page 82)

STUDY SESSION 14

The topical coverage corresponds with the following CFA Institute assigned reading:

27. Risk Management

The candidate should be able to:

a. discuss features of the risk management process, risk governance, risk reduction, and an enterprise risk management system. (page 97)

b. evaluate strengths and weaknesses of a company's risk management process. (page 99)

c. describe steps in an effective enterprise risk management system. (page 99)

d. evaluate a company's or a portfolio's exposures to financial and nonfinancial risk factors. (page 99)

e. calculate and interpret value at risk (VaR) and explain its role in measuring overall and individual position market risk. (page 102)

f. compare the analytical (variance–covariance), historical, and Monte Carlo methods for estimating VaR and discuss the advantages and disadvantages of each. (page 103)

g. discuss advantages and limitations of VaR and its extensions, including cash flow at risk, earnings at risk, and tail value at risk. (page 107)

h. compare alternative types of stress testing and discuss advantages and disadvantages of each. (page 108)

i. evaluate the credit risk of an investment position, including forward contract, swap, and option positions. (page 110)

j. demonstrate the use of risk budgeting, position limits, and other methods for managing market risk. (page 115)

k. demonstrate the use of exposure limits, marking to market, collateral, netting arrangements, credit standards, and credit derivatives to manage credit risk. (page 116)

l. discuss the Sharpe ratio, risk-adjusted return on capital, return over maximum drawdown, and the Sortino ratio as measures of risk-adjusted performance. (page 118)

m. demonstrate the use of VaR and stress testing in setting capital requirements. (page 119)

©2017 Kaplan, Inc.

STUDY SESSION 15

The topical coverage corresponds with the following CFA Institute assigned reading:

28. Risk Management Applications of Forward and Futures Strategies

The candidate should be able to:

a. demonstrate the use of equity futures contracts to achieve a target beta for a stock portfolio and calculate and interpret the number of futures contracts required. (page 138)

b. construct a synthetic stock index fund using cash and stock index futures (equitizing cash). (page 142)

c. explain the use of stock index futures to convert a long stock position into synthetic cash. (page 147)

d. demonstrate the use of equity and bond futures to adjust the allocation of a portfolio between equity and debt. (page 148)

e. demonstrate the use of futures to adjust the allocation of a portfolio across equity sectors and to gain exposure to an asset class in advance of actually committing funds to the asset class. (page 151)

f. explain exchange rate risk and demonstrate the use of forward contracts to reduce the risk associated with a future receipt or payment in a foreign currency. (page 153)

g. explain the limitations to hedging the exchange rate risk of a foreign market portfolio and discuss feasible strategies for managing such risk. (page 155)

The topical coverage corresponds with the following CFA Institute assigned reading:

29. Risk Management Applications of Option Strategies

The candidate should be able to:

a. compare the use of covered calls and protective puts to manage risk exposure to individual securities. (page 170)

b. calculate and interpret the value at expiration, profit, maximum profit, maximum loss, breakeven underlying price at expiration, and general shape of the graph for the following option strategies: bull spread, bear spread, butterfly spread, collar, straddle, box spread. (page 175)

c. calculate the effective annual rate for a given interest rate outcome when a borrower (lender) manages the risk of an anticipated loan using an interest rate call (put) option. (page 187)

d. calculate the payoffs for a series of interest rate outcomes when a floating rate loan is combined with 1) an interest rate cap, 2) an interest rate floor, or 3) an interest rate collar. (page 193)

e. explain why and how a dealer delta hedges an option position, why delta changes, and how the dealer adjusts to maintain the delta hedge. (page 199)

f. interpret the gamma of a delta-hedged portfolio and explain how gamma changes as in-the-money and out-of-the-money options move toward expiration. (page 205)

The topical coverage corresponds with the following CFA Institute assigned reading:

30. Risk Management Applications of Swap Strategies

The candidate should be able to:

a. demonstrate how an interest rate swap can be used to convert a floating-rate (fixed-rate) loan to a fixed-rate (floating-rate) loan. (page 214)

b. calculate and interpret the duration of an interest rate swap. (page 216)

    c. explain the effect of an interest rate swap on an entity's cash flow risk. (page 217)

    d. determine the notional principal value needed on an interest rate swap to achieve a desired level of duration in a fixed-income portfolio. (page 218)

    e. explain how a company can generate savings by issuing a loan or bond in its own currency and using a currency swap to convert the obligation into another currency. (page 222)

    f. demonstrate how a firm can use a currency swap to convert a series of foreign cash receipts into domestic cash receipts. (page 223)

    g. explain how equity swaps can be used to diversify a concentrated equity portfolio, provide international diversification to a domestic portfolio, and alter portfolio allocations to stocks and bonds. (page 224)

    h. demonstrate the use of an interest rate swaption 1) to change the payment pattern of an anticipated future loan and 2) to terminate a swap. (page 227)

©2017 Kaplan, Inc.

The following is a review of the Equity Portfolio Management principles designed to address the learning outcome statements set forth by CFA Institute. Cross-Reference to CFA Institute Assigned Reading #25.

EQUITY PORTFOLIO MANAGEMENT

EXAM FOCUS

Don't be misled. Candidates expect to see equity security valuation with lots of math and models, like Level II. Instead this is portfolio management. There is a little math to know, but pay attention to all the softer discussion issues. For example, there is a long discussion of index construction methodologies; the math could be tested, but the implications of the methodologies are as likely to be important. There is repetition of other topic areas on active versus passive management styles and benchmarks, as these are common exam topics. Also important are discussions of style and style analysis.

There is a lot of terminology and often passing references to complex techniques and issues which are not explained. A common mistake of Level III candidates is to fixate on things not explained in the CFA text. The exam focus has been on a working knowledge of terminology, the ability to assess the pros and cons of alternatives, and calculations that are taught. Focus on what is here, not on what the readings did not cover.

EQUITIES IN A PORTFOLIO

LOS 25.a: Discuss the role of equities in the overall portfolio.

CFA® Program Curriculum, Volume 4, page 255

Equities are a substantial portion of the investment universe, and U.S. equity typically constitutes about half of the world's equity. The amount of equity in an investor's portfolio varies by location. For example, U.S. institutional investors often exceed 50% of their portfolio invested in equities, while their European counterparts may be under 25% invested in equities. Regardless of these starting allocations, investing internationally provides diversification as well as the opportunity to invest in companies not available in the investor's home market.

An inflation hedge is an asset whose nominal returns are positively correlated with inflation. Bonds have been a poor inflation hedge because their future cash flows are fixed, which makes their value decrease with increased inflation. This drop in price reduces or eliminates returns for current bondholders. The historical evidence in the United States and in other countries indicates that **equities** have been a good inflation hedge. There are some important qualifiers, however. First, because corporate income and capital gains tax rates are not indexed to inflation, inflation can reduce the stock investor's return, unless this effect was priced into the stock when the investor bought it. Second, the ability of an individual stock to hedge inflation will depend on its industry and competitive position. The greater the competition, the less likely the firm will be able to pass inflation on to its consumers, and its stock will be a less effective hedge.

Examining the historical record in 17 countries from 1900–2005, equities have had consistently positive real returns. Equities have also had higher real returns than bonds in all 17 countries.[1]

ACTIVE, PASSIVE, AND SEMIACTIVE STRATEGIES

LOS 25.b: Discuss the rationales for passive, active, and semi-active (enhanced index) equity investment approaches and distinguish among those approaches with respect to expected active return and tracking risk.

CFA® Program Curriculum, Volume 4, page 257

Passive equity managers do not use forecasts to influence their investment strategies. The most common implementation of passive management is indexing, where the manager invests so as to mimic the performance of a security index. Though indexing is passive in the sense that the manager does not try to outperform the index, the execution of indexing requires that the manager buy securities when the security's weight increases in the index (e.g., the security is added to the index or the firm sells new stock) or sell stock when the security's weight decreases in the index (e.g., the security is dropped from the index or the firm repurchases stock). Indexing has grown in popularity since the 1970s and often constitutes an investor's core holding.

Active equity management is the other extreme of portfolio management. Active managers buy, sell, and hold securities in an attempt to outperform their benchmark. Even with the growth of indexing, active management still constitutes the vast majority of assets under management.

The middle road between the two previous approaches is **semiactive** equity management (a.k.a. enhanced indexing or risk-controlled active management). A semiactive manager attempts to earn a higher return than the benchmark while minimizing the risk of deviating from the benchmark.

There are not really three approaches, but a scale from pure passive to full blown unrestricted active management. The more a portfolio moves towards active management, the higher the expected active return should be, but the higher return will carry higher tracking risk. Where a portfolio falls on the scale is often reflected in how high or low the active return. This scale is summarized in Figure 1.

Active return is the excess return of a manager relative to the benchmark. *Tracking risk* is the standard deviation of active return and is a measurement of active risk (i.e., volatility relative to the benchmark).

---

1. Elroy Dimson, Paul Marsh, and Mike Staunton, "The Worldwide Equity Premium: A Smaller Puzzle," *EFA 2006 Zurich Meetings Paper* (April 7, 2006), http://papers.ssrn.com/sol3/papers.cfm?abstract_id=891620. Accessed June 2017.

©2017 Kaplan, Inc.

Figure 1: Active Return and Tracking Risk for Equity Investment Approaches

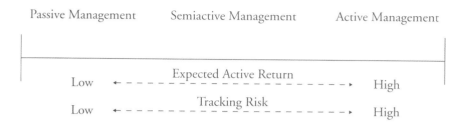

The **information ratio** combines expected active return and tracking risk into one risk-adjusted return measure. It is the expected active return divided by the tracking risk, so it shows the manager's active return per unit of tracking risk (a.k.a. tracking error). Historically, it has been highest for semiactive management and lowest for passive management with active management falling in the middle.

Example: Computing and interpreting information ratios

Suppose there are two managers, Cirrus Managers and Cumulus Managers. **Calculate** their information ratios and comment on their relative performance.

	Cirrus Managers	*Cumulus Managers*
Active return	0.40%	0.62%
Tracking risk	5.60%	9.20%

Answer:

The information ratio for Cirrus Managers is 0.40% / 5.60% = 0.071.

The information ratio for Cumulus Managers is 0.62% / 9.20% = 0.067.

Even though Cumulus has the higher active return, on a risk-adjusted basis, it slightly underperforms Cirrus as its information ratio is lower. For every 1% in tracking risk, Cirrus Managers delivered 0.071% in active return, whereas Cumulus delivered 0.067%.

THE IPS, MARKET EFFICIENCY, AND EQUITY STRATEGIES

LOS 25.c: Recommend an equity investment approach when given an investor's investment policy statement and beliefs concerning market efficiency.

CFA® Program Curriculum, Volume 4, page 258

If an investor's **investment policy statement** (IPS) states that the investor is taxable, the asset allocation is more likely to favor passive management. This is because active management requires higher portfolio turnover such that capital gains and their associated taxes are realized more frequently. Additionally, each particular investor will have required liquidity, time horizon, and/or ethical investing concerns that will provide direction on which investment strategy to follow.

If an investor believes that markets are **efficient**, he is likely to choose a passive strategy because he does not believe the returns of active management will justify the costs of research and trading. Historical data suggests that such investors would be justified in their thinking because active management, on average, does not outperform passive management after consideration of expenses. The level of active manager underperformance is about the same as their average expenses, which suggests that active manager performance before expenses is about the same level as passive management.

Passive strategies are appropriate in a wide variety of markets. When investing in large-cap stocks, indexing is suitable because these markets are usually informationally efficient. In small-cap markets, there may be more mispriced stocks, but the high turnover associated with active strategies increases transaction costs. In international equity markets, the foreign investor may lack information that local investors have. In this case, active investing would be futile and the manager would be wise to follow a passive strategy.

EQUITY INDEX WEIGHTING SCHEMES

LOS 25.d: Distinguish among the predominant weighting schemes used in the construction of major equity market indexes and evaluate the biases of each.

CFA® Program Curriculum, Volume 4, page 260

Stock indices are used to benchmark manager performance, provide a representative market return, create an index fund, execute technical analysis, and measure a stock's beta. The weighting schemes for stock indices are price-weighted, value-weighted, float-weighted, and equally weighted.

A *price-weighted index* is simply an arithmetic average of the prices of the securities included in the index. Computationally, a price-weighted index adds together the market price of each stock in the index and then divides this total by the number of stocks in the index. The divisor of a price-weighted index is adjusted for stock splits and changes in the composition of the index (i.e., when stocks are added or deleted), so the total value of the index is unaffected by the change. A price-weighted index implicitly assumes the investor holds one share of each stock in the index.

The primary advantage of a price-weighted index is that it is computationally simple. There is also a longer history of data for price-weighted indices, so they can provide a long record of performance.

A *market capitalization-weighted index* (or just *value-weighted*) is calculated by summing the total market value (current stock price times the number of shares outstanding) of all the stocks in the index. The value-weighted index assumes the investor holds each company in the index according to its relative weight in the index. This index better represents changes in aggregate investor wealth than the price-weighted index.

Unlike the price-weighted index where a stock's representation is determined by its price, the representation of a stock in the value-weighted index is determined by the stock's total market value. This method thus automatically adjusts for stock splits of individual firms so that high priced firms are not overrepresented in the index.

©2017 Kaplan, Inc.

A subtype of a value-weighted index is the *free float-adjusted market capitalization index*. The portion of a firm's outstanding shares that are actually available for purchase is known as the *free float*. A problem with some equity benchmarks is that market capitalization weighting can overstate the free float. For example, a large fraction of a firm's shares may be closely held by a small number of investors. This means that not all of the firm's shares are truly investable from the viewpoint of outside investors. A free float-adjusted market capitalization index is adjusted for the amount of stock that is actually available to the public.

A free float-adjusted market cap-weighted (e.g., value-weighted) index assumes the investor has bought all the *publicly available* shares of each company in the index. The major value-weighted indices in the world have been adjusted for free-float. The float-adjusted index is considered the best index type by many investors because it is more representative and can be followed with minimal tracking risk.

In an *equal-weighted index*, all stock returns are given the same weight (i.e., the index is computed as if an investor maintains an equal dollar investment in each stock in the index). These indices must be periodically rebalanced to maintain equal representation of the component stocks.

Biases in the Weighting Schemes

The price-weighted index has several biases. First, higher priced stocks will have a greater impact on the index's value than lower priced stocks. Second, the price of a stock is somewhat arbitrary and changes through time as a firm splits its stock, repurchases stock, or issues stock dividends. As a stock's price changes through time, so does its representation in the index. Third, the price-weighted index assumes the investor purchases one share (or the same number of shares) of each stock represented in the index, which is rarely followed by any investor in practice.

The primary bias in a value-weighted index and the free float-adjusted market capitalization index is that firms with greater market capitalization have a greater impact on the index than firms with lower market capitalization. This feature means that these indices are biased toward large firms that may be mature and/or overvalued. Another bias is that these indices may be less diversified if they are overrepresented by large-cap firms. Lastly, some institutional investors may not be able to mimic a value-weighted index if they are subject to maximum holdings and the index holds concentrated positions.

The equal-weighted index is biased toward small-cap companies because they will have the same weight as large-cap firms even though they have less liquidity. Many equal-weighted indices also contain more small firms than large firms, creating a further bias toward small companies. Secondly, the required rebalancing of this index creates higher transactions costs for index investors. Lastly, the emphasis on small-cap stocks means that index investors may not be able to find liquidity in many of the index issues.

The Composition of Global Equity Indices

The best-known price-weighted index in the United States is the Dow Jones Industrial Average. It was created in 1896 and has undergone many changes in composition through time. The Nikkei Stock Average is also a price-weighted index, and it contains 225 stocks listed on the Tokyo Stock Exchange.

There are many examples of value-weighted indices, and most of them are float-adjusted. They include the Standard & Poor's 500 Index Composite and the Russell Indices. International indices that are value-weighted include the Morgan Stanley Capital International Indices. Non-U.S. indices include the Financial Times Actuaries Share Indices, which represents stocks on the London Stock Exchange, and the Tokyo Stock Exchange Price Index (TOPIX). European examples include the CAC 40 in France and the DAX 30 in Germany.

An example of an equal-weighted index is the Value Line Composite Average, which is an equally weighted average of approximately 1,700 U.S. stock returns.

Regardless of the weighting scheme, the investor should be aware of differences in methodologies across indices. Index reconstitution refers to the process of adding and deleting securities from an index. Indices that are reconstituted by a committee may have lower turnover, and hence, lower transactions costs and taxes for the index investor. These indices may drift from their intended purpose, though, if they are reconstituted too infrequently. In contrast, an index regularly reconstituted by a mechanical rule will have more turnover and less drifting. Another difference in index methodologies concerns minimum liquidity requirements. The presence of small-cap stocks may create liquidity problems but also offers the index investor a potential liquidity risk premium.

METHODS OF PASSIVE INVESTING

LOS 25.e: Compare alternative methods for establishing passive exposure to an equity market, including indexed separate or pooled accounts, index mutual funds, exchange-traded funds, equity index futures, and equity total return swaps.

CFA® Program Curriculum, Volume 4, page 267

Index Mutual Funds and Exchange-Traded Funds

There are five main differences between **index mutual funds** and **exchange-traded funds** (ETFs). First, index mutual funds are less frequently traded. In the United States, a mutual fund's value (as calculated using the net asset value) is typically only provided once a day at the end of the day when trades are executed. In contrast, an ETF trades throughout the day.

Second, ETFs do not have to maintain recordkeeping for shareholders, whereas mutual funds do. These expenses can be significant, especially if the fund has many small shareholders. As a consequence, some mutual funds charge expenses to shareholders based on the amount they have invested. Note, however, that there are trading expenses associated with ETFs because they trade through brokers like ordinary shares.

©2017 Kaplan, Inc.

Third, index mutual funds usually pay lower license fees to Standard & Poor's and other index providers than ETFs do.

Fourth, ETFs are generally more tax efficient than index mutual funds. Typically, when an investor wants to liquidate their ETF shares, they sell to another investor, which is not a taxable event for the ETF, or when an ETF redeems a large number of ETF shares for an institutional investor, the ETF may exchange the shares for the actual basket of stocks underlying the ETF. This also is not a taxable event for the ETF. In an index mutual fund, redemptions by shareholders might require the sale of securities for cash, which could be a taxable event for the mutual fund that is passed on to shareholders. The bottom line is that an ETF structure is more tax efficient for the investor than a mutual fund structure.

Fifth, although ETFs carry brokerage commissions, the costs of holding an ETF long-term is typically lower than that for an index mutual fund. Due to the differences in redemption described previously, the management fees arising from taxes and the sale of securities in an ETF are usually much lower than that for a mutual fund. Thus, an ETF investor does not pay the cost of providing liquidity to other shareholders the way a mutual fund investor does.

Separate or Pooled Accounts

Many of the same managers who offer index mutual funds or ETFs may also offer separately managed index accounts for investors. The minimum portfolio size is very large in order to execute the large number of holdings in the index efficiently. Slightly smaller accounts can be grouped together and the manager will manage the pooled funds. Think of it as an informal (without the regulation) private mutual fund. With only one or a small number of investors, the fees for separately managed or pooled index funds can be very low.

Equity Futures

Futures contracts are available on many stock market indexes around the globe. The purchase of a futures contract and fully collateralizing the position with sufficient cash equivalents to pay the contract price at expiration provides a close approximation of purchasing the underlying stocks in the index. Often, the trading volume and liquidity of the contracts exceeds that of the underlying stock markets.

The link between the contract price and the underlying depends on arbitrage and this link is facilitated by **portfolio**, **basket**, or **program trades**. These trades allow a single trade to buy or sell all the underlying securities of the index. This has two benefits for futures contract users: (1) arbitrage keeps futures prices closely aligned with fair value and the price of the index and (2) the arbitrage trading creates trading volume and a more liquid market for all contract users.

There are two (minor) drawbacks to using futures rather than the underlying stock. Contracts have a finite life and the most liquid contracts are typically those that are closer to maturity. Thus, using contracts for extended periods of time will require rolling over the contracts. Also, there can also be restrictions on the ability to trade the underlying basket of stocks in markets with an "uptick" rule.

Professor's Note: As an example, in the U.S., stock cannot be shorted if the last trade movement was a down tick in price (trade price was below the last trading price). A short trade can only be done after there is a trade at a higher price. This can limit arbitrage and how well the contract price reflects the underlying index. ETFs are often exempt to the uptick rule giving a slight advantage to trading in ETFs.

Equity Total Return Swap

In an *equity total return swap*, an investor typically exchanges the return on an equity security or an interest rate for the return on an equity index. By doing so, the investor can synthetically diversify a portfolio in one transaction. This portfolio rebalancing can often be performed more cheaply than trading in the underlying stocks. Their lower costs makes equity swaps ideal for tactical asset allocation.

There are also tax advantages to equity swaps. Suppose a U.S. investor wanted to buy European stocks but did not want to be responsible for the withholding taxes on them. The investor would exchange the return on a security for the return on the foreign portfolio. The swap dealer would be responsible for the tax payments and may be tax-advantaged relative to the investor.

For the Exam: Swap and futures are discussed in more detail in the readings on derivatives.

INDEXING A PORTFOLIO

LOS 25.f: Compare full replication, stratified sampling, and optimization as approaches to constructing an indexed portfolio and recommend an approach when given a description of the investment vehicle and the index to be tracked.

CFA® Program Curriculum, Volume 4, page 271

Full Replication

To create an indexed portfolio using **full replication**, all the stocks in the index are purchased according to the weighting scheme used in the index. Full replication is more likely to be used when the number of stocks in the index is less than 1,000 and when the stocks in the index are liquid. A prime example of an index that can be replicated is the S&P 500. Replication is also more likely when the manager has more funds to invest.

The *advantage* of replication is that there is low tracking risk and the portfolio only needs to be rebalanced when the index stocks change or pay dividends. The return on a replicated fund should be the index returns minus the administrative fees, cash drag, and transactions costs of tracking the index. Cash drag results because a fund must set aside cash for shareholder redemptions. Transactions costs arise due to reinvesting dividends and changes in index composition. Note that a replicated fund will underperform the index to a greater extent when the underlying stocks are illiquid and, thus, have higher trading costs. The index does not bear the trading costs that the replicating fund does.

Stratified Sampling

As the number of stocks in the index increases and as the stocks decrease in liquidity, stratified sampling or optimization become more likely. In **stratified sampling** (a.k.a. representative sampling), the portfolio manager separates the stocks in an index using a structure of two or more dimensions. For example, the dimensions might be industry, size, and price-earnings ratio. The market caps for each cell in a matrix are calculated given the total market cap of all the stocks in that cell. Within each cell, the manager picks a few representative stocks and makes an investment in them equaling the total market cap for that cell.

The *advantage* of stratified sampling is that the manager does not have to purchase all the stocks in an index. This is particularly useful when the number of stocks in an index is large and/or when the stocks are illiquid. The tracking risk from stratified sampling decreases as the number of cells increases in the structure (i.e., the cells are differentiated into finer divisions). Note that some government regulations restrict funds from investing too much in any one security. A stratified sampling process can be used to mimic the performance of concentrated positions within an index without taking the actual concentrated positions.

Optimization

An **optimization** approach uses a factor model to match the factor exposures of the fund to those of the index. It can also incorporate an objective function where tracking risk is minimized subject to certain constraints. The advantage of an optimization is that the factor model accounts for the covariances between risk factors. In a stratified sampling procedure, it is implicitly assumed that the factors (e.g., industry, size, price-earnings ratios) are uncorrelated.

There are three main *disadvantages* of the optimization approach. First, the risk sensitivities measured in the factor model are based on historical data and may change once the model is implemented. Second, optimization may provide a misleading model if the sample of data is skewed by a particular security or time period of data. Third, the optimization must be updated to reflect changes in risk sensitivities, and this leads to frequent rebalancing.

Despite the complexity of optimization, it generally produces even lower tracking risk than stratified random sampling. Both optimization and stratified random sampling could be combined with replication. To do this, the largest security positions in the index would be replicated. The balance of the index would be mimicked with either optimization or stratified random sampling. This also tends to reduce tracking risk even further. Regardless of its limitations, the optimization approach leads to lower tracking risk than a stratified sampling approach. This is particularly true when optimization is combined with replication. In this case, a few of the largest securities are purchased and the rest of the securities in the index are mimicked using an optimization approach.

EQUITY STYLE

LOS 25.g: Explain and justify the use of equity investment-style classifications and discuss the difficulties in applying style definitions consistently.

CFA® Program Curriculum, Volume 4, page 276

LOS 25.h: Explain the rationales and primary concerns of value investors and growth investors and discuss the key risks of each investment style.

CFA® Program Curriculum, Volume 4, page 279

For the Exam: Equity style, equity style benchmarks, and tracking risk are important topics for the Level III exam. They are discussed in multiple study sessions.

There are three main categories of investment style: value, growth, and market-oriented. A value investor focuses on stocks with low price multiples [e.g., low price-earnings (P/E) ratio or low price-to-book value of assets (P/B) ratio]. A growth investor favors stocks with high past and future earnings growth. Market-oriented investors cannot be easily classified as value or growth. Equity investment styles can also be defined using market cap.

It is important to define a manager's style so that performance measurement is conducted fairly. It is generally more informative to compare a value manager to other value managers and a growth manager to other growth managers. However, the differentiation between a value and a growth manager is often not clear. For example, a stock may have respectable earnings growth that is expected to increase in the future. The current P/E ratio may be low because the market hasn't yet recognized the stock's potential. Based on the P/E ratio, it appears to be a value stock, but based on expectations, it appears to be a growth stock.

Value Investing

Value investors focus on the numerator in the P/E or P/B ratio, desiring a low stock price relative to earnings or book value of assets. The two main justifications for a value strategy are: (1) although a firm's earnings are depressed now, the earnings will rise in the future as they revert to the mean; and (2) value investors argue that growth investors expose themselves to the risk that earnings and price multiples will contract for high-priced growth stocks.

The philosophy of value investing is consistent with behavioral finance, where investors overreact to the value stock's low earnings and price them too cheaply. Market efficiency proponents argue, however, that the low price of value stocks reflects their risk. Still others argue that value stocks are illiquid and that the excess return earned by value investors is actually a liquidity risk premium. Regardless of the explanation, a value investor must realize that there may be a good reason why the stock is priced so cheaply.

The value investor should consider what catalyst is needed for the stock to increase in price and how long this will take.

There are three main *substyles* of value investing: high dividend yield, low price multiple, and contrarian. Value investors favoring high dividend yield stocks expect that their stocks will maintain their dividend yield in the future. The dividend yield has constituted a major part of equity return through time. Low price multiple investors believe that once the economy, industry, or firm improves, their stocks will increase in value. Contrarian investors look for stocks that they believe are temporarily depressed. They frequently invest in firms selling at less than book value.

Growth Investing

Growth investors focus on the denominator in the P/E ratio, searching for firms and industries where high expected earnings growth will drive the stock price up even higher. The risk for growth investors is that the earnings growth does not occur, the price-multiple falls, and stock prices plunge. Growth investors may do better during an economic contraction than during an expansion. In a contraction, there are few firms with growth prospects, so the growth stocks may see their valuations increase. In an expansion, many firms are doing well, so the valuation premiums for growth stocks decline.

There are two main *substyles* of growth investing: consistent earnings growth and momentum. A consistent earnings growth firm has a historical record of growth that is expected to continue into the future. Momentum stocks have had a record of high past earnings and/or stock price growth, but their record is likely less sustainable than that of the consistent earnings growth firms. The manager holds the stock as long as the momentum (i.e., trend) continues, and then sells the stock when the momentum breaks.

Market-Oriented Investing

The term market-oriented investing is used to describe investing that is neither value nor growth. It is sometimes referred to as blend or core investing. Market-oriented investors have portfolios that resemble a broad market average over time. They may sometimes focus on stock prices and other times focus on earnings. The risk for a market-oriented manager is that she must outperform a broad market index or investors will turn to lower cost indexing strategies.

The *substyles* of market-oriented investing are market-oriented with a value tilt, market-oriented with a growth tilt, growth at a reasonable price (GARP), and style rotation. Value and growth tilting is not full-blown value or growth, and these investors hold diversified portfolios. GARP investors search for stocks with good growth prospects that sell at moderate valuations. Style rotators adopt the style that they think will be popular in the near future.

Market Capitalization-Based Investing

Besides the three previous characterizations of investment style, investors can also be classified by the market cap of their stocks. *Small-cap* investors believe smaller firms are more likely to be underpriced than well-covered, larger cap stocks. They may also believe that small-cap stocks are likely to have higher growth in the future and/or that higher returns are more likely when an investor is starting from a stock with a small market cap. *Micro-cap* investors focus on the smallest of the small-cap stocks.

Mid-cap investors believe that stocks of this size may have less coverage than large-cap stocks but are less risky than small-cap stocks. *Large-cap* investors believe that they can add value using their analysis of these less risky companies. Investors in the different capitalization categories can be further classified as value, growth, or market-oriented.

STYLE IDENTIFICATION

LOS 25.i: Compare techniques for identifying investment styles and characterize the style of an investor when given a description of the investor's security selection method, details on the investor's security holdings, or the results of a returns-based style analysis.

CFA® Program Curriculum, Volume 4, page 282

One method of determining a portfolio manager's style is to ask the manager to explain their security selection methods. For example, if the manager focuses on stocks with minimal analyst coverage that are underpriced relative to their earnings, we would characterize the manager as a *small-cap value manager*.

However, managers do not always invest as stated. For this reason, we may want to examine a manager's portfolio returns or holdings to determine style. Style can be identified using either returns-based style analysis or through an examination of an investor's holdings. These methods can be used for performance evaluation or to predict a manager's future performance.

Returns-Based Style Analysis

In **returns-based style analysis**, the returns on a manager's fund are regressed against the returns for various security indices (e.g., large-cap value stocks, small-cap value stocks). The regression coefficients, which represent the portfolio's exposure to an asset class, are constrained to be nonnegative and to sum to one.

To demonstrate the use of returns-based style analysis, we regress the returns on a manager's portfolio against the returns on four indices: a small-cap growth index; a large-cap growth index; a large-cap value index; and a small-cap value index. As with any regression, the coefficients on the independent variables indicate the change in the dependent variable (in this case the return on the portfolio) given changes in the returns on the independent variables (in this case the returns on the four indices).

©2017 Kaplan, Inc.

Assume an analyst has run the following regression:

$$R_p = b_0 + b_1 SCG + b_2 LCG + b_3 SCV + b_4 LCV + e$$

where:

R_p = returns on our manager's portfolio
SCG = returns on a small-cap growth index
LCG = returns on a large-cap growth index
SCV = returns on a small-cap value index
LCV = returns on a large-cap value index

output: $b_1 = 0$; $b_2 = 0$; $b_3 = 0.15$; $b_4 = 0.85$
(SCG) (LCG) (SCV)   (LCV)

From the values of the regression coefficients, we would conclude that the manager's portfolio has no exposure to growth stocks ($b_1 = 0$ and $b_2 = 0$). The manager is primarily a large-cap value manager ($b_4 = 0.85$) with an exposure to small-cap value stocks ($b_3 = 0.15$). We would construct a custom benchmark for this manager consisting of 85% large-cap value stocks (i.e., a large-cap value index) and 15% small-cap value stocks (i.e., a small-cap value index). This custom benchmark is often called the manager's normal portfolio or benchmark.

The security indices used in the regression should be mutually exclusive of one another, be exhaustive in the sense that all the manager's exposures are represented, and represent distinct, uncorrelated sources of risk. If the indices don't have these characteristics, then the results of the returns-based style analysis can be misleading. In the previous example, if we had omitted the small-cap indices and just used the large-cap value and growth indices, then the regression might force the coefficient on the large value index to equal one. Using this misspecified regression, we could have mistakenly concluded that the investor had no exposure to small-cap stocks, when in fact he did.

Suppose that instead of four indices in the regression, we just used two broad indices: large-cap stocks and small-cap stocks. In this case, the regression would show some exposure to both indices, but there would be no indication as to whether the manager was a value manager or a growth manager. In that case, the indices (i.e., independent variables) are not well specified and the regression will not provide much useful information.

From the regression, we are also provided with the coefficient of determination (R^2). This provides the amount of the investor's return explained by the regression's style indices. It measures the *style fit*. One minus this amount indicates the amount unexplained by style and due to the manager's security selection. For example, suppose the style fit from the regression is 79%. This would mean that 21% of the investor's returns were unexplained by the regression and would be attributable to the manager's security selection (i.e., the manager made active bets away from the securities in the style indices). The error term in the regression, which is the difference between the portfolio return and the returns on the style indices, is referred to as the manager's *selection return*.

One of the benefits of returns-based style analysis is that it helps determine if the manager's reported style and actual style are the same. For a mutual fund, the investment objective of the manager is contained in the fund's prospectus, and in some cases the investment objective can be determined by the fund's name. However, not all aggressive growth funds invest in the same asset categories or even in the same proportions.

Returns-based style analysis helps to determine the reality—not what the manager says, but what she does.

Figure 2 shows the returns-based style analysis of two hypothetical funds, ABC and PDQ, which claim to be large-cap growth funds. The first column shows the indices (benchmarks) against which the portfolio returns were regressed. The second and third columns show the weights each manager has in each category. These are the coefficients from the regression analysis.

Figure 2: Returns-Based Style Analysis of ABC and PDQ Funds

Style Category	ABC Fund Weight %	PDQ Fund Weight %
Large-cap growth	52.0	86.0
Large-cap value	23.0	9.0
Mid-cap growth	11.0	1.5
Mid-cap value	5.0	0.0
Small-cap growth	1.9	1.7
Small-cap value	0.0	0.0
T-bond (1–10 yr.)	0.0	0.0
T-bond (10+ yr.)	0.0	0.0
Corporate bond	1.1	1.3
T-bills	6.0	0.5
Foreign equity	0.0	0.0
Total	100.0	100.0

The results show that although ABC has exposure to large-cap growth, it also has substantial exposure to large-cap value and mid-cap stocks. PDQ's main exposure is to large-cap growth (86%) and some exposure to large-cap value (9%).

Both ABC and PDQ funds claim to be large-cap growth funds. However, ABC fund has substantial exposure to large-cap value and mid-cap stocks. PDQ fund, on the other hand, has style exposure more consistent with its investment objective.

Multi-Period Returns-Based Style Analysis

A single regression in a returns-based style analysis provides the average fund exposures during the time period under analysis. A series of regressions can be used to check the style consistency of a manager. That is, does the manager pursue the same style consistently over time?

Consider a hypothetical fund—Spark Growth and Income Fund. There are five years of monthly data from January 2007 to December 2011 (i.e., T = 60 monthly data points).

©2017 Kaplan, Inc.

We use 36 months in each regression analysis and form 25 overlapping samples of 36 months each:

- The first sample starts at t = 1 (January 2007) and ends at t = 36 (December 2009).
- The second sample starts at t = 2 (February 2007) and ends at t = 37 (January 2010) and so forth.
- The last sample starts at t = 25 (January 2009) and ends at t = 60 (December 2011).

For each of the data samples, we run the returns-based style analysis regression and compute the weights (exposures) of each of the style asset categories. Thus, there are 25 regressions in total. Results for the first and the last samples are shown in Figure 3. Figure 4 shows the plot of all the changes in exposure over the five years, using the results of the 25 regressions.

Figure 3: 5-Year Rolling 36-Month Returns-Based Style Analysis

Style Category	Sample 1 (t = 1 to 36) Weight %	Sample 25 (t = 25 to 60) Weight %
Large-cap growth	12	8
Large-cap value	62	49
Mid-cap value	20	37
Cash	6	6
Total	100	100

Figure 4: Style Consistency of Spark Growth and Income Fund

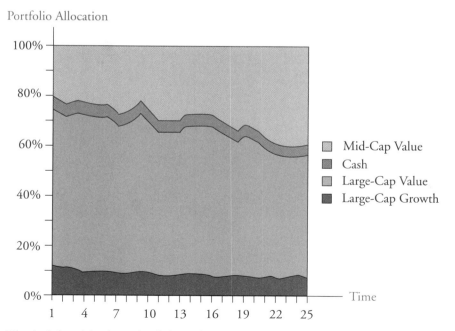

The heights (thickness) of the colored bands indicate that the fund's exposures have changed over time. The exposures to large-cap growth and large-cap value have declined, while the exposure to mid-cap value increased, and the exposure to cash stayed the same. This type of analysis helps to check the manager's style consistency over time. If the manager was hired to focus on large-cap investments, the investor should be concerned about the manager's increasing focus on mid-cap stocks.

Holdings-Based Style Analysis

A second method of verifying a portfolio manager's style is to evaluate the characteristics of the securities in the manager's portfolio. This method is referred to as holdings-based style analysis or composition-based style analysis. The manager would characterize securities based on the following attributes:

Value or growth: Does the manager invest in low P/E, low P/B, and high dividend yield stocks? If so, the manager would be characterized as a value manager. A manager with high P/E, high P/B, and low dividend yield stocks would be characterized as a growth manager. A manager with average ratios would be characterized as market-oriented.

Expected earnings per share growth rate: Does the manager have a heavy concentration in firms with high expected earnings growth? If so, the manager would be characterized as a growth manager.

Earnings volatility: Does the manager hold firms with high earnings volatility? If so the manager would be characterized as a value manager because value managers are willing to take positions in cyclical firms.

Industry representation: Value managers tend to have greater representation in the utility and financial industries because these industries typically have higher dividend yields and lower valuations. Growth managers tend to have higher weights in the technology and health care industries because these industries often have higher growth. Although industry representation can be used as a guide, it should be used with the other characteristics described here. Individual firms within industries do not always fit the industry mold, and the value/growth classification of an industry will vary as the business cycle varies.

©2017 Kaplan, Inc.

Example: Identifying a fund's style

In the following table, the characteristics of a mutual fund and a broad market index are provided. Using only the data provided, **identify** the style of the fund.

Investment Characteristics for a Mutual Fund and Broad Market

	Mutual Fund	*Broad Market*
P/E ratio	18.47	22.33
P/B ratio	2.27	4.09
Dividend yield	2.2%	1.7%
EPS growth for 1 year	11.9%	22.7%
EPS growth for 5 years	6.0%	11.0%
Median market cap ($ billion)	$8.5	$47.9
Industry Weight		
Basic industries	13%	12%
Business services	7%	5%
Consumer goods	5%	8%
Consumer services	9%	8%
Energy	3%	10%
Financials	37%	21%
Information technology	7%	17%
Health	2%	13%
Media	2%	3%
Utilities	15%	3%
Total	100%	100%

Answer:

The manager appears to be a *value manager* because the P/E and P/B ratio are below that of the broad market, and we would expect the portfolios of value managers to have higher dividend yields than that of the broad market. The manager is also invested in stocks with lower EPS growth and overweighted in financials and utilities, which is also characteristic of a value style. The manager is underweighted in technology and health care stocks, which are favored by growth managers. Additionally, we would conclude that the manager has a small-cap focus, because the median market cap is much lower than that of the broad market.

Returns-based style analysis is compared to holdings-based style analysis in Figure 5. Note that both methods can be performed on the same portfolio. By doing so, the analyst can gain further insight into the portfolio manager's processes and holdings. For example, whereas returns-based analysis is useful for easily characterizing an entire portfolio, it will not detect changes in style (i.e., style drift) as quickly as holdings-based analysis. The reason is that the regression in returns-based analysis typically uses monthly returns over the past several years. Thus, a portion of the analysis is based on data that may no longer reflect the manager's emphasis. In contrast, holdings-based style analysis uses the portfolio's current contents to characterize the portfolio and provides a more up-to-date picture of the portfolio's contents.

Figure 5: Advantages/Disadvantages of Returns-Based Analysis and Holdings-Based Style Analysis

Advantages of Returns-Based Analysis	*Advantages of Holdings-Based Analysis*
Characterizes an entire portfolio	Characterizes each security
Enables comparisons of entire portfolios	Enables comparisons of securities
Summarizes the result of the investment process	Can detect style drift more quickly than returns-based analysis
Methodology backed by theory	
Low information requirements	
Different models usually result in the same conclusions	
Low cost and can be executed rapidly	

Disadvantages of Returns-Based Analysis	*Disadvantages of Holdings-Based Analysis*
May be inaccurate due to style drift	Is not consistent with the method used by many managers to select securities
Misspecified indices can lead to misleading conclusions	Requires subjective judgment to classify securities
	Requires more data than returns-based analysis

EQUITY STYLE INDICES

LOS 25.j: Compare the methodologies used to construct equity style indexes.

CFA® Program Curriculum, Volume 4, page 291

There are several providers of style indices, each of whom competes to earn the business and licensing fees of ETFs and others who would like to create a financial product based on their index. Some providers differentiate their style using just a few variables whereas others use several. Style may be differentiated using price multiples, earnings growth rates, dividends, and other variables. Most indices use holdings-based style analysis to characterize securities.

There are three different methods used to assign a security to either a value or growth index. In the first method the stock is assigned to value or growth. In the second method, the stock can be assigned to value, growth, or to a third neutral category. In the third method, a stock can be split between categories. For example, if its predominant characteristics are value but there are also some features of the stock that suggest growth, the stock may be classified as 70% value and 30% growth. In the first two methods, style is perceived as a category, whereas in the third method style is perceived as a quantity.

Viewing style as a category means that there will be no *overlap* when a style index is constructed (i.e., an individual security will be assigned to only one style). Viewing style as a quantity means that there will be overlap. Some of a stock's market cap may be assigned to value and another part could be assigned to growth. This occurs when a stock is not clearly value or growth.

Examples of style indices with style overlap are the Russell value and growth indices, where the growth ranking is determined by the price/book ratio as well as by a long-term growth estimate. There is no neutral category, just value or growth. Some stocks are split between the growth and value indices, with, for example, 20% of the stock's market capitalization in the Russell Growth and 80% in the Russell Value Index.

Most indices are constructed with no overlap. Additionally, most indices have just two categories, value and growth (i.e., there is no neutral style index). The justification for just two categories is that many investment managers have a clear value or growth directive they must follow.

Another distinguishing characteristic among index methodologies is the presence of **buffering**. When an index has buffering rules, a stock is not immediately moved to a different style category when its style characteristics have changed slightly. The presence of buffering means there will be less turnover in the style indices and, hence, lower transactions costs from rebalancing for managers tracking the index.

THE EQUITY STYLE BOX AND STYLE DRIFT

LOS 25.k: Interpret the results of an equity style box analysis and discuss the consequences of style drift.

CFA® Program Curriculum, Volume 4, page 294

Another method of characterizing a portfolio's style is to use a **style box**. This method is used by Morningstar to characterize mutual funds and stocks. In this approach, a matrix is formed with value/growth characteristics across the top and market cap along the side. Morningstar uses holdings-based style analysis to classify securities.

In Figure 6, we have provided the Morningstar style box for a hypothetical small-cap value fund. The numbers in each cell represent the percent of the fund's market cap in each category (total of the cells = 100%). Note that most of the fund's component stocks are classified as small-cap value, although other categories are represented as well.

Figure 6: Morningstar Style Box for a Hypothetical Small-Cap Value Fund

	Value	Core	Growth
Large-cap	2%	1%	0%
Mid-cap	17%	12%	1%
Small-cap	60%	5%	2%

Categorizing portfolios by size is fairly standard in that market cap is the usual metric for evaluating size. However, different providers use different categorizations of value and growth attributes. For this reason, the categorization of portfolios can differ a great deal depending on the provider. Usually, price multiples are used to define value stocks, whereas earnings or sales growth rates are used to define growth stocks.

Style drift is when a portfolio manager strays from his original, stated style objective. There are two reasons why this can be problematic for an investor. First, the investor will not receive the desired style exposure. This is a concern because value and growth stocks will perform quite differently over time and over the course of business cycles. Second, if a manager starts drifting from the intended style, she may be moving into an area outside her expertise.

As mentioned previously, returns-based style analysis and holdings-based style analysis can both be used to evaluate style drift, with holdings-based style analysis considered to be the more effective of the two methods. To determine whether a manager has drifted using holdings-based style analysis, we would evaluate the same factors mentioned earlier (i.e., the portfolio's value or growth characteristic, expected earnings growth, earnings volatility, and industry representation).

SOCIALLY RESPONSIBLE INVESTING

LOS 25.l: Distinguish between positive and negative screens involving socially responsible investing criteria and discuss their potential effects on a portfolio's style characteristics.

CFA® Program Curriculum, Volume 4, page 296

Socially responsible investing (SRI), also known as ethical investing, is the use of ethical, social, or religious concerns to screen investment decisions. The screens can be negative, where the investor refuses to invest in a company they believe is unethical; or positive, where the investor seeks out firms with ethical practices. An example of a negative screen is an investor who avoids tobacco and alcohol stocks. An example of a positive screen would be when the investor seeks firms with good labor and environmental practices. Most SRI portfolios utilize negative screens, some use both negative and positive screens, and even less use only positive screens. An increasing number of portfolio managers have clients with SRI concerns.

A SRI screen may have an effect on a portfolio's style. For example, some screens exclude basic industries and energy companies, which typically are value stocks. SRI portfolios thus tend to be tilted toward growth stocks. SRI screens have also been found to have a bias toward small-cap stocks. There are two main benefits to monitoring the potential style bias resulting from SRI screens. First, the portfolio manager can take steps to minimize the bias, if it is inconsistent with the investor's risk and return objectives. Second, with knowledge of the portfolio's style bias, the manager can determine the appropriate benchmark for the SRI portfolio. Returns-based style analysis can detect the presence of style bias and monitor the success of its remedy.

LONG-SHORT AND LONG-ONLY INVESTMENT STRATEGIES

LOS 25.m: Compare long–short and long-only investment strategies, including their risks and potential alphas, and explain why greater pricing inefficiency may exist on the short side of the market.

CFA® Program Curriculum, Volume 4, page 297

Long-only strategies focus on using fundamental analysis to find undervalued stocks. In contrast, **long-short** strategies focus on exploiting the constraints many investors face. Specifically, many investors such as institutions are unable to take short positions, which may lead to overvalued stocks.

Whereas long-only strategies can only buy undervalued stocks and avoid overvalued stocks, long-short strategies can both buy undervalued stocks and short overvalued stocks. In essence, the long-short strategy can earn **two alphas**, one on long positions and one on short sales. A long-only strategy can only earn the long alpha through security selection (the excess return relative to its benchmark).

Another way of viewing the advantage of long-short strategies is to consider an investor who is attempting to outperform a market index. If he would like to express a negative view of an index security in a long-only strategy, he is limited to avoiding the stock. For example, if a stock's market cap constitutes 4% of an index, the minimum possible underweighting is 4%, created by not holding the stock. Here the *active weight* is –4%. If the investor wanted an active weight of 6%, on the other hand, the investor would overweight the stock, and it would constitute 10% of the market cap in the investor's portfolio. Thus, the distribution of potential active weights in a long-only portfolio is asymmetric (i.e., underweighting is limited to the security's weight in the portfolio, whereas overweighting is unlimited).

In contrast, a long-short investor can create a symmetric distribution of active weights, provided there is sufficient information regarding the stock's under or overvaluation. The long-short investor can create as short a position as desired (i.e., he is not limited to just avoiding the stock).

In regard to *risk*, a long-only investor is potentially exposed to both systematic and unsystematic risk. In contrast, the long-short investor can eliminate expected systematic risk by using a pair trade (also known as pairs arbitrage) in a *market neutral strategy*. In a pair trade, the investor buys one stock and shorts another in the same industry, thus eliminating exposure to marketwide risk. Systematic risk can be added, if desired, through the use of equity futures or ETFs, which is discussed in the next LOS. The investor, however, still has company specific risk, and if the short position rises in value while the long falls, the results could be disastrous for the long-short investor.

The potential returns and risks of a long-short trade are also magnified by leverage (borrowed funds). Many long-short investors, for example hedge funds, will use leverage of two to three times their capital in a long-short trade. Leverage increases the investor's potential alpha but also increases the likelihood that an investor will have to unwind her position early and at a loss in order to satisfy a margin call.

Pricing Inefficiencies on the Short Side

There are **four reasons for pricing inefficiencies** on the short side of equity trades:

1. There are barriers to short sales that do not exist for long trades. Because of these barriers, some investors do not pursue short strategies. One barrier is that to short a stock, the short seller must find someone who will lend the shares. When the lender requests the shares to be returned, the short seller may have to buy the shares in the open market at an adverse price.

2. Firm management is more likely to promote their firm's stock through accounting manipulations and other means than they are to disparage it. Thus, stock is more likely to be overvalued than undervalued.

3. Analysts on the sell-side are more likely to issue buy recommendations than sell recommendations. The reason is that there is a larger pool of potential buyers of a stock than sellers. Potential sellers are limited to those investors who already own the stock or short sellers. Additionally, analysts will anger large stockholders if they issue a sell recommendation.

4. Sell-side analysts face pressure from firm management against issuing sell recommendations because managers often have stock holdings and options in their firm and may threaten analysts with a cutoff of communications and lawsuits, if the analysts issue sell recommendations. The analyst's firm may also be shut out from investment banking and other corporate finance business if the analyst issues a sell recommendation. Note that such corporate actions are inconsistent with the Best Practice Guidelines Governing Analyst/Corporate Issue Relations supported by the CFA Centre for Financial Market Integrity and the National Investor Relations Institute. Additionally, CFA members, candidates, and charterholders are bound to independence and objectivity by Standard I(B) of the Code of Ethics and Standards of Professional Conduct.

EQUITIZING A LONG-SHORT PORTFOLIO

LOS 25.n: Explain how a market-neutral portfolio can be "equitized" to gain equity market exposure and compare equitized market-neutral and short-extension portfolios.

CFA® Program Curriculum, Volume 4, page 299

By definition, a market-neutral strategy has no systematic risk exposure to the market. Neither the direction nor magnitude of movement in the overall market is expected to affect the portfolio's return.

©2017 Kaplan, Inc.

Long-short is one way to achieve market neutrality. A manager would own stocks (long) believed to be undervalued and short stocks believed to be overvalued. The long and short positions are sized to remove any exposure to overall market direction. For example, if the long and short positions have the same beta, then their size will be equal. The short sales fund the long positions and the portfolio holds cash. To add market exposure, long equity futures equivalent to the portfolio's cash holdings are purchased and the cash fully collateralizes the contract position. The portfolio return is:

- The risk-free rate earned on the cash (equivalent) holdings.
- The market return on the futures contracts.
- The spread earned on the long-short positions. (Assuming the misvaluations correct, both the long and short positions earn positive alpha. This is pure stock picking, the ability to buy undervalued and sell overvalued securities.)

As an alternative to holding cash and long contract positions, the cash could be used to purchase ETFs, producing comparable results.

As another alternative, the long-short spread (the stock picking alphas) can be transported to other markets. For example, take long and short stock positions to capitalize on identifying misvalued stocks and buy bond contracts (or any other security type available) fully collaterlized by the cash to earn bond market return and stock alpha. There is no limit to how this concept can be applied. A bond expert could take long and short positions in bonds to capture individual bond misvaluation and buy contracts on foreign stock ETFs to transport bond value added to foreign stock returns.

Short Extension Strategies

Short extension strategies (also called partial long-short strategies) are seen by the market as extensions to long-only investing. In a short extension strategy, the manager shorts an amount of securities equal to a set percentage of his long portfolio and then purchases an equal amount of securities. For example, in a 120/20 short extension strategy on a $100 million portfolio, the manager would purchase 120% of $100 million in long stock positions and short 20% of $100 million in stocks for a net investment of $100 million. The long positions would be under- or neutral-valued stocks and the short positions would be over-valued stocks.

This is not market-neutral or hedging, an important distinction because it leads to the strategy being classified and evaluated versus long only equity portfolios and not against hedge funds which are typically classified as alternative investments. To illustrate the distinction, a market-neutral portfolio might have equal betas and position sizes in long and short positions for a zero beta and no systematic risk exposure. In contrast, a short-extension strategy (extension meaning it is just a small variation from long only equity) will typically have a beta of 1.0. The manager could be long 120% at a beta of 1.0 and short 20% at 1.0 for a portfolio weighted average beta of 1.0. Just like a long only stock portfolio, the manager could choose to have a higher or lower beta. For example, if the manager is bullish on the market, the manager could go long 120% with a beta of 1.1 and short 20% with a beta of .9 for a weighted average beta of $(1.20 \times 1.1) + (-.2 \times .9)$ = 1.14. Inherently short-extension strategies tend to have a beta of 1.0 while market-neutral strategies tend to have a beta closer to 0.0.

Study Session 12

Advantages of short-extension strategies include:

- Perceived as an equity strategy, not as an alternative investment.
- Lets a manager better exploit information; under-valued securities can be purchased and over-valued can be shorted. Long only portfolios can avoid buying over-valued stocks but cannot short them.
- The short position frees up additional funds for investing in under-valued positions (120% of capital in our 120/20 example). The long only manager can only invest 100%.
- Short-extension strategies can be implemented without a derivatives market. Many market-neutral strategies utilize futures or swaps for part of their execution.
- The short-extension strategy is a more efficient and coordinated portfolio of long and short positions. Long positions are only taken in under-valued (or at least neutral-value) stocks and short positions are in over-valued stocks. In contrast, a separate 100/0 plus 20/20 strategy would first invest 100% of capital in the market portfolio (and nothing short, hence the 100/0 designation). Then it would take 20% of capital in offsetting long and short positions in under- and over-valued stocks (the 20/20). There is inherent inefficiency in this approach as the 100% long market portion will involve buying some of the same over-valued stocks which are shorted in the 20% short position.

There are also inherent disadvantages versus other approaches:

- Higher transaction costs due to the larger quantity of trades executed—120% of capital long and 20% of capital short in our example. In addition, there are borrowing fees on stocks borrowed to cover the short position versus a long only portfolio.
- All of the potential added value comes from the managers' ability to identify under- and over-valued stocks. In contrast, equitizing a market-neutral long-short portfolio (EMNLSP) earns returns from the gain/loss on long and short positions, long futures positions, and interest on the cash equivalent collateral (the long futures are generally 100% collateralized with cash). EMNLSP inherently has more varied sources of return and often allows positions in assets other than stocks. As a market-neutral strategy, EMNLSP is generally compared to cash equivalent returns while short-extension strategies are compared to equity returns.

> *Professor's Note: It is easy to over-study this material and try to create false distinctions. You are expected to know the key essence of each idea and realize they can overlap:*
>
> - *Long/short holds long positions that gain if the security's price increases and short positions that gain if the security's price decreases.*
> - *Market neutral is long/short, and the size of long and short positions are set to leave the portfolio theoretically unaffected by the direction of market movement.*
> - *Pairs trading is the same idea, but matching up a single long position with an offsetting short position.*
> - *Short extension is another variation on long/short, but instead of being market neutral it is net 100% long.*
> - *Equitizing, portable alpha, and transportable alpha are all the same thing.*
>
> *If we have not yet gotten to all these terms, they are coming.*

SELL DISCIPLINES

LOS 25.o: Compare the sell disciplines of active investors.

CFA® Program Curriculum, Volume 4, page 302

An investor may need to sell holdings to rebalance the portfolio, to alter the asset allocation for liquidity, or to update the portfolio's security selection. The use of various strategies can help the investor decide when to sell.

Substitution is replacing an existing security with another with brighter prospects. Considering the transactions costs and tax consequences of the sale of the existing security and the purchase of the new security, this approach is referred to as an *opportunity cost sell discipline*. After careful research, a manager may also conclude that a firm's business will worsen in the future. This is referred to as a *deteriorating fundamentals sell discipline*.

Other, more technical, selling disciplines are based on rules. For example, in a *valuation-level sell discipline*, a value investor may sell a stock if its P/E or P/B ratio rises to the ratio's historical mean. In a *down-from-cost sell discipline*, the manager may sell a stock if its price declines more than say 20% from the purchase price. In an *up-from-cost sell discipline*, the manager may sell a stock once it has increased, for example, either a percentage or a dollar amount from the purchase price. In a *target price sell discipline*, the manager determines the stock's fundamental value at the time of purchase and later sells the stock when it reaches this level.

These sell disciplines are not mutually exclusive within an investor's portfolio, as different stocks may call for different disciplines. Also, the consequences of sell disciplines should be appraised on an after-tax basis according to the investors' tax status.

The frequency of buying and selling in a portfolio is driven by the manager's style. Value investors are typically long-term investors, who buy undervalued stocks and hold them until they appreciate. Annual turnover for value managers varies from 20% to 80%. Growth managers base their decisions on earnings growth and are less patient. They often sell after the next quarterly, semiannual, or annual earnings statement comes out (the frequency of the statements depends on the country of the firm's incorporation). Thus, it is not unusual to see annual turnover of 60% to several hundred percent for these investors.

ENHANCED INDEXING

LOS 25.p: Contrast derivatives-based and stock-based enhanced indexing strategies and justify enhanced indexing on the basis of risk control and the information ratio.

CFA® Program Curriculum, Volume 4, page 303

As discussed previously, semiactive or enhanced indexing strategies attempt to earn an active return (a return greater than a benchmark) while minimizing deviations in performance from the benchmark (tracking risk or active risk). Enhanced indexing strategies have resulted in higher information ratios (active return divided by tracking risk) than passive or active strategies.

Stock-Based and Derivatives-Based Enhanced Indexing Strategies

An enhanced indexing strategy can be executed using either actual stocks or derivative contracts such as equity futures. Using a **stock-based enhanced indexing strategy**, the manager underweights or overweights index stocks based on beliefs about the stocks' prospects. Risk is controlled by monitoring factor risk and industry exposures. The portfolio resembles the index, except where the manager has a specific belief about the value of an index security.

To understand a stock-based enhanced indexing strategy, it may help to compare it to full-blown active management. If the manager does not have an opinion about an index stock in full-blown active management, she doesn't hold the stock. If the manager does not have an opinion about an index stock in a stock-based enhanced indexing strategy, she holds the stock at the same level as the benchmark.

In a **derivatives-based enhanced indexing strategy**, the manager obtains an equity exposure through derivatives. A common method of doing so is to *equitize cash*. Here the manager holds a cash position and a long position in an equity futures contract. The manager can then attempt to generate an excess return by altering the duration of the cash position. If the yield curve is upward sloping, the manager invests longer-term, if she thinks the higher yield is worth it. If, on the other hand, the yield curve is flat, the manager invests in short-duration, fixed-income securities because there would be no reward for investing on the long end. In these derivative-based strategies, the value added (alpha) is coming from the non-equity portion of the portfolio and the equity exposure is coming through derivatives.

There are two *limitations* to enhanced indexing in general. First, successful managers will be copied and their alpha will disappear, unless they change their strategy through time. Second, models obtained from historical data may not be applicable to the future, if the economy changes.

The Fundamental Law of Active Management

The **fundamental law of active management** states that an investor's information ratio (IR) is a function of his depth of knowledge about individual securities (the information coefficient—IC) and the number of investment decisions (the investor's breadth—IB).[2]

More formally:

$$IR \approx IC\sqrt{IB}$$

where:
IR = information ratio
IC = information coefficient
IB = investor breadth

The IC is measured by comparing the investor's forecasts against actual outcomes. The closer they are, the higher the correlation between them, and the greater the IC. More skillful managers will have a higher IC.

Note that investor breadth measures the number of *independent* decisions an investor makes, which does not necessarily increase with the number of securities followed. For example, if an investor buys ten energy stocks because she thinks the sector will do well, the IB equals one, not ten.

The narrower an investor's breadth, the greater her knowledge of each security must be to produce the same information ratio. Unfortunately, it is difficult for most investors to realize a high IC. A stock-based enhanced indexing strategy can produce higher information ratios because the investor can systematically apply her knowledge to a large number of securities, each of which would have different attributes requiring independent decisions.

Example: Using the fundamental law of active management

Manager X follows the stocks in a broad market index and has made independent forecasts for 400 of them. Her IC is 0.05.

Manager Y has made independent forecasts for 150 stocks. His IC is 0.07.

Which manager has the best performance as measured by the information ratio?

Answer:

The information ratio for each manager can be approximated as:

$$IR_X = 0.05\sqrt{400} = 1.00$$
$$IR_Y = 0.07\sqrt{150} = 0.86$$

Although manager X's depth of knowledge is not as great, she has better performance because she has a greater breadth of decisions. Performance here is measured by the information ratio, so Manager X earns more excess return per unit of active risk.

---

2. Richard C. Grinold and Ronald N. Kahn. *Active Portfolio Management*. (McGraw Hill, 1995).

Note that a derivatives-based enhanced indexing strategy will have less breadth than a stock-based enhanced indexing strategy because the investor uses a derivatives contract to gain exposure to equity *and* earns an excess return with non-equity strategies (duration management by moving out the yield curve in the previous discussion) using the duration strategy described earlier. Due to its lower breadth, it will require a higher information coefficient to earn as high an information ratio as a stock-based strategy.

ALLOCATING TO MANAGERS

LOS 25.q: Recommend and justify, in a risk-return framework, the optimal portfolio allocations to a group of investment managers.

CFA® Program Curriculum, Volume 4, page 306

Given funds to invest, an investor has a series of decisions to make. The investor must first decide which asset classes to allocate the funds to and in what weights. At this level, the focus is on maximizing expected return for a given level of risk.

Once an equity allocation is made, the investor needs to focus on choosing passive or active equity management. Passive equity management has zero active return and zero active risk. Think of passive equity management as the *baseline*. As one moves from passive management to enhanced indexing to active management, the expected active return and active risk increase.

So just as in asset allocation, the investor must choose the tradeoff between risk and return. However, once the investor has made a decision to invest in equity, the tradeoff focuses on **active risk** and **active return**.

The gist of the steps to follow is that the investor must decide how much active risk he is willing to accept and what the best combination of equity managers is to achieve that active risk while maximizing active return.

The investor will seek to maximize utility with an optimal allocation among managers. The utility function for active return is similar to the utility function for expected return. The utility of the active return increases as active return increases, as active risk decreases, and as the investor's risk aversion to active risk decreases. Maximize utility through manager selection using the following equation:

$$U_A = R_A - \lambda_A \sigma_A^2$$

where:

U_A = utility of active return (risk adjusted active return) of the mix of managers
R_A = expected active return of the mix of managers

λ_A = The investors' risk aversion trade-off between active risk and active return

σ_A^2 = variance of active return

Next, given his utility function, the investor needs to investigate the performance characteristics of available equity managers. An efficient frontier analysis is useful here, except instead of using expected return and risk, this efficient frontier plots expected active return and active risk using combinations of available equity managers.

Investors are usually more risk averse when facing active risk than they are when dealing with total risk for the following three reasons. First, if an investor were willing to accept zero active return, it would be easy enough to just index. However, to believe that a positive active return is possible, the investor must think that an active manager can deliver an active return, and the investor must believe they can pick that active manager. Second, an investor who must answer to a superior (e.g., a pension plan) for their equity managers' performance will be judged relative to a passive benchmark. It is difficult to produce a positive alpha, and investors are reluctant to take risk positions away from the index. Third, if an investor wants higher active return positions, they must be willing to invest more in the highest active return manager. This results in less diversification across managers. Most institutional investors have an active risk target in the range of 1.5% to 2.5%.[3]

CORE-SATELLITE AND COMPLETENESS FUND APPROACHES

LOS 25.r: Explain the core-satellite approach to portfolio construction and discuss the advantages and disadvantages of adding a completeness fund to control overall risk exposures.

CFA® Program Curriculum, Volume 4, page 309

In a **core-satellite approach** to managing active equity managers, the investor has a core holding of a passive index and/or an enhanced index that is complemented by a satellite of active manager holdings. The idea behind a core-satellite approach is that active risk is mitigated by the core, while active return is added by the satellites. The core is benchmarked to the asset class benchmark, whereas the satellites are benchmarked to a more specific benchmark.

A core-satellite approach can be executed using an informal approach or using a more formal approach as described in LOS 25.q. As part of the latter process, a manager targets an active risk and return and then uses optimization to find the best mix of equity managers to deliver that performance. In the following example, the manager has a 50% core in the passive index and the enhanced indexed portfolio, with satellites of 25%, 15%, and 10% in the active managers.

> *Professor's Note: This example specifically states that the correlation between manager's active returns is zero. If nothing were said, this should be the default assumption. It is likely that there is positive correlation between manager returns; in other words, most managers do well or do poorly at the same time because each manager's return is related to how well the market is doing. But, it is likely that active returns are uncorrelated (0.0). Active return is return less a benchmark return and it is likely that some managers are generating positive active return and others are generating negative active return. That would be a zero correlation of active return. This is even more true among a group of managers pursuing the same style or approach.*

---

3. Barton Waring, Duane Whitney, John Pirone, and Charles Castille. "Optimizing manager structure and budgeting manager risk." *Journal of Portfolio Management*. Vol. 26, Iss. 3; p. 90. (New York, Spring 2000).

Example: Applying the core-satellite approach

The investor has an active risk target of no more than 1.75% and a target information ratio of at least 0.9. The investor can choose from passive management, enhanced indexing, or three active managers (X, Y, and Z) in the figure below. Given the targeted active risk, the investor makes the allocations to maximize return. Note that, by definition, the active return and risk to passive indexing is 0%. Assume that the correlations between the equity managers' active returns are zero.

Active Return, Active Risk, and Allocations to Equity Managers

	Expected Active Return	Expected Active Risk	Allocations
Passive index	0.00%	0.00%	10%
Enhanced indexing	1.40%	2.20%	40%
Active Manager X	1.70%	2.80%	25%
Active Manager Y	3.00%	5.10%	15%
Active Manager Z	3.70%	7.00%	10%

Calculate the investor's active return given the above allocations. **Determine** if the investor has met the targeted active risk and information ratio.

Answer:

To calculate the investor's active return given the equity manager allocations listed in the figure above, we would calculate a weighted average return using the following formula. Note that it is similar to the formula for portfolio expected return except now we use active return instead of total return.

$$\text{expected active portfolio return} = \sum_{i=1}^{n} w_{a,i}(\hat{R}_{a,i})$$

where:
$w_{a,i}$ = weight invested with ith manager
$\hat{R}_{a,i}$ = expected active return of ith manager

Using the active returns and allocations in the figure above, we calculate an expected active portfolio return of 1.81%:

expected active portfolio return =
$(0.10 \times 0\%) + (0.40 \times 1.4\%) + (0.25 \times 1.7\%) + (0.15 \times 3.0\%) + (0.10 \times 3.7\%) = 1.81\%$

To calculate the portfolio active risk, we assume that the correlations between the equity managers' active returns are zero. Assuming zero correlation, the formula for portfolio active risk is:

$$\text{portfolio active risk} = \sqrt{\sum_{i=1}^{n} w_{a,i}^2 \sigma_{a,i}^2}$$

Using the active risks and allocations, we calculate the portfolio active risk:

portfolio active risk
$$= \sqrt{(0.10)^2(0)^2 + (0.40)^2(0.022)^2 + (0.25)^2(0.028)^2 + (0.15)^2(0.051)^2 + (0.10)^2(0.07)^2}$$
$$= \sqrt{0.000234} = 0.0153 = 1.53\%$$

The investor's information ratio is 1.81% / 1.53% = 1.18. The investor has satisfied the active risk target of no greater than 1.75% and the information ratio of at least 0.9.

The Completeness Fund Approach

In contrast to the formalized process followed for the core-satellite approach, many managers use a less exact approach. Given that the resulting portfolio will still be benchmarked against a broad market index, the manager's portfolio will have a number of industry or other biases relative to the benchmark. This is particularly true when examining the portfolios of bottom-up managers, where industry exposures are not given a priority in stock selection.

To minimize the differences in risk exposures between the portfolio and the benchmark, the investor can use a **completeness fund**. The completeness fund is combined with the active portfolio, so that the combined portfolios have a risk exposure similar to the benchmark. The advantage of the completeness fund approach is that the active return from the managers can be maintained while active risk is minimized. The completeness fund must be rebalanced regularly as the active manager's exposures change. The fund can be managed passively or semiactively.

The disadvantage of a completeness fund is that it may result in a reduction of active returns arising from misfit risk. (As described in the next LOS, misfit risk results from differences between the manager's normal portfolio and the broader asset class benchmark.)

Professor's Note: Both core-satellite and completeness have a similar objective, a total portfolio that meets the client's overall risk and return exposure characteristics. The distinction is the core-satellite starts with a desired index-like portfolio and then adds actively managed funds, seeking + value added. The completeness portfolio starts with an existing position that does not have the desired overall characteristics and adds positions that are specifically intended to make the total portfolio better reflect the desired risk and return exposure characteristics.

COMPONENTS OF TOTAL ACTIVE RETURN

LOS 25.s: Distinguish among the components of total active return ("true" active return and "misfit" active return) and their associated risk measures and explain their relevance for evaluating a portfolio of managers.

CFA® Program Curriculum, Volume 4, page 311

Recall that a manager's *normal portfolio* or normal benchmark reflects the securities she normally chooses from for her portfolio. It is an appropriate benchmark for the manager, because it reflects the manager's style. For example, the normal portfolio for a value manager might be an index of value stocks.

In contrast, an investor who hires a manager may use a broad-based benchmark for the manager's asset class that does not reflect the manager's style. This portfolio would be referred to as the **investor's benchmark**.

Using these two benchmarks, we can then decompose the manager's total active return into two parts, the true active return and the misfit active return, as follows:

manager's true active return = manager's total return – manager's normal portfolio return

manager's misfit active return = manager's normal portfolio return – investor's benchmark return

The **true active return** is *true* in the sense that it measures what the manager earned relative to the correct benchmark. The **misfit active return** is *misfit* in the sense that it measures that part of the manager's return from using a benchmark that is not suited to the manager's style.

Using these components of return, we can decompose the manager's total active risk into the true risk and misfit risk. The total active risk is the volatility of the manager's portfolio relative to the investor's benchmark.

$$\text{total active risk} = \sqrt{(\text{true active risk})^2 + (\text{misfit active risk})^2}$$

Using the true active return and true active risk, we can define an information ratio that better represents the manager's skills:

$$\text{true information ratio} = \frac{\text{true active return}}{\text{true active risk}}$$

There are two uses of the decomposition of the manager's performance into true and misfit components. The first use is to more accurately evaluate the manager's performance using the manager's true return as in the following example.

Example: Decomposing performance into true and misfit components

Bob Davis is a small-cap growth manager who invests in U.S. equities. He was hired by a pension fund that benchmarks him against a broad U.S. market index. Using the information in the following figure, **calculate** the manager's information ratio that most accurately reflects his abilities.

Decomposing Active Risk and Return

Manager return	18.0%
Broad market return	15.0%
Normal portfolio return	20.0%
Total active risk	5.0%
Misfit active risk	3.5%

Answer:

Comparing the manager's return to the broad market, the manager appears to have generated an excess return of 3% (18% – 15%). That is an inappropriate benchmark. If one uses the normal portfolio as the benchmark, the manager has actually underperformed the appropriate benchmark by 2% (18% – 20%). The true and misfit active returns are measured as follows:

$$\text{true active return} = 18\% - 20\% = -2\%$$
$$\text{misfit active return} = 20\% - 15\% = 5\%$$

The true active risk is backed out of the total and misfit risk:

$$\text{total active risk} = \sqrt{(\text{true active risk})^2 + (\text{misfit active risk})^2}$$

$$5\% = \sqrt{(\text{true active risk})^2 + (3.5\%)^2}$$

$$(5\%)^2 = (\text{true active risk})^2 + (3.5\%)^2$$

$$(5\%)^2 - (3.5\%)^2 = (\text{true active risk})^2$$

$$\sqrt{(5\%)^2 - (3.5\%)^2} = \text{true active risk}$$

$$\text{true active risk} = 3.57\%$$

The true information ratio demonstrates underperformance as it is negative, resulting from the negative true active return:

$$\text{true information ratio} = \frac{-2\%}{3.57\%} = -0.56$$

The decomposition of the total active performance into true and misfit components is also useful for optimization. The objective is to maximize the total active return for a given level of total active risk while allowing for an optimal amount of misfit risk. Note that misfit risk is not optimized at zero because a manager may be able to generate a level of true active return for some level of misfit risk. In other words, if you let the manager concentrate in the style he is familiar with, the manager is more likely to generate an excess return relative to his normal portfolio.

ALPHA AND BETA SEPARATION

LOS 25.t: Explain alpha and beta separation as an approach to active management and demonstrate the use of portable alpha.

CFA® Program Curriculum, Volume 4, page 313

In an **alpha and beta separation approach**, the investor gains a systematic risk exposure (beta) through a low-cost index fund or ETF, while adding an alpha through a long-short strategy. This strategy may be particularly suitable for markets that are highly efficient and difficult to generate an alpha from.

For example, the investor may pick up a beta exposure in an S&P 500 index fund. The stock prices in this large-cap index are highly efficient with respect to information, and it would be difficult to generate an alpha with this index. The investor could pick up alpha by hiring a manager who specializes in long-short strategies in less efficient small-cap markets. If the manager decides to take a different index exposure, she could keep the small-cap alpha and pick up the beta exposure in some index (e.g., an MSCI World Index ETF). This strategy is referred to as a portable alpha strategy.

An advantage of this approach is that the investor can gain access to equity styles and asset classes outside of a systematic risk class. The investor can also better understand and manage the risks in an alpha and beta separation approach because they are more clearly defined. In contrast, in a long-only strategy, the risks are not as clearly delineated. Lastly, by partitioning the alpha and beta, the investor has a better idea of the costs of investing. A passive beta exposure is typically cheaper than an active alpha exposure.

A limitation of the alpha and beta separation approach is that it may be difficult or costly to implement short positions in markets such as emerging markets or small-cap markets. Secondly, some long-short strategies are not truly market neutral and may have a degree of systematic risk. Lastly, long-short investing may be off-limits to some investors. These investors, however, could create an alpha and beta separation approach exposure using equity futures. For example, suppose the investor wants a beta from large-cap U.S. stocks and an alpha from European equities. The investor can take a long position in the S&P 500 index futures contract and invest with a European equity manager to generate the alpha. To become market neutral in the European equity market, the investor would then short a futures contract based on European equities.

 Professor's Note: Alpha and beta separation is not one specifically designated technique, but an intent. Any strategy that seeks to provide (low cost) index-like return (beta risk) from one set of decisions and positive value added from other decisions is alpha and beta separation.

©2017 Kaplan, Inc.

SELECTING EQUITY MANAGERS

LOS 25.u: Describe the process of identifying, selecting, and contracting with equity managers.

CFA® Program Curriculum, Volume 4, page 314

The process of selecting investment managers is particularly important for institutions and high net worth individuals. The process may be performed in-house or by outside consultants. Consultants research performance records and interview investment managers to determine which managers are worthy of consideration. Qualitative considerations are the strength of the firm's investment approach and research as well as the manager's personnel. Quantitative considerations include the manager's fees, performance, and style. The manager should also have consistency between stated and actual investment approaches.

Past Performance

Past performance is often no guarantee of future performance. In fact, a contrarian strategy often works as well with managers as it does with stocks. Although consistency in superior performance is rare, managers with poor historical performance are unlikely to be hired. That is, without some evidence that a manager can generate an alpha, the investor will passively index. Additionally, a manager who achieves superior performance with a consistent staff and investment philosophy is more likely to be hired.

Manager Questionnaires

In the hiring process, a manager questionnaire is used to screen potential managers. If the manager's responses to the questionnaire are promising, the questionnaire will be followed by personal interviews with the manager.

There are five sections of the questionnaire. The first section regards the manager's staff and organizational structure. Investing is a labor-intensive process, and having the right people and compensation structure in place is key to a manager's potential success. This part of the questionnaire also covers topics such as the vision of the firm, the qualifications and experience of the staff, and how long the staff has worked as a team.

The second section of the questionnaire concerns investment philosophy and procedures. This section provides details on the firm's investment philosophy, how it intends to capture alpha, how research is conducted, how risk is managed and monitored, the firm's stock selection techniques, and how portfolios are composed.

The third section focuses on resources and how research is conducted and used. Other details provided here include portfolio turnover, how quantitative models are utilized, and how trading functions.

The fourth section concerns performance: the manager's benchmark, the expected alpha, the sources of risk, and portfolio holdings.

The fifth section provides details on the fee schedule, which are discussed in the next section.

Fee Schedules

Fees can be charged on an *ad valorem* basis or based on performance. Ad valorem fees are also referred to as asset under management fees (AUM) and are charged based on the asset value managed and may be on a sliding schedule (e.g., 0.50% for the first $10 million managed and 0.40% for asset amounts over $10 million).

A *performance-based fee* is often charged as a base fee plus some percentage of the alpha. For example, the fee may be 0.40% of all assets managed plus 10% of any profit above the benchmark. The performance-based fee may also include *fee caps* and *high water marks*. A fee cap specifies a maximum performance fee. The intent is to prevent managers from undertaking too much risk to earn higher fees. A high water mark is designed to prevent the manager from collecting a performance fee twice for the same outperformance. For example, in period one a manager generates positive incremental performance and is paid an incentive fee. In period two, the manager generates negative incremental performance. The manager still receives their base fee but no incentive fee. In period three, any incremental performance must first earn back the negative incremental return of period two before performance fees are paid on the new incremental performance.

The *advantage* of ad valorem fees is that they are straightforward and known in advance. This is useful when the investor is budgeting investment fees. Their *disadvantage* is that they do not align the interests of managers and investors the way performance-based fees do.

Performance-based fees have two *disadvantages*. First, performance-based fees are more complicated and require detailed specifications. Second, they also increase the volatility of the manager's compensation, which may create problems for a manager attempting to retain staff and provide consistent performance. This is particularly true in years when the manager has underperformed its competitors.

The advantage of performance-based fees is that they align the interests of the manager and the investor, especially if they are *symmetric* (i.e., contain penalties for poor performance and rewards for good performance). This should motivate the manager to work harder on the investor's behalf.

©2017 Kaplan, Inc.

STRUCTURING EQUITY RESEARCH

LOS 25.v: Contrast the top-down and bottom-up approaches to equity research.

CFA® Program Curriculum, Volume 4, page 322

Some investors begin their investment process by examining an economy to determine its future state. If, for example, the investor determines the economy is going to expand, cyclical stocks would be favored. Next, specific firms within cyclical industries are examined for attractiveness. This approach is known as a **top-down approach** because the investor starts at the economy level and works her way down. Using a global perspective, the investor would also look at global economic factors and the projections for currencies.

In a **bottom-up approach**, the investor starts at the individual stock level. Stocks are chosen on the basis of their individual characteristics and valuation. For this type of approach, the investor is more concerned with security and industry conditions and less concerned with macro and overall economic conditions.

Some investors use a combination of the two approaches. For example, the investor forecasting an economic expansion may select cyclical stocks based on their valuations.

Another way to differentiate investment approaches is by whether the research is conducted by sell-side or buy-side analysts. A *buy-side* analyst works for and builds a portfolio for an investment management firm. The analyst in this case usually must present recommendations to and get approval from a committee. Buy-side research is not usually available to those outside the firm because this is how the firm hopes to establish their competitive advantage.

In contrast, *sell-side* analysts often work for an investment bank that uses the research to promote stocks the bank is selling. Sell-side research is also conducted by independent firms available for hire by investment managers. Thus, sell-side research is available to those outside the firm. It is the research that the public is most familiar with, as sell-side analysts often appear in the financial news or on investment television shows. This research is often organized by industry or sector and provides a buy, sell, or hold recommendation.

KEY CONCEPTS

LOS 25.a
Equities are a good inflation hedge in the long run. But in the short run, the correlation of their return with inflation is imperfect because companies vary in their ability to pass through inflation with higher product prices and the tax code does not adjust for the effects of inflation.

LOS 25.b
Passive managers do not use forecasts to influence their investment strategies. Indexing is a common form of passive management.

Active managers use expectations to try and anticipate market changes that can be exploited to add value.

Semiactive (enhanced indexing) managers attempt to earn a higher return than the benchmark while minimizing the risk of deviating from the benchmark.

Active return is the excess return of a manager relative to the benchmark. *Tracking risk* is the standard deviation of active return and is a measurement of active risk. Passive managers have the lowest active return and tracking risk whereas active managers have the highest, with semiactive managers between the two.

LOS 25.c
Passive strategies may be preferable when the investor is taxable, has an informational disadvantage in global markets, is investing in informationally efficient large-cap markets, or wants to avoid high transaction costs.

LOS 25.d
A price-weighted index is the arithmetic average price of the securities in the index. It reflects owning an equal number of shares of each security. It is biased towards the performance of the highest priced securities. To avoid distortion when stocks split or pay a stock dividend, the divisor for the average is adjusted.

A value-weighted index is based on the total market cap of all securities in the index. It is the most commonly used type of index and reflects what is in aggregate owned by all investors. If significant numbers of shares are not tradable, free-float adjusted (based on tradable shares) are used in the computation of the index's value. It is biased towards the performance of the largest market cap stocks.

In an equal-weighted index, return reflects the average return of all the securities in the index. It is as if the same amount were invested in each security. Replicating this could be expensive as it would have to be rebalanced continually.

LOS 25.e

Mutual funds and ETFs both offer passive index portfolios. Mutual funds allow investors to purchase or redeem shares daily at NAV. ETFs do not offer cash redemption, but the shares trade continuously. A redemption-in-kind (in underlying securities) mechanism keeps market price near NAV.
*   ETFs do not provide shareholder recordkeeping.
*   ETFs may have to pay a licensing fee to use the index name (as would mutual funds).

 ©2017 Kaplan, Inc.

- ETFs are generally more tax efficient, as they do not trade securities and therefore do not pass through realized gains and losses each year.
- ETF investors pay a brokerage commission to buy or sell ETF shares, but costs are usually lower for long-term investors in ETFs because annual fees are lower than in mutual funds.

The same managers who offer index mutual funds and ETFs may manage separate indexed portfolios for large individual clients or a pool (small group) of clients. The fees are very low.

Holding long equity futures contracts plus cash equivalents can replicate the performance of the index at very low cost. Over long periods the expense does increase as contracts must be rolled over. Holding cash equivalents and a total return equity swap (pay the floating rate and receive the equity return) is another, derivatives-based indexing approach.

LOS 25.f
In full replication, all index weights and positions are matched. Tracking error is minimized, but expenses are increased if there are more and illiquid securities in the index.

In stratified sampling, securities are chosen to replicate index weights by cell, but not by individual positions. Tracking error will be slightly higher, but costs can be reduced by avoiding illiquid securities.

Optimization uses a factor model to match the factor exposures of the index. Exposures must be monitored and rebalanced; it is more complicated, but tracking error can be lower than for stratified sampling.

LOS 25.g
- A value investor focuses on stocks with low price multiples [e.g., P/E, P/B, and price/ dividends (P/D)].
- A growth investor favors stocks with high or increasing earnings growth.
- Market-oriented investors cannot be easily classified as value or growth.

LOS 25.h

Value investors focus on buying undervalued stocks that are often out of favor. Low P/B, P/E, and P/D are typical. Behavioral finance could explain why out-of-favor stocks can be unpopular and therefore underpriced. Value investors argue that growth investors pay too much and their risk is too high. The risk in the value style is the stock price stays low or gets worse.

Growth investors favor higher growth in earnings and expect the stock price to track the high growth rate. The primary risk is that if earnings growth is disappointing, both E and P/E decline, resulting in a large price decline.

Market-oriented investing is commonly done through indexing or quasi-indexing. It can also be tilted towards the value or growth style.

Market capitalization strategies tilt the portfolio towards small, mid, or large-cap stocks. Some evidence supports the notion that small and mid-cap tend to outperform, perhaps reflecting that they are less followed and therefore underpriced and/or earn an illiquidity premium.

LOS 25.i

Returns-based style analysis regresses historical returns versus various style indexes to determine a best fit weighting that would have replicated the past performance progression. It is simple to do (with software), but does not consider the actual portfolio holdings or the manager's investment approach.

Holdings-based style analysis categorizes the portfolio holdings as of a moment in time. It is more time-consuming to do, and there can be various opinions about the most important variables to categorize or where a particular holding should be categorized.

Observing how the results of either analysis change over time can reveal style drift, though holdings-based analysis will reveal it more quickly.

LOS 25.j

Most style indexes use P/E, P/B, and P/D to categorize themselves as value or growth style. Most style indexes exclude stocks that are ambiguous to style. Buffering rules are often employed to reduce the frequency with which securities are moved into and out of the index.

LOS 25.k

A style box categorizes portfolio holdings across two dimensions, often market cap and growth/value style. Tracking how the weights in each cell change over time can indicate style drift.

Style drift can mean the client is not exposed to the expected risk and return characteristics that meet his objectives and/or the manager is moving out of her area of expertise.

LOS 25.l

Socially responsible investing (SRI) uses positive screens to select securities with desirable social and ethical (not economic) characteristics, and negative screens to exclude securities with undesirable characteristics. Typically, screening may tilt the portfolio away from older, large cap basic industry and therefore towards smaller cap.

LOS 25.m

Long-only investment strategies seek to select undervalued securities that provide both market (beta) and value added (alpha) return. The portfolios are exposed to both systematic and unsystematic risk. Only long positions are allowed, so the opportunity to exploit overvalued securities is limited.

Long-short can buy undervalued and short overvalued securities to potentially earn two sources of alpha. Shorting allows the investor to profit from overvalued securities, while a long-only investor can only choose to not own those securities. In theory, the portfolio can be market neutral and only face unsystematic risk, but that can be high. The portfolio is inherently leveraged, as short positons fund long positions.

The short side may be inefficient because many investors are not allowed to short and there is expense involved in shorting. A sell recommendation can anger the company's management, therefore many analysts are reluctant to make sell recommendations. Finally, companies generally emphasize favorable (and not unfavorable) information about their companies.

©2017 Kaplan, Inc.

LOS 25.n

With the short positions funding the long positions in a market neutral strategy, the investor's capital can be equitized by investing in stocks, equity index funds, or equity futures. The latter provide market return and the long-short positions alpha. Alternatively, the investor's capital can be invested in any other type of market, and the equity alphas transported to that other market's return.

A short-extension strategy also uses long and short positions but is net 100% long (e.g., 130/30). The sources of market return and alpha are combined, not separate decisions. The portfolios are typically compared to long-only portfolios.

LOS 25.o

Investors often spend too little time deciding when to sell. Rules could be used to overcome this tendency:

*   Estimate and compare projected total return of the existing position versus its proposed replacement.
*   Use mechanical rules to sell at a predetermined price, P/E, or after a specified percentage increase or decrease.

LOS 25.p

Stock-based enhanced indexing owns the securities in the index but slightly over/ underweights under/overvalued securities.

Derivatives-based enhanced indexing could use long equity futures positions to earn the market return and aggressively manage the cash position to add value.

The information ratio (IR) is active return/standard deviation of active return. The fundamental law of active management states the IR is driven by IC (the value of what is known) and IB (the number of things that are known):

$$IR \approx IC\sqrt{IB}.$$

Higher IR is better.

LOS 25.q

When selecting managers, investors should focus on active return (value added) and its variability (not on total return and its variability). The market return is available at lower cost and with more certainty through indexing strategies.

LOS 25.r

Core-satellite starts with allocating funds to index strategies to provide the desired market return, then allocates funds to active strategies to add value.

Completeness starts with an existing position that does not provide the desired market characteristics and adds allocations, such that the total portfolio better matches the desired market characteristics.

LOS 25.s

Clients often make tactical decisions (e.g., style benchmarks) to deviate away from long term strategic allocations (e.g., market benchmarks). In such cases active return, risk, and IR can be decomposed into client and manager sources.

true active return = manager's total return – manager's normal portfolio return

misfit active return = manager's normal portfolio return – investor's benchmark return

$$\text{total active risk} = \sqrt{(\text{true active risk})^2 + (\text{misfit active risk})^2}$$

$$\text{true information ratio} = \frac{\text{true active return}}{\text{true active risk}}$$

LOS 25.t

In alpha and beta separation strategies, one set of portfolio decisions provide low cost market return (beta) and other decisions provide value added (alpha) (e.g., market neutral long-short (alpha) equitized with an equity index fund holding (beta)).

LOS 25.u

Manager evaluation should include quantitative analysis of results and manager style, as well as qualitative assessment of what they say they do and their resources. Questionnaires are generally used as a first step to gather standardized information from an initial group of managers being considered.

LOS 25.v

The top-down approach uses macroeconomic considerations to identify attractive and unattractive markets and sectors. The bottom-up approach aggregates the forecast for individual securities to make those decisions.

 ©2017 Kaplan, Inc.

CONCEPT CHECKERS

1.   **Critique** the following statement: "Equities are a better inflation hedge than bonds."

2.   Many U.S. media outlets have recommended investing in global stocks because there may be more opportunities to exploit mispriced stocks. **Identify** the conditions under which this advice would be correct.

3.   A market-value weighted index is considered the most representative of market conditions, especially when it is adjusted for free float. Some practitioners, however, have suggested moving away from this weighting scheme to one based on fundamentals such as the price-earnings ratio. **Explain** their reasoning.

4.   Suppose a taxable investor has a large amount to invest and would like to invest long term. Would he be *more likely* to use an ETF or an index mutual fund?

5.   A manager would like to create a fund that tracks the performance of a prominent developed and emerging country European index. There are 1,500 stocks in the index. The manager has $10 million initially to invest. Should the manager use replication, stratified sampling, or optimization?

6. Many researchers have found that value stocks have higher returns than growth stocks, on average over time. What would market efficiency proponents say about this performance differential?

7. An analyst wants to evaluate a manager who claims that she invests in mid-cap value stocks. The analyst uses both returns-based style analysis and holdings-based style analysis.

    Explain why the manager would pursue these stocks. **Describe** the indices the analyst should include in the returns-based style analysis. **Describe** the expected characteristics using the holdings-based style analysis.

8. A manager's portfolio has gradually shifted from high P/E, high P/B, and high earnings growth rate stocks into stocks with more moderate levels of the variables. **Discuss** the problem with this movement.

9. **Describe** the potential style bias in socially responsible portfolios.

10. **Explain** how a pair trade can go awry.

11. Why would an investor want to equitize a long-short portfolio?

©2017 Kaplan, Inc.

12.   Manager A has made independent forecasts for 450 stocks. Her IC is 0.03.

Manager B has made independent forecasts for 200 stocks. His IC is 0.05.

Which manager has the better performance as measured by the information ratio?

13.   Are investors more risk averse when facing total risk or active risk? **Explain** why.

14.   An investor uses a core-satellite approach to allocate funds amongst equity managers. The equity manager's active risk, active return, and allocations are shown as follows.

	Expected Active Return	Expected Active Risk	Allocations
Passive Index	0.00%	0.00%	15%
Enhanced Indexing	1.70%	2.50%	45%
Active Manager X	1.90%	3.00%	25%
Active Manager Y	3.30%	5.50%	10%
Active Manager Z	3.90%	7.20%	5%

Describe the investor's core. **Calculate** the investor's active return, active risk, and information ratio given the above allocations. Assume that the correlations between the equity managers' active returns are zero.

15.   Using the following figures, **evaluate** the manager's performance.

Manager return	15.0%
Investor's benchmark	11.0%
Normal portfolio return	8.0%
Total active risk	5.2%
Misfit active risk	3.8%

16.   An investor places funds with a small-cap growth stock manager. The investor believes the manager can outperform other small-cap growth managers to generate alpha but also wants exposure (beta) to the broad S&P 500 market. **Explain** how the investor can retain the alpha of the manager but gain the desired beta using equity contracts.

17.   **Explain** how a fee cap and a high water mark affect a manager's incentive fee.

18.   Maria Castillo is an investment manager who is promoting the Japanese equity market to her investment management committee because she forecasts that the Japanese economy is finally rebounding from a decade long slump. She also thinks the Japanese yen will stay strong relative to other major currencies. What type of investment approach is Castillo using?

For more questions related to this topic review, log in to your Schweser online account and launch SchweserPro™ QBank; and for video instruction covering each LOS in this topic review, log in to your Schweser online account and launch the OnDemand video lectures, if you have purchased these products.

     ©2017 Kaplan, Inc.

ANSWERS – CONCEPT CHECKERS

1. Generally, this is true. Equity is a claim on company assets and future earnings, which tend to increase with inflation. In contrast, increasing inflation generally increases interest rates, lowering bond prices and their realized return. However, equities are not a perfect inflation hedge. In the shorter run, equity return and inflation may be less positively correlated as company profits are not fully indexed to inflation. For example, depreciation expense is based on historical cost and not replacement value, leading to higher reported profits and taxes with lower after-tax cash flow. In addition, companies vary in their ability to pass through price increases to cover inflation.

2. This advice would be correct if the U.S. investor or her portfolio manager can gain access to the same information that investors have in the country they are considering. This may difficult to achieve. Additionally, smaller cap markets typically have higher transactions costs. The investor should be sure that the higher transactions costs in these markets do not offset the potentially higher returns.

   For these reasons, the U.S. investor may want to consider a passive indexing strategy in these markets.

3. A value-weighted index may overweight overvalued stocks because the overvalued stocks will have a higher market cap. By weighting by price-earnings ratio, these practitioners hope to avoid overweighting overvalued stocks. Stocks with high price-earnings ratios would have lower weights in such an index.

4. The large investor would be more likely to use an ETF because in a mutual fund, he would pay record-keeping costs for smaller investors. Given that the investor pays taxes, an ETF would be more appropriate because there are fewer taxes realized that are passed on to shareholders. If they are a long-term investor, they are more likely to use ETFs because in a mutual fund, they would pay for the costs of supplying liquidity to shorter-term investors.

5. Given that there are 1,500 stocks, the manager should consider a method other than replication. Furthermore, the manager has only $10 million to invest and many of the stocks, especially in the emerging countries, are likely to be illiquid.

   Optimization will provide lower tracking risk compared to stratified sampling, but it requires more frequent rebalancing. If tracking risk is not highly important, the manager may want to consider stratified sampling since the trading costs in some emerging countries can be particularly high. Stratified sampling also does not require or depend on the use of a model.

6. Market efficiency proponents would argue that these stocks have higher returns because investors expect their risk to be higher. As such, they have lower prices and the higher future returns (on average) are compensation for the increased risk.

   Indeed, the risk for value investors is that these stocks' low prices are justified (i.e., their weak earnings never recover). The value investor must have an expectation of how and when these stocks will recover before he invests in them.

7. The manager would pursue mid-cap stocks because mid-cap stocks may have less coverage than large-cap stocks but are less risky than small-cap stocks. Value stocks have excess returns on average over time, but the manager must understand that these stocks may be priced cheaply for a reason (i.e., they have higher risk).

The analyst should include six indices for the returns-based style analysis: value and growth indices for small-, mid-, and large-cap stocks. This will help identify if the manager has any exposure to growth or to other capitalization stocks.

From the holdings-based style analysis for the mid-cap value manager, the manager should expect low P/E and P/B ratios, below-average expected earnings growth, higher earnings volatility, and representation in the financial and utility industries. The manager should also find a market cap that reflects mid-cap.

8.   The manager's style is drifting. The portfolio is shifting from a growth orientation into a market orientation. When a manager's style drifts, the investor does not receive the intended exposure and the manager moves outside his area of expertise.

9.   Socially responsible portfolios have a potential bias towards growth stocks because they tend to shun basic industries and energy stocks, which are typically value stocks. Socially responsible portfolios also have a bias towards small-cap stocks.

10. A pair trade can go awry if the stock that was shorted rises in price and the stock that was bought decreases in price. The probability of a pair trade performing poorly increases if the investor uses leverage, receives a margin call, and has to liquidate the position early at adverse prices.

11. An investor would equitize a long-short portfolio if she thought the stock market was going to do well in the future. A market neutral strategy has no systematic risk, but a broad market exposure can be added by taking a long position in a futures contract, index fund, or an ETF. Note that exposures to other asset classes can also be added using an index security for them.

12. The approximate information ratio for each manager is:

$$IR_A = 0.03\sqrt{450} = 0.64$$
$$IR_B = 0.05\sqrt{200} = 0.71$$

Manager B's depth of knowledge is greater, which accounts for his greater information ratio.

13. Investors are more risk averse when facing active risk. To obtain an active return—a return higher than a passive benchmark—the investor must accept active risk. To believe that an active return is possible, the investor must believe that there are active managers who can produce it and that the investor will be able to pick those successful managers. Second, an active equity style will also be judged against a passive benchmark. It is difficult to generate alpha and those who don't face pressure from their superiors. Lastly, higher active returns mean that more is invested with the high return active manager, and this results in less diversification.

14. The investor has a core of 15% passive equity and 45% enhanced indexed funds for a total core of 60%. The satellites are 25%, 10%, and 5% around the core.

The investor's active return is calculated as a weighted average return:

expected active portfolio return
= (0.15 × 0%) + (0.45 × 1.7%) + (0.25 × 1.9%) + (0.10 × 3.3%) + (0.05 × 3.9%) = 1.77%

To calculate the portfolio active risk, we use the active risks and allocations:

portfolio active risk

$$= \sqrt{(0.15)^2(0)^2 + (0.45)^2(0.025)^2 + (0.25)^2(0.03)^2 + (0.10)^2(0.055)^2 + (0.05)^2(0.072)^2}$$

$$= \sqrt{0.000226} = 0.0150 = 1.50\%$$

The investor's information ratio is then: 1.77% / 1.50% = 1.18.

15.   The manager's style (as measured by the normal portfolio) underperformed the investor's benchmark by 3% (8% − 11%). But the manager outperformed the normal portfolio by 7% (15% − 8%). We use this true active return of 7% to more accurately evaluate the manager. More formally:

true active return = 15% − 8% = 7%

misfit active return = 8% − 11% = −3%

The true active risk is backed out of the total and misfit risk:

$$\text{total active risk} = \sqrt{(\text{true active risk})^2 + (\text{misfit active risk})^2}$$

$$5.2\% = \sqrt{(\text{true active risk})^2 + (3.8\%)^2}$$

true active risk = 3.55%

The manager's performance generates a true information ratio of:

$$\text{true information ratio} = \frac{7\%}{3.55\%} = 1.97$$

16.   To separate the alpha and beta, the investor could pick up the desired beta by taking a long position in a large-cap U.S. equity index futures contract, such as the S&P 500 contract. To create the market-neutral alpha, the investor would then invest with the small-cap growth manager and short a small-cap growth equity index futures contract.

17.   Both potentially reduce the fee a manager can earn. A fee cap limits the total fee a manager can collect. This cap on additional reward for the manager may reduce the incentive of the manager to take excessive risk. A high water mark prevents a manager from collecting an incentive fee twice. Suppose a fund increases 10% in value to 1,000 and the manager receives a performance fee on this increase. Then the fund declines. Any subsequent incentive fees are earned from 1,000 and up.

18.   Castillo is using a top-down approach. She starts at the top of the economy to determine its prospects before moving down to the individual stock level.

SELF-TEST: EQUITY PORTFOLIO MANAGEMENT

Use the following information for Questions 1 through 6.

Kathy Berg is the private wealth adviser to Caroline Corbin, a woman in her 40s who has recently come into a large inheritance. Corbin feels her age enables her to take on significant risk, so Berg has suggested a fairly substantial equity allocation to the portfolio.

Berg and Corbin have assessed a variety of approaches to equity investing, both passive and active. They have now reached the point of beginning to identify, assess, select, and contract with the appropriate equity managers to implement their strategic asset allocation.

Berg explains to Corbin that she investigated a variety of managers for potential addition to the portfolio stable of managers. "We use manager questionnaires to gather quantitative and qualitative data," Berg says. "If the two disagree, we rely on the quantitative data."

Berg elaborates that she also considers it important that the manager's style not conflict with her own analytic views. "Because I start my asset allocation process by assessing the overall economy, I don't want our asset managers to make their own economic decisions. I want asset managers who focus on individual securities and don't use overall macroeconomic analysis. I want them to ignore the big picture and start with the top line for the individual company. For that reason, I only considered managers who use a top-down approach to research."

Berg informs Corbin that she initially investigated a wide range of managers and narrowed the field by assessing them with a manager questionnaire. Berg provides Corbin with the following list of topics included in the manager questionnaire:

Topic 1: Staff and organizational structure, including staff résumés and how long the staff has worked together as a team.

Topic 2: Investment philosophy and procedures, including how they intend to capture alpha, how risk is managed and monitored, and how portfolios are composed.

Topic 3: Manager performance, including benchmark, expected alpha, and portfolio holdings.

Topic 4: Competitive position in the investment management industry, including comparative analysis of firm performance against leading competitive firms, decomposed into alpha and beta.

Topic 5: Fees, including performance-based components, with fee caps and high-water marks, if any.

Corbin specifies, "I want to make sure that any manager we consider has a strong performance history. Even though we all know that past performance is no guarantee of future results, statistics show that the managers with the best recent performance are most likely to outperform going forward." She also adds, "We should only hire managers who charge fees on an ad-valorem basis. I prefer to pay for performance and not merely for the value of assets under management."

Corbin asks Berg about implementing an alpha and beta separation in the portfolio. Corbin says, "I want to have exposure to large-cap U.S. equities, like the S&P 500, but I am unconvinced that a manager will be able to add alpha to such an efficient market. Instead, I'd prefer to have the beta of the S&P 500 through a passive index and pick up alpha by hiring a manager who specializes in long-short strategies in a less efficient sector of the market, such as micro-cap equities."

Berg argues against such an approach, pointing out, "The risks in an alpha and beta separation approach are less clearly defined than the risks in a long-only active strategy." She recommends instead that Corbin consider equitizing a long-short portfolio.

1.   Is Berg correct in her description of manager questionnaires and of a top-down research approach?
     A.   Berg is correct regarding both statements.
     B.   Berg is incorrect regarding both statements.
     C.   Berg is incorrect regarding only one of the statements.

2.   Which of the following statements about equitizing a long-short portfolio is *least accurate*?
     A.   The benchmark for the equitized strategy should be the index underlying the futures contract or ETF.
     B.   It can be accomplished by taking a long position in an equity futures contract with a notional principal equal to the cash from the short sales.
     C.   The investor's total return equals the net profit or loss from the long/short position plus the profit or loss from the futures contract, all divided by the equity the investor put up for the transaction.

3.   Are Corbin and Berg correct in their descriptions of an alpha and beta separation approach?
     A.   Only one is correct.
     B.   Both Berg and Corbin are correct.
     C.   Both Berg and Corbin are incorrect.

4.   Is Corbin correct in her descriptions of manager fees and the likelihood that managers who performed best recently will perform best going forward?
     A.   Corbin is correct regarding both statements.
     B.   Corbin is incorrect regarding both statements.
     C.   Corbin is incorrect regarding only one of the statements.

5.   Which of the following statements about manager fee schedules is *least accurate*?
     A.   The principal purpose of a fee cap is to prevent managers from taking unnecessary risk in order to enhance fees.
     B.   The principal disadvantage of ad-valorem fees is that they do not effectively align the interests of managers and investors.
     C.   A principal advantage of performance-based fees is that they help managers retain staff because they reward good performance.

6.   Of the topics in Berg's manager questionnaire, the topic that is *least likely* to be found in a typical manager questionnaire is:
     A.   Topic 4, competitive position.
     B.   Topic 2, investment philosophy.
     C.   Topic 1, staff and organizational structure.

SELF-TEST ANSWERS: EQUITY PORTFOLIO MANAGEMENT

1. **B** Berg is incorrect on both counts. A conflict between quantitative and qualitative data is worrisome and would lead to a need for more investigation or the exclusion of that manager from consideration. Regarding top-down versus bottom-up approaches, Berg is performing the top-down macroeconomic analysis and then relying on managers to add value with individual security selection. She is using the managers for bottom-up security selection.

2. **C** The first two are true. The portfolio results are typically compared to the market in which the investor's capital is invested. The short sale proceeds could be invested in a long position in equity futures. This is unusual, as the only potential alphas would be from shorting overvalued securities. Usually individual undervalued securities would be purchased to earn alpha on the long positions as well. But C is possible and not inconsistent with equitizing long/short. The last statement is partially false. It is true the profits and losses on the individual securities and futures contract are aggregated. But if contracts are used to create the equity market exposure, the investor's capital is invested in cash equivalents to fully collateralize the contract position. Thus, the risk-free rate is also earned.

3. **A** Berg is incorrect because the risks are more clearly defined in an alpha and beta separation approach than in a long-only strategy. Corbin is correct that an alpha and beta separation strategy could be implemented by taking a long passive position in an index such as the S&P 500 for beta and picking up alpha in a long-short active strategy in a less efficient market.

4. **B** Corbin is incorrect on both points. A contrarian strategy (e.g., investing in recent losers) often works as well with managers as it does with stocks. Ad-valorem fees are also referred to as asset under management (AUM) fees and depend on asset value managed, not manager performance.

5. **C** A principal disadvantage of performance-based fees is that the increased volatility of a manager's compensation can create problems with retaining staff. The other statements are accurate.

6. **A** Topic 4, competitive position, is not typically included in a manager questionnaire. The section not listed in Berg's questionnaire that would usually be listed is resources and research.

©2017 Kaplan, Inc.

The following is a review of the Alternative Investments Portfolio Management principles designed to address the learning outcome statements set forth by CFA Institute. Cross-Reference to CFA Institute Assigned Reading #26.

ALTERNATIVE INVESTMENTS PORTFOLIO MANAGEMENT[1]

EXAM FOCUS

There is an immense amount of supporting detail for a simple topic that is usually about 5% of the exam. Focus on the common characteristics of alternative investments and their resulting role in the portfolio. Then, know the main issues associated with each type of alternative investment. Throughout this reading, you will see data tables representing historical performance in specific time periods. Consider this raw data. Any one time period may well be distorted by random events in that period. The data tables generally support the final conclusions of the reading, but not always. Do not study the data tables. We recommend you read this section of the SchweserNotes on alternative investments and then watch the OnDemand videos to solidify the main points for each alternative investment type. The Schweser Weekly Class Workbook will also focus on the issues to know by alternative investment type.

ALTERNATIVE INVESTMENT FEATURES

LOS 26.a: Describe common features of alternative investments and their markets and how alternative investments may be grouped by the role they typically play in a portfolio.

CFA® Program Curriculum, Volume 5, page 7

Alternative investments offer diversification benefits and the potential for active management. There are six basic groups. Traditional alternative investments include *real estate, private equity,* and *commodities*. The more modern alternative investments include *hedge funds, managed futures*, and *distressed securities*.

Alternative investments can also be grouped by their role in portfolio management:

1. Real estate and long-only commodities offer exposure to risk factors and return that stocks and bonds cannot provide.

2. Hedge funds and managed futures offer exposure to special investment strategies and are heavily dependent on manager skill.

3. Private equity and distressed securities are seen as a combination of 1 and 2.

---

1. The terminology used throughout this topic review is industry convention as presented in Reading 26 of the 2018 Level III CFA exam curriculum. Empirical results are referenced in that reading as well.

Alternative investments can be highly unique and there are differences of opinion on how to group them. But they do share some common features:

1. *Low liquidity.* Their general lack of liquidity requires careful attention to determine if they are suitable for a given investor. The alternative investment should also be associated with a liquidity premium and higher return.

2. *Diversification.* They generally have low correlation with and offer significant diversification to traditional stock and bond portfolios.

3. *Due diligence costs.* Costs associated with researching and monitoring alternative investments can be high. Specialized expertise and specific business skills are often required. These markets frequently lack transparency, making information difficult to obtain.

4. *Difficult performance evaluation.* The lack of transparency and unique features of many strategies make it difficult to identify appropriate valuation benchmarks.

DUE DILIGENCE CHECKPOINTS

LOS 26.b: Explain and justify the major due diligence checkpoints involved in selecting active managers of alternative investments.

CFA® Program Curriculum, Volume 5, page 10

The lack of transparency and unique strategies of many alternative investment managers makes due diligence in manager selection crucial:

1. *Assess the market opportunity offered.* Are there exploitable inefficiencies in the market for the type of investments in which the manager specializes? Past returns do not justify selecting a manager unless there are understandable opportunities available for the manager to exploit. (This one would have stopped anyone from investing with Bernie Madoff.)

2. *Assess the investment process.* What is the manager's competitive edge over others in that market? How does the manager's process identify potential opportunities?

3. *Assess the organization.* Is it stable and well run? What has been the staff turnover?

4. *Assess the people.* Meet with them and assess their character, both integrity and competence.

5. *Assess the terms and structure of the investment.* What is the fee structure? How does it align the interest of the manager with the investors? What is the lock-out period? Many funds do not allow withdrawals for an initial period. What is the exit strategy for redeeming the funds invested?

6. *Assess the service providers.* Investigate the outside firms that support the manager's business (e.g., lawyers, brokers, ancillary staff).

©2017 Kaplan, Inc.

7. *Review documents.* Review the prospectus or private-placement memorandum, the audits of the manager's reports, and other available documents. Seek legal and other expert advice where needed.

8. *Write-up.* Document the above review process.

Issues for Private Wealth Clients

LOS 26.c: Explain distinctive issues that alternative investments raise for investment advisers of private wealth clients.

CFA® Program Curriculum, Volume 5, page 11

Institutional investors are presumed to be more knowledgeable and dispassionate investors. Individuals can be less knowledgeable, more emotional, and have real issues that must be considered to determine suitability.

1. *Taxes.* Most individuals must pay taxes. Many alternative investments are structured as limited partnerships which require specialized tax expertise.

2. *Suitability.* Many alternative investments require that funds stay invested for a minimum time period. Is this compatible with the investor's time horizon and liquidity needs? What happens if the investor's situation changes? Individuals may have emotional feelings that draw them towards or repel them from some investments.

3. *Communication.* Discussing complex strategies with the client is not easy. When a client is excited about a unique opportunity, how do you make sure they really do understand a ten-year lock-out means they cannot get the money back for ten years? How do you explain the diversification benefit of a very complex strategy to someone with no investment training?

4. *Decision risk.* This could be defined as the risk of emotionally abandoning a strategy right at the point of maximum loss. Carefully communicating the expected ups and downs of a strategy and being prepared for the emotional response to the downside is hard. Some strategies offer frequent small returns but the occasional large loss. They maximize the chance of an emotional investor making the wrong decision to cash out after a loss. Other strategies offer wild swings between large gains and losses with an attractive long term average return.

5. *Concentrated positions.* Wealthy individuals' portfolios frequently contain large positions in closely held companies or private residences. Such ownership should be considered as a preexisting allocation before deciding to add additional private equity or real estate exposure. These existing positions may also have large unrealized taxable gains which add complexity to any rebalancing decision.

One approach to incorporating alternative investments into a traditional portfolio is *core-satellite*. The traditional core of the portfolio would remain as stocks and bonds to provide market exposure and return. However, it is difficult to add value in such efficient markets. More informationally inefficient alternative investments would be added to provide excess return (alpha) as the satellite.

ALTERNATIVE INVESTMENT CLASSES

LOS 26.d: Distinguish among types of alternative investments.

CFA® Program Curriculum, Volume 5, page 13

Real Estate

One way to classify real estate investment is between *direct* and *indirect*. *Direct* real estate investment includes ownership of residences, commercial real estate, or agricultural land. The ownership involves direct management of the assets. *Indirect* investment in real estate generally means there is a well-defined middle group that manages the properties. Indirect real estate investments include:

- Companies that develop and manage real estate.
- Real estate investment trusts (REITs), which are publicly traded equity shares in a portfolio of real estate. Equity REITS own and operate properties while mortgage REITS hold mortgages on real estate. REITS can be purchased in small sizes and are liquid.
- Commingled real estate funds (CREFs), which are pooled investments in real estate that are professionally managed and privately held. They can be open-end and allow in new investors or closed-end and not allow in new investors after an initial offering period. They are restricted to wealthy investors and institutions.
- Separately managed accounts for wealthy investors are usually offered by the same managers who manage CREFs.
- **Infrastructure funds** specialize in purchasing public infrastructure assets (e.g., airports, toll roads) from cities, states, and municipalities. Because infrastructure assets typically provide a public service, they tend to produce relatively stable long-term returns. They tend to be regulated by local governments which adds to the predictability of cash flows. Their low correlation with equity markets means infrastructure assets provide diversification, and their long-term nature provides a good match for institutions with long-term liabilities (e.g., pension funds). Their relatively low risk, however, means that infrastructure returns are low.

The advantages of real estate investment typically include low correlation with stocks and bonds (providing a portfolio diversification benefit), low volatility of return, and often an inflation hedge. Real estate may also offer tax advantages and the potential to leverage return.

Disadvantages include high information and transaction costs, political risk related to the potential for tax law changes, high operating expenses, and the inability to subdivide direct investments. Real estate as an asset class and each individual real estate asset can have a large idiosyncratic risk component.

Private Equity

Private equity investment is an ownership interest in a non-publically-traded private company. Legal restrictions generally limit ownership to high-net-worth individuals or institutions. Often, the investing is done through pooling funds with other investors

©2017 Kaplan, Inc.

in a **private equity fund**. There are numerous subcategories of private equity. The two most important are **venture capital**, which provides funding to start or grow a private company, and **buyout funds**, which provide funds to buy existing public companies from their shareholders and then take the company private.

Two important segments of buyout funds are *middle-market buyout funds* and *mega-cap buyout funds*. Middle-market buyout funds concentrate on divisions spun off from larger, publicly traded corporations and private companies that, due to their relatively small size, cannot efficiently obtain capital. Mega-cap buyout funds concentrate on taking publicly traded firms private.

Buyout funds add value through some combination of: 1) restructuring company operations and management, 2) buying companies for less than intrinsic value, and 3) creating value by adding leverage or restructuring existing debt of the company. The exit strategies include selling the companies through private placements or IPOs or through *dividend recapitalizations*. In a dividend recapitalization, the company (under direction of the buyout fund) issues substantial debt and pays a large special dividend to the buyout fund and other equity investors. The debt effectively replaces some or most of the equity of the company, while allowing the investors to recoup some or all of their original investment. *Recapitalization* increases the company's leverage but does not change the owner. The buyout fund retains control but extracts cash from the company.

Private equity is a highly diverse class that typically involves high risk with a significant number of investments that fail. The venture capitalist is often expected to bring not only funding but business expertise to operate the company. The entrepreneurs who start the company often lack the capital and management skills to grow the company. The company may employ agents to solicit private equity investors through a private placement memorandum which describes the business plan, risk, and many other details of the investment.

Commodities

Commodity investments can include *direct* purchase of the physical commodity (e.g., agricultural products, crude oil, metals) or the purchase of derivatives (e.g., futures) on those assets. *Indirect* investment in commodities can include investment in companies whose principal business is associated with a commodity (e.g., investing in a metal via ownership of shares in a mining company). Direct investment through derivatives is more common as indirect investment has not tracked well with commodity price changes and direct investment by buying the commodities creates issues to consider such as storage costs.

Investments in both commodity futures and publicly traded commodity companies are fairly liquid, especially when compared to many other alternative investments. Investments in commodities have common risk features such as *low correlation with stocks and bonds* and *business-cycle sensitivity*, and most have a *positive correlation with inflation*. These risk characteristics are the reasons commodities provide good diversification to an investor's portfolio.

Hedge Funds

Hedge funds are a diverse group and the terminology used to describe them is flexible. Initially they were private pools of money that were both long and short the market. Hence, they were not exposed to market risk. Many hedge funds still target an absolute level of return that is not dependent on market returns. Hedge funds are generally structured to avoid regulation which also allows them to charge substantial incentive fees. Each fund is designed to exploit a perceived market opportunity, often taking both long and short positions on a leveraged basis. Many hedge funds describe themselves as exploiting arbitrage opportunities. In the case of hedge funds the term "arbitrage" is used very loosely to mean lower-risk and not to mean risk-free.

Hedge fund classifications include: *equity market neutral, convertible arbitrage, fixed-income arbitrage, distressed securities, merger arbitrage, hedged equity, global macro, emerging markets*, and *fund-of-funds (FOF)*.

Managed Futures

Managed futures funds are sometimes classified as hedge funds. Others classify them as a separate alternative investment class. In the United States, they generally use the same limited partnership legal structure and base fee plus performance fee compensation structure as hedge funds. A 2% base fee plus a 20% share of the profits is a common fee structure. Like hedge funds, they are often considered to be skill based and not an asset class, per se; they depend on the skill of the manager to find and exploit opportunities and as such have no inherent return and risk characteristics of their own.

The primary feature that distinguishes managed futures from hedge funds is the difference in the assets they hold. For example, managed futures funds tend to trade only in derivatives markets, while hedge funds often trade in spot and futures markets. Also, managed futures funds generally take positions based on indices, while hedge funds tend to focus more on individual asset price anomalies. In other words, hedge funds tend to have more of a micro focus, while managed futures tend to have a macro focus. In some jurisdictions they are more regulated than hedge funds.

Investment in managed futures can be done through: *private commodity pools, managed futures programs as separately managed accounts* (called CTA managed accounts), and *publicly traded commodity futures funds* that are available to small investors. *Liquidity* will be lower for private funds than for publicly traded commodity futures funds.

Trading strategies and *classifications* used include:

- *Systematic trading strategies* follow rules. *Trend following rules* are common and may focus on short-, medium-, or long-term trends. *Contrarian strategies* exist but are less common.
- *Discretionary trading strategies* depend on the judgment of the manager and could be based on economic or other criteria.
- Managed futures may invest in all *financial* markets, *currency* markets only, or a *diversified* mix of derivatives and underlying commodities.

©2017 Kaplan, Inc.

The *risk characteristics* of managed futures will vary, as they do for hedge funds. The standard deviation of managed futures is generally less than that of equities but greater than that of bonds. The correlation between managed futures and equities is low and often negative. With bonds, the correlation is higher but still less than 0.30.

Distressed Securities

Distressed securities are securities of companies that are in or near bankruptcy. They are another type of alternative investment where the risk and return depend upon skill-based strategies. Some analysts consider distressed securities to be part of the hedge fund class or of the private equity class.

One way to construct subgroups in distressed securities is by structure, which determines the level of liquidity. The hedge fund structure for distressed security investment is more liquid. The private equity fund structure describes funds that are less liquid because they have a fixed term and are closed-ended. The latter structure is more appropriate when the underlying securities are too illiquid to overcome the problem of determining a net asset value (NAV).

Figure 1 presents a summary of alternative investment characteristics.

Figure 1: Alternative Investment Characteristics

	Types of Investments	Risk/Return Features	Liquidity
Real estate	Residences; commercial real estate; raw land.	Large idiosyncratic risk component; provides good diversification.	Low.
Private equity	Preferred shares of stock; venture capital; buyout funds.	Start-up and middle-market private companies have more risk and lower returns than investments in established companies via buyout funds.	Low.
Buyout funds	Well-established private firms and corporate spin-offs.	Less risk than venture capital funds; good diversification.	Low.
Infrastructure funds	Public infrastructure assets.	Low risk, low return; good diversification.	Low.
Commodities	Agricultural products; crude oil; metals.	Generally low correlation with stocks/bonds. Non-agricultural have the additional benefit of positive correlation with inflation.	Fairly liquid.
Managed futures	Tend to trade only in derivatives market. Private commodity pools; publicly traded commodity futures funds.	Risk is between that of equities and bonds. Negative and low correlations with equities and low-to-moderate correlations with bonds.	Lower for private funds than for publicly traded commodity futures funds.
Distressed securities	May be part of hedge fund class or private equity class. Investments can be in debt and/or equity.	Depends on skill-based strategies. Can earn higher returns due to legal complications and the fact that some investors cannot invest in them.	Hedge fund structure more liquid; private equity structure less liquid.

©2017 Kaplan, Inc.

ALTERNATIVE INVESTMENT BENCHMARKS

LOS 26.e: Discuss the construction and interpretation of benchmarks and the problem of benchmark bias in alternative investment groups.

CFA® Program Curriculum, Volume 5, page 15

> *Professor's Note: There are two main types of RE indices (REIF and REIT). Plus, each has an "adjusted" version. You should notice that based on the previous discussion of direct versus indirect real estate, both REIF and REIT can be classified as indirect investment in RE. However, that is a trivial issue. The more important issue is that unsmoothed NCREIF provides the best data for representing the performance of direct investment in RE.*

- **National Council of Real Estate Investment Fiduciaries (NCREIF) Property Index:** *These are the performance results of commingled portfolios making direct, unleveraged investment in real estate properties. However, that means the underlying properties are not regularly traded and, therefore, the reported results are biased by the* **smoothing problem** *discussed after this professor's note.*
  - *Unsmoothed REIF is adjusted to remove the distortions of smoothing.* **Unsmoothed NCREIF is considered to provide the most accurate representation of the true investment characteristics of direct RE investing.**
- **National Association of Real Estate Investment Trusts (NAREIT) Index:** *This is an index of traded stocks of companies that invest in RE or RE-related assets.* **As such, it reflects blended characteristics of public equity and RE, not the true investment characteristics of direct RE investing.**
  - *Like most public companies, those in the NAREIT use financial leverage on their balance sheet. This further distorts the data and makes NAREIT data less reflective of the underlying RE assets.* **"Hedged" REIT** *data removes the equity-like effects of leverage but still does not provide the best reflection of underlying RE characteristics because the REITs are still publicly traded companies.*

Appropriate benchmarks for a given alternative investment manager can be difficult to establish. The following list describes the more common benchmarks available and some of the issues that arise.

- **Real estate** has the National Council of Real Estate Investment Fiduciaries (NCREIF) Property Index as its principal benchmark for *direct investments*. The NCREIF Index is a *value-weighted* index of commercially owned properties that uses samples based both on geographic location and type (e.g., apartment and industrial). The values are obtained periodically, usually by annual appraisal, so the volatility of the index is *downward biased*. The index is published quarterly.

  For *indirect* real estate investment, the primary benchmark is the National Association of Real Estate Investment Trusts (NAREIT) Index. The NAREIT Index is cap-weighted and includes all REITs traded on the NYSE or AMEX. Similar to other indices based upon current trades, the monthly NAREIT Index is "live" (i.e., its value represents current values).

The biggest problem is the infrequent trading of most real estate investments and the resulting understatement of actual volatility. Various techniques have been used to *unsmooth* or "correct" this bias. The unsmoothed data raises the standard deviation and reduces the Sharpe ratio of real estate, making real estate less attractive but still a valuable addition to stock and bond portfolios due to its low correlation. Another problem is that many real estate indices reflect leveraged investments. When leverage effects are removed, returns and Sharpe ratios are lower, but the low correlation with other asset classes still leaves real estate as an attractive addition to portfolios. Finally, in the case of REITS, the returns are more correlated with equity while other types of real estate investment are less correlated with equity, meaning REITS offer less of a diversification benefit.

- **Private equity** indices are provided by Cambridge Associates, Preqin, and LPX. Indices are constructed for the buyout and venture capital (VC) segments of the private equity markets. Because private equity values are not readily available, the value of a private equity index depends upon events like IPOs, mergers, new financing, and so on to provide this information. Thus, the indices might present dated values as *repricing* occurs infrequently. Note that private equity investors also often construct custom benchmarks.

  The primary problems are the lack of pricing data, forcing a heavy reliance on appraisal values for investments, and the resulting smoothing of returns and understatement of volatility. In addition, private equity shows a strong vintage year effect. The economic conditions of the year in which the fund was launched have a significant effect on subsequent performance for the life of the fund. As a result, comparisons are often made to other funds launched in the same year.

- **Commodity markets** have many indices for use as benchmarks. Most of them assume a futures-based strategy. For example, the Reuters/Jefferies Commodity Research Bureau (RJ/CRB) Index, the S&P Goldman Sachs Commodity Index (GSCI), and the Bloomberg Commodity Index (BCOM) represent returns associated with passive long positions in futures.

  The indices include exposures to most types of commodities and are considered *investable*. They can vary widely, however, with respect to their purpose, composition, and method of weighting the classes. Given the zero-sum nature of futures, the indices cannot use a market-cap method of weighting. Two methods of weighting are 1) basing weights on world production of the underlying commodities and 2) basing weights on the perceived relative worldwide importance of the commodity. The various indices use either arithmetic or geometric averaging to calculate component returns.

©2017 Kaplan, Inc.

- **Managed futures** have several investable benchmarks. Some common benchmarks, such as the Mount Lucas Management Index (MLMI), replicate the return to a *mechanical, trend-following strategy*. The strategies usually include utilizing both long and short positions using trading rules based upon changes in technical indicators. Other benchmarks, such as the BarclayHedge and CISDM CTA, are indices based upon *peer-group commodity trading advisors (CTAs) using equal-weighted* returns from databases of separately managed accounts. The Barclay Traders indices are benchmarks based upon the level of discretionary management and the underlying market, as well as systematic strategies.

- **Distressed securities** funds are often considered a hedge fund subgroup. Most of the index providers for hedge funds have a sub-index for distressed securities. Benchmarks in this area have the same characteristics as long-only hedge fund benchmarks.

Figure 2 presents a summary of these alternative investment benchmarks, their construction, and their associated biases. Hedge fund benchmarks are then discussed separately.

Figure 2: Alternative Investment Benchmarks

	Benchmarks	*Construction*	*Biases*
Real estate	NCREIF; NAREIT.	NCREIF is value weighted; NAREIT is cap weighted.	Measured volatility is downward biased. The values are obtained periodically (annually).
Private equity	Provided by Cambridge Associates, Preqin, and LPX.	Constructed for buyout and venture capital. Value depends upon events. Often construct custom benchmarks.	Repricing occurs infrequently which results in dated values.
Commodities	RJ/CRB, GSCI, and BCOM indices.	Assume a futures-based strategy. Most types considered investable.	Indices vary widely with respect to purpose, composition, and method of weighting.
Managed futures	MLMI; CTA Indices.	MLMI replicates the return to a trend-following strategy. CTA Indices use returns based on equal-weighted, systematic, discretionary, or market strategies.	Requires special weighting scheme.
Distressed securities	Characteristics similar to long-only hedge fund benchmarks.	Weighting either equally weighted or based upon assets under management. Selection criteria can vary.	Self-reporting; backfill or inclusion bias; popularity bias; survivorship bias.

Hedge Fund Benchmarks

Hedge fund benchmarks vary a great deal in composition and even frequency of reporting. Also, there is no consensus as to what defines hedge fund strategies and this leads to many differences in the indices, as style classifications vary from company to company. The following points summarize the ways index providers compose their respective indices.

- *Selection criteria* can vary, and methods include assets under management, the length of the track record, and the restrictions imposed on new investment.
- *Style classification* also varies as to how they classify a fund by style and whether it is included in a given index.
- *Weighting schemes* are usually either equally weighted or based upon assets under management.
- *Rebalancing rules* must be defined for equally weighted indices, and the frequency can vary from monthly to annually.
- *Investability* often depends upon frequency of reporting (e.g., daily reporting allows for investability while monthly reporting tends not to). Some indices are not explicitly investable, but independent firms modify the index to produce an investable proxy.

Some indices explicitly report the funds they include in the composition of the index, and some do not. Some indices report monthly and some report daily. Of the major index providers, only the Hedge Fund Research (HFR) provides a daily return series.

The following lists providers of *monthly indices* with a few of their general characteristics:

- *CISDM:* several indices that cover both hedge funds and managed futures (equally weighted).
- *Credit Suisse:* provides various benchmarks for different strategies and uses a weighting scheme based upon assets under management.
- *EACM Advisers:* provides the EACM100® Index, a wide range of equally weighted index of 100 funds that span many categories.
- *Hedge Fund Intelligence:* provides a wide range of equally weighted hedge fund indexes including those that invest in Europe and Asia.
- *HedgeFund.net:* provides an equally weighted index that covers more than 40 strategies.
- *HFR*: provides the HFRI equally and asset weighted composite hedge fund indexes and equally weighted sub-indexes based on managers' reporting of their hedge fund returns. FOFs are reported in a separate index.
- *Morningstar MSCI*: Indexes are classified according to five basic categories including a composite index. Within each category indexes are separated according to geographical region and asset class. Equally weighted and asset weighted indexes are available.

Hedge fund benchmark selection includes several issues:

- **Relevance of past data** may be questionable. If hedge funds are a reflection of manager skill, then past returns for indices is less relevant to future returns since hedge fund indices frequently change composition and thus managers within the index. The empirical evidence shows that funds within a particular style do have similar returns and that individual managers do not consistently beat their style group. The data also suggests volatility of past returns tends to persist even when return does not. This makes selection of the relevant comparison benchmark very important.

- **Popularity bias** can result if one of the funds in a value-weighted index increases in value and then attracts a great deal of capital. The inflow of investment to that fund will have a misleading effect on the index. Research has shown that indices can easily suffer from a popularity bias of a particular style, which is caused by inflows and not the actual return on investment. Even without the popularity bias, a dramatic increase in one style can bias an index. The problem with equally weighted indices is that they are not rebalanced often and effectively. This lowers their investability.

- **Survivorship bias** is a big problem for hedge fund indices. Indices may drop funds with poor track records or that fail, causing an upward bias in reported values. Studies have shown that the bias can be as high as 1.5–3% per year. The degree of survivorship bias varies among the hedge fund strategies. It is lower for event-driven strategies and higher for hedged equity strategies.

- **Stale price bias** varies depending on the markets used by the hedge fund. If the fund operates in markets with infrequent trading, the usual issues of appraisal or infrequent pricing and the resulting understatement of volatility can arise. The evidence suggests this is not a large problem.

- **Backfill or inclusion bias** is a similar problem but arises from filling in missing past data. It tends to be directionally biased, as only managers who benefit from the missing data have an incentive to supply the data. It seems to be an issue with some indices.

RETURN ENHANCEMENT AND DIVERSIFICATION

LOS 26.f: Evaluate the return enhancement and/or risk diversification effects of adding an alternative investment to a reference portfolio (for example, a portfolio invested solely in common equity and bonds).

CFA® Program Curriculum, Volume 5, page 18

Real Estate

Real estate is an asset class as well as an alternative investment. High risk-adjusted performance is possible because of the low liquidity, large lot sizes, immobility, high transactions costs, and low information transparency that usually means the seller knows more than the buyer.

Real estate typically reacts to macroeconomic changes differently than other asset classes, and each investment has a large idiosyncratic (unsystematic) risk component. Because of both of these characteristics, real estate has provided diversification. Using data for the period 1996–2015, Figure 3 compares the returns of the indicated portfolios based on benchmarks for the indicated asset classes.

Figure 3: Portfolio Returns From 1996–2015

Portfolios[1]	A	B	C	D
Annual return	7.26%	7.70%	7.26%	7.69%
Annual standard deviation	7.83%	8.36%	8.11%	8.62%
Average return-to-volatility ratio[2]	0.93	0.92	0.89	0.89

1. Portfolio A = 50/50 stocks and bonds, portfolio B = 10% REITs + 90% portfolio A, portfolio C = 75% stocks and bonds + 25% alternative investments (hedge funds, private equity, commodities, managed futures), portfolio D = 10% REITs + 90% portfolio C.
2. Risk-adjusted performance ratio of the mean return for the period divided by the standard deviation of return.

Some conclusions from Figure 3 and past data include:

- Comparing portfolios A and B: REITs provided no diversification benefits relative to a stock and bond portfolio due to the high volatility of REITs for the time period studied. (Later in the reading, other alternative investments, e.g., hedge funds, will be shown to have provided diversification benefits to a stock and bond portfolio.)
- Comparing portfolios C and D: Real estate may become a redundant asset in the presence of other alternative investments.

Private Equity

Private equity is less of a diversifier and more a long-term return enhancer. Private equity investments (both venture capital and buyout funds) are usually illiquid, require a long-term commitment, and have a high level of risk with the potential for complete loss. In addition, there is often a minority discount associated with the investment. Because of these issues, investors require a high expected internal rate of return (IRR). Venture capital investments have lower transparency than buyout funds, which can actually add to the potential for large profits.

The difference in transparency between venture capital funds and buyout funds is caused by the different natures of the investments. Venture capital, for example, is provided to new, non-public companies in need of capital for growth. By definition, the managers of firms receiving the funds have considerably more information on the true value of the firm than the investing public. This adds to the risk faced by venture capital funds but, at the same time, increases the possible return to venture capitalists, who make it a point to learn as much about the firm as possible before investing. Buyout funds, on the other hand, usually provide capital to managements and others to purchase the equity of publicly traded firms.

©2017 Kaplan, Inc.

Private equity returns typically move with stock market returns. Computed correlations are often positive and low, but some attribute the low correlation to the infrequently updated (i.e., "stale") prices of the private equity. Each investment has a large idiosyncratic risk component, however, which can provide moderate diversification.

Because the primary benefit from private equity is return enhancement, Figure 4 gives the most important information for comparison. From the figure, we see that in the most recent years, venture capital funds had a lower return than Growth Equity, NASDAQ, and S&P 500. Over the longer 10- and 20-year periods however, private equity had higher returns.

Professor's Note: In our opening comments for this reading, we included a warning not to "overstudy" the data tables. The data tables represent historical performance in specific time periods. Consider this raw data. Any one time period may well be distorted by random events in that period. The data tables generally support the final conclusions of the reading, but not always. Do not study the data tables. We recommend you read this section of the SchweserNotes on alternative investments and then watch the OnDemand videos to solidify the main points for each alternative investment type. The Schweser Weekly Class Workbook will also focus on the issues to know by alternative investment type.

Figure 4: Returns to Private Equity and Equity Markets

Period	NASDAQ	S&P 500	Growth Equity	VC Multi-Stage funds[1]
2011–2014	23.0	23.0	17.9	15.0
2009–2014	16.2	15.7	17.2	13.3
2004–2014	9.0	8.1	14.0	10.0
1994–2014	9.3	9.6	n/a	13.4

1. VC funds that comprise both early and late stage investments

Commodities

Commodities chiefly offer *diversification* to a portfolio of stocks and bonds. Correlations of commodity indices with stocks have been moderately positive and with bonds have been low and even slightly negative. Most commodity indices have a positive correlation with inflation. That is a benefit to the investor because they provide a hedge against unexpected inflation, while bonds are hurt by inflation.

The returns on commodities have generally been lower than stocks and bonds over the period 1996–2015, both on an absolute and risk-adjusted basis. The poor performance of the energy subgroup had a negative impact on the S&P GSCI over the time period shown due to the heavy weighting of energy related futures in the index. Figure 5 gives the statistics for 1996–2015.

Figure 5: Index Returns From 1996–2015

Stock, Bond, and Commodity Index Performance	S&P 500	Bloomberg Barclays US Aggregate[1]	S&P GSCI TR[2]
Annual return	8.51%	5.37%	−1.01%
Annual standard deviation	15.31%	3.47%	22.79%
Average return-to-volatility ratio[3]	0.56	1.55	−0.04
Correlation with commodity index	0.25	−0.01	1.0

1. Market capitalized weighted intermediate term index of U.S.-traded investment grade bonds which includes: Treasuries, government agency, MBS, corporate bonds, and some foreign.
2. S&P Goldman Sachs Commodity Index total return (long commodity futures with collateral invested at the risk free rate).
3. Risk-adjusted performance ratio of the mean return for the period divided by the standard deviation of return.

Figure 6 shows the role commodities played in a portfolio context over the 1996–2015 time periods.

Figure 6: Index Returns From 1996–2015

Portfolios[1]	A	B	C	D
Annual return	7.26%	6.65%	7.92%	7.22%
Annual standard deviation	7.83%	7.91%	8.38%	8.50%
Average return-to-volatility ratio[2]	0.93	0.84	0.94	0.85

1. Portfolio A = 50% S&P 500 and 50% Bloomberg Barclays U.S. Aggregate Bond Index, portfolio B = 10% commodity index + 90% portfolio A, portfolio C = 25% alternative investments (hedge funds, private equity, CTA, real estate) + 75% portfolio A, portfolio D = 10% commodity index + 90% portfolio C.
2. Risk-adjusted performance ratio of the mean return for the period divided by the standard deviation of return.

The results show that over the period studied when commodities were added to a portfolio (portfolios B and D), they underperformed U.S. equity and bond markets both on an absolute and risk adjusted basis. Due to the low correlation of the returns of the S&P GSCI with the S&P 500 (0.25) and negative correlation with the Bloomberg Barclays U.S. Government Bond Index (−0.10), we would expect to see diversification benefits with improving average return-to-volatility ratios but the results do not support those conclusions.

Study Session 13

Professor's Note: The overall conclusion in the CFA text is that commodities offer diversification benefits due to their low correlation with stocks and slightly negative correlation and bonds even though the results of the time period studied suggests otherwise.

Hedge Funds

In aggregate, hedge funds generated higher absolute returns compared to other asset classes with the exception of real estate over the period 1996–2015. The CISM Equal Weighted Hedge Fund Index return, standard deviation, and average return-to-risk ratio were 9.15%, 7.36%, and 1.24, respectively. Hedge funds had the highest average return-to-volatility ratio compared to other asset classes with the exception of bonds.

A 45/45/10 stock/bond/hedge fund portfolio had a higher return and lower standard deviation than the 50/50 stock/bond portfolio over the 2001–2015 period.

Hedge funds vary widely, however, so the benefits of investing in one of any given style will differ. Figure 7 provides a representative list of the best and worst performing funds with their correlations with the S&P 500 and the Bloomberg Barclays US Aggregate Bond Index. The last two rows in Figure 7 indicate how a lower correlation of each index's return with stocks and bonds added diversification over the period 1996–2015.

Figure 7: Hedge Fund (HF) Strategy and Traditional Assets Index Performance From 1996–2015

Measure (Annualized)	Global Macro HF	Merger Arbitrage HF	Equity Long/Short HF	Equal Weighted HF	S&P 500	Bloomberg Barclays U.S. Aggregate Bonds
Return	6.29%	7.12%	8.88%	9.15%	8.51%	5.37%
Standard deviation	3.93%	3.26%	7.47%	7.36%	15.31%	3.47%
Average return-to-volatility ratio	1.60	2.19	1.19	1.24	0.56	1.55
Correlation with S&P 500	0.39	0.58	0.75	0.74	1.0	−0.01
Correlation with bonds	0.22	0.02	-0.06	0.00	−0.01	1.0

Managed Futures

Managed futures are usually considered a category of hedge funds and are usually compared to stocks and bonds, but their record has been similar to that of hedge funds. Over the period 1996–2015, the equal-weighted index of separately managed accounts (CISDM CTA EW) had a return, standard deviation, and average return-to-volatility ratio equal to 7.2%, 8.5%, and 0.85, respectively, which is about the same as stocks but with a better average return-to-volatility ratio. They also had a higher return than bonds but with a lower average return-to-volatility ratio.

During the major equity market collapse of 2008 the CISDM CTA EW Index far outperformed all other asset classes studied including stocks and bonds. During that time period the CISDM CTA EW index return was 21.8% with a standard deviation of 10.6% compared to the S&P 500 return of –37.0% and standard deviation of 21.0% while the Bloomberg Barclays US Aggregate Bond Index return was 5.2% with a standard deviation of 6.1%.

For the 1996–2015 period, a portfolio comprising 10% CISM CTA EW Index and equal weights S&P 500 and Bloomberg Barclays US Aggregate Bond Index, outperformed a similar portfolio comprised of equal weights S&P 500 and bond index on an absolute and risk adjusted basis. Likewise, when adding 10% CISM CTA EW Index to a portfolio constructed of equal weights stocks and bonds plus 25% alternative investments (hedge funds, commodities, private equity, and real estate), this outperformed a similar portfolio constructed of stocks, bonds, and alternative investments.

Note that actively managed separate accounts are those where the managers seek to take advantage of mispricing opportunities. There is some evidence that short-term momentum and other strategies can produce excess returns. Managed futures seem to provide unique returns and diversification benefits. This is made evident from the zero correlation (0.00) between the index of separately managed accounts and a 50/50 stock/bond fund.

Distressed Securities

Distressed security returns have had a relatively high average return but a large negative skew, so the comparisons using averages and Sharpe ratios or average return-to-volatility ratios can be misleading. Based on comparisons of the average return and average return-to-volatility ratio, the HFRX Distressed/Restructuring Index for the 1995–2015 period underperformed both stocks and bonds, both on an absolute and on a risk-adjusted basis. The returns are often event-driven, so they are uncorrelated with the overall stock market.

©2017 Kaplan, Inc.

REAL ESTATE EQUITY INVESTING

LOS 26.g: Describe advantages and disadvantages of direct equity investments in real estate.

CFA® Program Curriculum, Volume 5, page 20

Direct equity real estate investing has the following advantages and disadvantages.

Advantages:

- Many expenses are tax deductible.
- Ability to use more leverage than most other investments.
- Direct control of the properties.
- Ability to diversify geographically.

Disadvantages:

- Lack of divisibility means a single investment may be a large part of the investor's portfolio.
- High information costs.
- High commissions.
- High operating and maintenance costs plus hands-on management requirements.
- Special geographical risks, such as neighborhood deterioration.
- Political risks, such as changing tax codes.

VENTURE CAPITAL INVESTING

LOS 26.h: Discuss the major issuers and suppliers of venture capital, the stages through which private companies pass (seed stage through exit), the characteristic sources of financing at each stage, and the purpose of such financing.

CFA® Program Curriculum, Volume 5, page 27

In a typical sequence, the venture capitalist brings capital to start a company based on an attractive business plan and/or to fund and grow an existing private company. The typical exit plan involves an IPO (initial public offering) to sell stock to the public and pay off the early private investors. This can take years to execute.

There is an extensive vocabulary to describe venture capital. The issuers (companies seeking capital) of venture capital include *formative-stage companies* that are either new or young and *expansion-stage companies* that need funds to expand their revenues or prepare for an IPO.

The investors (suppliers) include:

- **Venture capitalists** are specialists who identify pools of capital available for investing in and find the promising private companies to invest in. They may pool investor's capital into **venture capital funds or trusts**.

- **Corporate venturing** refers to large companies that invest in venture capital opportunities in their own area of business expertise.
- *Angel investors* are considered to be knowledgeable, accredited individuals who are often the first outsiders (non-founders or relatives) who invest in the company.

The **stages** through which private companies pass are early stage, expansion stage, and exit stage. The *early stage* includes *seed money* often put up by the entrepreneur or other family members to begin prototype work, then *start-up funds* to begin product development and marketing, and *first-stage funding* to begin manufacturing and sales.

The *expansion stage* can include very young companies with an established product looking to expand sales, more established companies seeking to fund growth, or even companies soon to launch an IPO. *Second-stage* financing supports further expansion of production and sales, while *third-stage* financing can support additional major expansion. *Mezzanine or bridge financing* is used to prepare for an IPO and may include both debt and equity capital.

The *exit stage* could involve an IPO, merger with another company, or acquisition by another company (which might be a venture capital fund specializing in such activity).

LOS 26.i: Compare venture capital funds and buyout funds.

CFA® Program Curriculum, Volume 5, page 40

In contrast to venture capital funds, **buyout funds** usually have:

- A higher level of leverage.
- Earlier and steadier cash flows.
- Less error in the measurement of returns as more of the return is from cash flow return.
- Less frequent losses.
- Less upside potential.

These differences are the natural consequence of buyout funds purchasing entities in later stages of development or established companies and corporate spin-offs, where the risks are lower.

CONVERTIBLE PREFERRED STOCK

LOS 26.j: Discuss the use of convertible preferred stock in direct venture capital investment.

CFA® Program Curriculum, Volume 5, page 34

Direct investors in private equity often use convertible preferred stock (CPS) rather than common stock. The CPS has first claim on cash flow ahead of the founder, who typically retains the common stock. CPS can be structured to receive a minimum return before the common shareholders are paid. It also has prior claim in bankruptcy if the company fails. The conversion to common feature provides upside participation.

©2017 Kaplan, Inc.

There are typically subsequent financing rounds required, and these subsequent rounds may have priority over receiving cash flows before earlier financing rounds. Priority induces the later investors to provide funds. With all other features the same, these later financing rounds with priority will be more valuable than earlier rounds.

Private Equity Investing

LOS 26.k: Explain the typical structure of a private equity fund, including the compensation to the fund's sponsor (general partner) and typical timelines.

CFA® Program Curriculum, Volume 5, page 34

Private equity funds usually take the form of **limited partnerships** or **limited liability companies** (LLCs). These legal structures limit the loss to investors to the initial investment and avoid corporate double taxation. For limited partnerships, the sponsor is called the *general partner*; for LLCs, the sponsor is called the *managing director*. The sponsor constructs and manages the fund and selects and advises the investments.

The **time line** starts with the sponsor getting commitments from investors at the beginning of the fund and then giving "capital calls" over the first five years (typically). This is referred to as the *commitment period*. The expected life of these funds is seven to ten years, and there is often an option to extend the life up to five more years.

The sponsor can receive *compensation* in several ways. First, the sponsor has capital invested that earns a return. This is usually required, as it helps keep the sponsor's interests in line with those of the limited partners. As a manager, the sponsor typically gets a *management fee* and *incentive fee*.

The **management fee** is usually 1.5% to 2.5% and is based upon the *committed funds*, not just funds already invested. The percent may decline over time based upon the assumption that the manager's work declines over time.

The **incentive fee** is also called the *carried interest*. It is the share of the profits, usually around 20%, that is paid to the manager after the fund has returned the outside investors' capital—often after a minimum required return or hurdle rate has been paid on the cash from the outside investors. In some cases, the manager can receive early distributions based on expectations, but a *claw-back* provision may be in place that requires the manager to give back money if the expected profits are not realized.

PRIVATE EQUITY INVESTMENT STRATEGY

LOS 26.l: Discuss issues that must be addressed in formulating a private equity investment strategy.

CFA® Program Curriculum, Volume 5, page 42

Any strategy for private equity investment must address the following issues:

- *Low liquidity:* the portfolio allocation to this class should typically be 5% or less with a plan to keep the money invested for seven to ten years.
- *Diversification through a number of positions:* direct private equity is generally for very large portfolios. The total portfolio allocation may be only 5%, but each private equity position is large and multiple positions are needed for diversification. Smaller portfolios for which private equity is otherwise suitable can consider private equity funds.
- *Diversification strategy:* knowing the unique aspects of a proposed private equity investment as they relate to the overall portfolio.
- *Plans for meeting capital calls:* committed funds are called as needed, and the investor needs to be prepared to meet the calls.

COMMODITY INVESTING

LOS 26.m: Compare indirect and direct commodity investment.

CFA® Program Curriculum, Volume 5, page 45

Direct commodity investment entails either purchasing the actual commodities or gaining exposure via derivatives. **Indirect commodity investment** is the purchase of indirect claims (e.g., shares in a corporation) that deal in the commodity.

Direct investment gives more exposure, but cash investment in commodities can incur carrying costs. Indirect investment may be more convenient, but it may provide very little exposure to the commodity, especially if the company is hedging the risk itself.

The increase in the number of investable indices in commodities and their associated futures is indicative of the advantages of investing via derivatives. These indices also make investing in commodities available to smaller investors.

©2017 Kaplan, Inc.

COMMODITIES AND INFLATION

LOS 26.n: Describe the principal roles suggested for commodities in a portfolio and explain why some commodity classes may provide a better hedge against inflation than others.

CFA® Program Curriculum, Volume 5, page 53

Commodities generally provide a diversification benefit to traditional portfolios. Some commodities also provide specific diversification and protection against unexpected increases in inflation. Two factors affect whether a commodity is a good hedge against unexpected inflation: *storability* and demand relative to *economic activity*.

Whether a commodity is *storable* is a primary determinant in its value providing a hedge against unexpected inflation. For example, the values of storable commodities such as industrial metals (e.g., zinc, aluminum, copper) are positively related to unexpected changes in inflation. That is, they tend to increase (decrease) in value with unexpected increases (decreases) in inflation. They have provided good diversification against unexpected inflation.

Another factor to consider with respect to inflation hedging capability is whether the commodity's demand is linked to economic activity. Those that enjoy a more or less constant demand regardless of the level of economic activity, for example, seem to provide little hedge against unexpected changes in inflation. Those commodities that are most affected by the level of economic activity tend to be better hedges.

HEDGE FUND CLASSIFICATIONS

LOS 26.o: Identify and explain the style classification of a hedge fund, given a description of its investment strategy.

CFA® Program Curriculum, Volume 5, page 57

Hedge funds are classified in various ways by different sources. Because hedge funds are a "style-based" asset class, strategies can determine the subgroups. Within the strategies, there can be even more precise subgroups such as long/short and long-only strategies. The following is a list of nine of the more familiar hedge fund strategies.

1. *Convertible arbitrage* seeks to exploit mispricings or anomalies in the price of convertible securities such as convertible bonds, convertible preferred stock, or warrants. Both long and short positions are taken to hedge the risks. A common example is to buy undervalued convertible bonds and short the stock. The investor owns the convertible which includes a "call option" on the stock and shorts the stock which should leave the position hedged against changes in the stock price. Interest is earned from the bond coupons and from investing the proceeds of the short-sale. The strategy would benefit if stock volatility increases and the convertible rises in value. (The value of the embedded call option in the convertible should rise with increasing volatility.) If the yield curve is upward sloping, making the yield on the

bond higher than short term borrowing rates, the strategy might also be leveraged to enhance returns.

2. *Distressed securities* are fundamentally different investments than conventional debt and equity investments. Many investors are not allowed to or do not want to deal with the legal complications for these securities. The resulting securities may be undervalued and offer superior returns. Distressed securities are generally illiquid, making it difficult or impossible to short the securities. These funds are generally long (not hedged) portfolios.

3. *Emerging markets* generally only permit long positions, and often there are no derivatives to hedge the investments.

4. *Equity market neutral* typically combines long and short positions in under-valued and over-valued securities (pairs trading) to eliminate systematic risk while capitalizing on mispricing.

5. *Hedged equity strategies* take long and short positions in under- and over-valued securities to exploit mispricings. Unlike market neutral funds, they do not seek to remove systematic risk. They might be net long, short, or hedged based on the manager's view of the markets.

6. *Fixed-income arbitrage* involves taking long and short positions in fixed-income instruments based upon expected changes in the yield curve and/or credit spreads.

7. *Global macro strategies* take positions in major financial and non-financial markets through various means (e.g., derivatives and currencies). The distinguishing feature is that they tend to focus on an entire group or area of investment instead of individual securities or classes of securities.

8. *Merger arbitrage* or *deal arbitrage* focuses on returns from mergers, spin-offs, takeovers, and so on. For example, if Company X announces it will acquire Company Y, the manager might buy shares in Y and short X.

9. *Fund-of-funds (FOF)* describes a hedge fund that invests in many hedge funds. The idea is to get diversification among hedge fund managers or styles, but there is a fee paid to the manager of the fund-of-funds, as well as to the managers of the funds in the fund-of-funds.

As a skill-based investment class, the risk and return of a hedge fund depends heavily upon the skill of the manager. We can make a distinction concerning risk, however, in that styles that are mainly long-only (e.g., distressed securities) tend to offer less potential for diversification than long/short styles.

Hedge Fund Structure

LOS 26.p: Discuss the typical structure of a hedge fund, including the fee structure, and explain the rationale for high-water mark provisions.

CFA® Program Curriculum, Volume 5, page 58

The most common **compensation structure** of a hedge fund consists of an *assets-under-management (AUM)* fee of about 1% to 2% and an *incentive fee* of 20% of profits. The definition of *profit* should be spelled out in the terms of the investment. It could be the dollar return over the initial investment, for example, or the dollar return above the initial investment increased by some hurdle rate.

High water marks (HWMs) are typically employed to avoid incentive fee double-dipping. For example, assume a fund is valued and opened for subscription on a quarterly basis. Each quarter, the increase in value over the previous quarter is determined and investors pay incentive and management fees accordingly. This is fine, as long as the fund's value is higher at each successive valuation. If the value of the fund is lower than the previous quarter, however, the manager receives only the management fee, and the previous high value of the fund (i.e., the last fund value at which incentive fees were paid) is established as a HWM. Investors are then required to pay incentive fees only if and when the value of the fund rises above the HWM. Note that HWMs are investor- and subscription-date specific. For those who subscribe while the fund value is below the previously established HWM, that HWM is not relevant. They will pay management fees each quarter, as well as incentive fees, for increases in value above the value at their subscription date.

A **lock-up period** is a common provision in hedge funds. Lock-up periods limit withdrawals by requiring a minimum investment period (e.g., one to three years) and designating exit windows. The rationale is to prevent sudden withdrawals that could force the manager to have to unwind positions.

Incentive fees are paid to encourage the manager to earn ever-higher profits. There is some controversy concerning incentive fees because the manager should have goals other than simply earning a gross return. For example, the manager may be providing limited downside risk and diversification. An incentive fee based upon returns does not reward this service.

Managers with good track records often demand higher incentive fees. The concern for investors is whether the manager with a good historical record can continue to perform well enough to truly earn the higher fees.

FUND-OF-FUNDS

LOS 26.q: Describe the purpose and characteristics of fund-of-funds hedge funds.

CFA® Program Curriculum, Volume 5, page 58

A **fund-of-funds** (FOF) is a hedge fund that consists of several, usually 10 to 30, hedge funds. The point is to achieve diversification, but the extra layer of management means an extra layer of fees. Often, an FOF offers more liquidity for the investor, but the cost is cash drag caused by the manager keeping extra cash to meet potential withdrawals by other investors. Despite the drawbacks, FOF are *good entry-level investments.*

An FOF may be a better indicator of aggregate hedge fund performance than the typical hedge fund index because it suffers from less survivorship and backfill bias. If an FOF includes a hedge fund that dissolves, it includes the effect of that failure in its return, while an index may simply drop the failed fund along with its historical performance.

An FOF can, however, suffer from style drift. This can produce problems because the investor may not know what she is getting. Over time, individual hedge fund managers may tilt their respective portfolios in different directions. Also, it is not uncommon for two FOF that claim to be of the same style to have returns with a very low correlation.

FOF returns have been more highly correlated with equity markets than those of individual hedge funds. This characteristic has important implications for their use as diversifiers in an equity portfolio.

HEDGE FUND PERFORMANCE EVALUATION

LOS 26.r: Discuss concerns involved in hedge fund performance evaluation.

CFA® Program Curriculum, Volume 5, page 62

The hedge fund industry views hedge fund performance appraisal as a major concern with many special issues and conventions to address. One special issue is that some claim that hedge funds are **absolute-return vehicles**, which means that no direct benchmark exists. Instead, the fund targets some absolute return per period. That target return is not really a benchmark because it is not investable. The question (and problem) is how to determine alpha. The problem is especially perplexing given that most performance evaluation techniques are based on long-only positions and hedge funds use various combinations of long and short positions and leverage. To create comparable portfolios, analysts might 1) use a single- or multi-factor model or 2) create tracking portfolios that have comparable return and risk characteristics. In either case, the resulting customized benchmark is used for subsequent evaluation.

©2017 Kaplan, Inc.

Conventions to consider in hedge fund performance evaluation are the impact of performance fees and lock-up periods, the age of funds, and the size of funds. Empirical studies have found that:

- Funds with longer lock-up periods tend to produce higher returns than those with shorter lock-up periods.
- Younger funds tend to outperform older funds.
- Large funds underperform small funds.

Returns. By convention, hedge funds report monthly returns by comparing the ending value of the fund to the beginning value [i.e., $(V_1 / V_0) - 1$]. These simply-calculated monthly returns are then compounded to arrive at annual returns. Note that returns are often biased by entry into and exit from the fund, which are allowed on a quarterly or less frequent basis, and by the frequency of the manager's trading (i.e., cash flows).

To smooth out variability in hedge fund returns, investors often compute a *rolling return*, such as a 12-month moving average. A 12-month moving average is the average monthly return over the most recent 12 months, including the current month. The next moving average return is calculated by adding the next month and dropping the most distant month. In this fashion, the average return is always calculated using returns for 12 months.

Leverage. The convention for dealing with leverage is to treat an asset as if it were fully paid for (i.e., effectively "look through" the leverage). When derivatives are included, the same principle of *deleveraging* is applied.

Risk. Using standard deviation to measure the risk of a hedge fund can produce misleading results. For example, hedge fund returns are usually skewed with significant leptokurtosis (fat tails), so standard deviation fails to measure the true risk of the distribution (i.e., standard deviation does not accurately measure the probability of returns in the tails).

Downside deviation. Downside deviation measures only the dispersion of returns below some specified threshold return. The most common formula for downside deviation is:

$$\text{downside deviation} = \sqrt{\frac{\sum_{1}^{n}\left[\min\left(\text{return}_t - \text{threshold}, 0\right)^2\right]}{n-1}}$$

The threshold return in the formula is usually either zero or the risk-free rate of return. If the threshold is a recent average return, then we call the downside deviation the **semivariance**. The point of these measures is to focus on the negative returns and not penalize a fund for high positive returns, which increases measured standard deviation.

The Sharpe Ratio

Annual hedge fund Sharpe ratios are calculated using annualized measures, as discussed earlier:

$$\text{Sharpe}_{HF} = \frac{\text{annualized return} - \text{annualized risk-free rate}}{\text{annualized standard deviation}}$$

In addition to concerns associated with the way returns are calculated, the Sharpe ratio has the following *limitations* with respect to hedge fund evaluation:

- *Time dependency:* The annual Sharpe ratio is typically estimated using shorter time periods. For example, to estimate the annual Sharpe ratio for a hedge fund using quarterly returns, the analyst multiplies the quarterly return by 4 and multiplies the quarterly standard deviation by the square root of 4. Thus, the *annualized* Sharpe ratio is biased upward by the square root of 4.
- *Assumes normality:* Measures that incorporate standard deviation are inappropriate for skewed return distributions.
- *Assumes liquidity:* Because of infrequent, missing, or assumed return observations, illiquid holdings have upward-biased Sharpe ratios (i.e., downward-biased standard deviations).
- *Assumes uncorrelated returns:* Returns correlated across time will artificially lower the standard deviation. For example, if returns are trending for a period of time, the measured standard deviation will be lower than what may occur in the future. Serially-correlated returns also result when the asset is illiquid and current prices are not available (e.g., private equity investments).
- *Stand-alone measure:* Does not automatically consider diversification effects.

In addition to these statistical shortcomings, the Sharpe ratio has been shown to have little power for predicting winners (i.e., it uses historical data). Also, research has found evidence that managers can manipulate their reported returns to artificially inflate their Sharpe ratio.

MANAGED FUTURES

LOS 26.s: Describe trading strategies of managed futures programs and the role of managed futures in a portfolio.

CFA® Program Curriculum, Volume 5, page 85

Managed futures programs are typically run by **Commodity Pool Operators** (CPOs). CPOs can themselves be **commodity trading advisors** (CTAs) or will hire CTAs to actually manage all or part of the pool. In the United States, both must be registered with the U.S. Commodity Futures Trading Commission and the National Futures Association.

Managed futures (CTAs) are typically classified by style, the markets in which they specialize, or by strategy. Because they often seek performance in major markets, managed futures are sometimes thought of as a subset of global macro hedge funds that specialize in trading derivatives.

CTA strategies can be described as systematic or discretionary. CTAs that specialize in **systematic trading strategies** typically apply sets of rules to trade according to short-, intermediate-, and/or long-term trends. They may also trade counter to trends in a contrarian (against the trend) strategy.

A **discretionary trading strategy** is much as it sounds. The strategy is based on the discretion of the CTA (commodity trading advisor), in the same way that any active manager seeks value.

Managed futures can also be classified according to the markets in which they trade. They apply systematic or discretionary trading strategies in financial markets, currency markets, or diversified markets.

In *financial markets*, they trade in financial (i.e., interest rate) and currency futures, options, and forward contracts. Those that specialize in *currency markets* trade exclusively in currency derivatives. A fund that trades in *diversified markets* trades in all the financial derivatives markets described as well as commodity derivatives.

Role in the Portfolio

The primary benefit to managed futures is the diversification potential (i.e., improved average return-to-risk ratios) due to their low correlation (0.00) with a portfolio of stocks and bonds. Research has shown the performance of managed futures is investment-vehicle dependent. In particular, private funds seem to add value whereas publicly traded funds have performed less well, both stand-alone and in portfolios.

In selecting a CTA to include in the portfolio, the manager should consider risk. For example, even though CTAs often exhibit negative correlations with equities, correlations among CTAs themselves can range anywhere from significantly positive (i.e., close to 1.0) to only modestly positive. In addition, the beta that relates the performance of an individual CTA to a fund of CTAs can be a good indicator of future risk-adjusted performance. Just as equity beta relates the volatility (risk) of an individual equity security or portfolio to the overall equity market, the CTA beta measures the risk of the individual CTA relative to a fund of CTAs.

DISTRESSED SECURITIES INVESTING

LOS 26.t: Describe strategies and risks associated with investing in distressed securities.

CFA® Program Curriculum, Volume 5, page 94

The major types of **distressed securities investing strategies** are long-only value investing, distressed debt arbitrage, and private equity.

Long-only value investing basically tries to find opportunities where the prospects will improve and, of course, tries to find them before other investors do. *High-yield investing* is buying publicly traded, below-investment grade debt. *Orphan equities investing* is the purchase of the equities of firms emerging from reorganization. The reason these present a market opportunity is that some investors cannot participate in this market and many do not wish to do the necessary due diligence.

Study Session 13
Cross-Reference to CFA Institute Assigned Reading #26 – Alternative Investments Portfolio Management

Study Session 13

Distressed debt arbitrage is the purchasing of a company's distressed debt while short selling the company's equity. The investment can earn a return in two ways: 1) if the firm's condition declines, the debt and equity will both fall in value; the equity should decline more in value, though, because debt has seniority; and 2) if the company's prospects improve, because of the priority of interest over dividends, the returns to bondholders should be greater than that of equity holders, including dividends paid on the short position. The possibility of returns from the two events provides a good market opportunity.

Private equity is an "active" approach where the investor acquires positions in the distressed company, and the investment gives some measure of control. The investor can then influence and assist the company as well as acquire more ownership in the process of any reorganization. By providing services and obtaining a strategic position, the investors create their own opportunities. *Vulture funds*, which specialize in purchasing undervalued distressed securities, engage in this type of strategy.

CONCERNS OF DISTRESSED SECURITIES INVESTING

LOS 26.u: Explain event risk, market liquidity risk, market risk, and "J-factor risk" in relation to investing in distressed securities.

CFA® Program Curriculum, Volume 5, page 99

Distressed securities can have event risk, market liquidity risk, market risk, J-factor risk, and other types of risk.

- **Event risk** refers to the fact that the return on a particular investment within this class typically depends on an event for the particular company. Because these events are usually unrelated to the economy, they can provide diversification benefits.
- **Market liquidity risk** refers to low liquidity and the fact that there can be cyclical supply and demand for these investments.
- **Market risk** from macroeconomic changes is usually less important than the first two types mentioned.
- **J-factor risk** refers to the role that courts and judges can play in the return, and this involves an unpredictable human element. By anticipating the bankruptcy court judge's rulings (the J-factor), the distressed security investor knows whether to purchase the distressed company's debt or equity.

 ©2017 Kaplan, Inc.

KEY CONCEPTS

LOS 26.a

Common features of alternative investments include:
- Low liquidity.
- Good diversification potential.
- High due diligence costs.
- Difficult to value.
- Limited access to information.

Alternative investments can provide:
- Exposure to asset classes that stocks and bonds cannot provide.
- Exposure to special investment strategies (e.g., hedge and venture capital funds).
- Special strategies and unique asset classes (e.g., funds that invest in private equity and distressed securities).

LOS 26.b

- Assess the market opportunity offered. Are there exploitable inefficiencies in the market for the type of investments in which the manager specializes?
- Assess the investment process. Does the manager seem to have a competitive edge over others in that market?
- Assess the organization of the manager and its operations. Is it stable and well run? What has been the staff turnover?
- Assess the people by meeting with them and assessing their character.
- Assess the terms and structure (amount and time period) of the investment.
- Assess the service providers (i.e., lawyers, brokers, ancillary staff, etc.) by investigating the outside firms that support the manager's business.
- Review documents such as the prospectus or private-placement memorandum and the audits.

LOS 26.c

- Taxes. Tax issues can be unique to the individual because the characteristics of private-wealth clients and their investments can vary greatly. For individuals, there can be partnerships, trusts, and other situations that make tax issues complex.
- Suitability. Time horizons and wealth of individuals can vary a great deal. With individuals, there is also the emotional aspect, like preferences for, or aversion to, certain types of assets.
- Communication. Communication with the client helps determine suitability of recommendations and the overall management process.
- Decision risk. Decision risk is the risk of irrationally changing a strategy. For example, the adviser must be prepared to deal with a client who wants to get out of a position that has just declined in value.
- Concentrated positions. Wealthy individuals' portfolios frequently contain large positions in closely held companies. Such ownership should be considered with the overall allocation to alternative investments, like private equity.

LOS 26.d

Real estate can be broken down into direct and indirect investment. Examples of direct investment in real estate include ownership of residences, commercial real estate, or agricultural land, and it involves direct management of the assets. Indirect real estate investments include:

- Companies that develop and manage real estate.
- Real estate investment trusts (REITs).
- Commingled real estate funds (CREFs).
- Separately managed accounts.
- Infrastructure funds.

Private equity subgroups include start-up companies, middle-market private companies, and private investment in public entities. A direct investment in private equity is when the investor purchases a claim directly from the firm (e.g., preferred shares of stock). Indirect investment is usually done through private equity funds, which include venture capital (VC) and buyout funds.

Commodity investments can also be grouped into direct and indirect subgroups. Direct investment is either through the purchase of the physical commodity or the purchase of derivatives (e.g., futures) on those assets. Indirect investment in commodities is usually done through investment in companies whose principal business is associated with a commodity (e.g., investing in a metal via ownership of shares in a mining company). Many commodities have a low correlation with stocks and bonds and a positive correlation with inflation.

Managed futures funds share many characteristics with hedge funds. The primary feature that distinguishes managed futures from hedge funds is the difference in the assets they hold. Managed futures funds tend to trade only in derivatives markets, while hedge funds tend to trade in spot markets and use futures for hedging. Also, managed futures funds generally take positions based on indices, while hedge funds tend to focus more on individual asset price anomalies. In other words, hedge funds tend to have more of a micro focus, while managed futures tend to have a macro focus.

Buyout funds are the largest segment of the private equity market. Middle-market buyout funds concentrate on divisions spun off from larger, publicly traded corporations and private companies that, due to their relatively small size, cannot efficiently obtain capital. Mega-cap buyout funds concentrate on taking publicly traded firms private. In either case, the target represents an investment opportunity through the identification of under-valued assets, the ability to restructure the debt of the firm, and/or improved (i.e., more efficient) management and operations.

Infrastructure funds specialize in purchasing public infrastructure assets (e.g., airports, toll roads) from cities, states, and municipalities. Distressed securities are securities of companies that are in or near bankruptcy. As with managed futures, analysts often consider distressed securities to be part of the hedge fund class of alternative investments. It may also be part of the private equity class.

©2017 Kaplan, Inc.

LOS 26.e

Real Estate: *Benchmarks:* NCREIF, NAREIT. *Construction:* NCREIF is value weighted, NAREIT is cap weighted. *Biases:* Measured volatility is downward biased. The values are obtained periodically (annually).

Private Equity: *Benchmarks:* Provided by Cambridge Associates, Preqin, and LPX. *Construction:* Constructed for buyout and venture capital. Value depends upon events. Often construct custom benchmarks. *Biases:* Repricing occurs infrequently, which results in dated values.

Commodities: *Benchmarks:* S&P GSCI, BCOM, and RJ/CRB Index. *Construction:* Assume a futures-based strategy. Most types considered investable. *Biases:* Indices vary widely with respect to purpose, composition, and method of weighting.

Managed Futures: *Benchmarks:* MLMI, CTA Indices include the CISDM, BarclayHedge, and Barclay Traders. *Construction:* MLMI replicates the return to a trend-following strategy. CTA Indices use equal-weighted returns. *Biases:* Requires special weighting scheme.

Distressed Securities: *Benchmarks:* Characteristics similar to long-only hedge fund benchmarks. *Construction:* Weighting either equally weighted or based upon assets under management. Selection criteria can vary. *Biases:* Self-reporting, backfill or inclusion bias, popularity bias, and survivorship bias.

LOS 26.f

Over the 1996–2015 time period, adding managed futures to a portfolio of stocks, bonds, and other alternative investments (commodities, private equity, real estate, hedge funds) increased the return and average return-to-volatility ratio. During the equity market collapse of 2008, managed futures far outperformed all other asset classes studied. Private equity provided return enhancement over the long term. Hedge funds have been found to provide both diversification and return enhancement.

LOS 26.g

Advantages of direct equity real estate investing:
- Many expenses are tax deductible.
- Ability to use more leverage than most other investments.
- Provides more control than stock investing.
- Ability to diversify geographically.

Disadvantages of direct equity real estate investing:
- Lack of divisibility means a single investment may be a large part of the investor's portfolio.
- High information cost, high commissions, high operating and maintenance costs, and hands-on management requirements.
- Special geographical risks, such as neighborhood deterioration and the political risk of changing tax codes.

LOS 26.h
Venture capital issuers include formative-stage companies and expansion-stage companies.

Venture capital buyers include angel investors, venture capitalists, and large companies (i.e., strategic partners).

A private company typically goes through the following stages.
- The early stage consists of three phases:
  - Seed.
  - Startup.
  - First stage.
- The later stage occurs after revenue has started and funds are needed to expand sales.
- The exit stage is the time when the venture capitalist realizes the value of the investment. It can occur through a merger, an acquisition, or an IPO.

LOS 26.i
In contrast to venture capital funds, buyout funds usually have:
- A higher level of leverage.
- Earlier and steadier cash flows.
- Less error in the measurement of returns.
- Less frequent losses.
- Less upside potential.

These differences are the natural consequence of buyout funds purchasing entities in later stages of development or even established companies where the risks are lower.

LOS 26.j
Convertible preferred stock is a good vehicle for direct venture capital investment. Preferred stock has first claim on company cash flow while operating and in bankruptcy. The conversion feature provides upside potential. Later financing rounds may have priority and be more valuable.

LOS 26.k
Private equity funds usually take the form of limited partnerships or limited liability companies (LLCs). These legal structures limit the loss to investors to the initial investment and avoid corporate double taxation. For limited partnerships, the sponsor is called the general partner; for LLCs, the sponsor is called the managing director.

The time line starts with the sponsor getting commitments from investors at the beginning of the fund and then giving "capital calls" over the first five years (typically), which are referred to as the commitment period. The expected life of these funds is seven to ten years, and there is often an option to extend the life up to five more years.

The sponsor can receive compensation in several ways. First, the sponsor has capital invested that earns a return. This is usually required as it helps keep the sponsor's interests in line with those of the limited partners. As a manager, the sponsor typically gets a management fee of around 2% and an incentive fee of about 20% of the profits.

©2017 Kaplan, Inc.

LOS 26.l

Any strategy for private equity investment must address the following issues:

- Low liquidity: Portfolio allocation to this class should be 5% or less with a plan to keep the money invested for 7 to 10 years.
- Diversification through a number of positions: Only very large portfolios have sufficient funds to support diversified, direct PE investing. Other portfolios can consider PE funds.
- Diversification strategy: Know how the proposed private equity investment relates to the overall portfolio.
- Plans for meeting capital calls: Committed funds are only called as needed, and the investor needs to be prepared to meet the calls.

LOS 26.m

Direct commodity investment entails either purchasing the actual commodities or gaining exposure via derivatives. Indirect commodity investment is the purchase of indirect claims (e.g., shares in a corporation) that deal in the commodity.

Direct investment gives more exposure, but cash investment in commodities can incur carrying costs. Indirect investment may be more convenient, but it may provide very little exposure to the commodity, especially if the company is hedging the risk itself.

The increase in the number of investable indices in commodities and their associated futures is indicative of the advantages of investing via derivatives. These indices also make investing in commodities available to smaller investors.

LOS 26.n

It appears that whether a commodity is *storable* is a primary determinant in its value providing a hedge against unexpected inflation. For example, the values of storable commodities such as industrial metals are positively related to unexpected changes in inflation. That is, they tend to increase (decrease) in value with unexpected increases (decreases) in inflation.

Another factor to consider with respect to inflation hedging capability is whether the commodity's demand is linked to economic activity. Those that enjoy a more or less constant demand regardless of the level of economic activity, for example, seem to provide little hedge against unexpected changes in inflation.

LOS 26.o

Hedge funds are classified in various ways by different sources. Because hedge funds are a "style-based" asset class, strategies can determine the subgroups. The following is a list of nine of the more familiar hedge fund strategies.

1. Convertible arbitrage commonly involves buying undervalued convertible bonds, preferred stock, or warrants, while shorting the underlying stock to create a hedge.

2. Distressed securities investments can be made in both debt and equity; because the securities are already distressed, shorting can be difficult or impossible.

3. Emerging markets generally only permit long positions, and often there are no derivatives to hedge the investments.

Study Session 13
Cross-Reference to CFA Institute Assigned Reading #26 – Alternative Investments Portfolio Management

Study Session 13

4. Equity market neutral (pairs trading) combines long and short positions in under-valued and over-valued securities, respectively, to eliminate systematic risk while capitalizing on mispricing.

5. Fixed-income arbitrage involves taking long and short positions in fixed-income instruments based upon expected changes in the yield curve and/or credit spreads.

6. Fund-of-funds describes a hedge fund that invests in many hedge funds to get diversification; there is a fee paid to the manager of the fund-of-funds, as well as to the managers of the funds in the fund-of-funds.

7. Global macro strategies take positions in major financial and non-financial markets through various means (e.g., derivatives and currencies), focusing on an entire group or area of investment instead of individual securities.

8. Hedged equity strategies (i.e., equity long-short) represent the largest hedge fund classification in terms of assets under management. These strategies take long and short positions in under- and over-valued securities, respectively. Hedged equity strategies do not focus on balancing the positions to eliminate systematic risk and can range from net long to net short.

9. Merger arbitrage (i.e., deal arbitrage) focuses on returns from mergers, spin-offs, takeovers, and so on.

LOS 26.p
The most common compensation structure of a hedge fund consists of an assets-under-management (AUM) fee of about 1% to 2% and an incentive fee of 20% of profits.

High water marks (HWMs) are typically employed to avoid incentive fee double-dipping. For example, each quarter the increase in value over the previous quarter is determined, and investors pay incentive and management fees accordingly. If the value of the fund is lower than the previous quarter, however, the manager receives only the management fee, and the previous high value of the fund is established as a HWM.

A lock-up period limits withdrawals by requiring a minimum investment period (e.g., one to three years), preventing sudden withdrawals that could force the manager to have to unwind positions.

Incentive fees are paid to encourage the manager to earn ever higher profits. There is some controversy concerning incentive fees because the manager should have goals other than simply earning a gross return.

LOS 26.q
A fund-of-funds (FOF) consists of approximately 10 to 30 hedge funds. The point is to achieve diversification, but the extra layer of management means an extra layer of fees. Often, an FOF offers more liquidity for the investor, but the cost is cash drag. Despite the drawbacks, FOF are *good entry-level investments* because the manager of the FOF exercises due diligence.

An FOF may serve as a better *benchmark* because it suffers from less survivorship bias.

An FOF can suffer from style drift. Often two FOF that are classified as having the same style have a low correlation of returns.

FOF returns have been more highly correlated with equity markets than those of individual hedge funds. This characteristic has important implications for their use as a diversifier in an equity portfolio (i.e., as correlation increases, diversification decreases).

LOS 26.r
One special issue is that some claim that hedge funds are absolute-return vehicles, which means that no direct benchmark exists. The question (and problem) is how to determine alpha. Conventions to consider in hedge fund performance evaluation are the impact of performance fees and lock-up periods, the age of funds, and the size of funds.
* Funds with longer lock-up periods tend to produce higher returns than those with shorter lock-up periods.
* Younger funds tend to outperform older funds.
* Large funds underperform small funds.

By convention, hedge funds report monthly returns by comparing the ending value of the fund to the beginning value. These simply-calculated monthly returns are then compounded to arrive at annual returns. The convention for dealing with leverage is to treat an asset as if it were fully paid for. When derivatives are included, the same principle of deleveraging is applied.

Using standard deviation to measure the risk of a hedge fund can produce misleading results. Hedge fund returns are usually skewed with significant leptokurtosis (fat tails), so standard deviation fails to measure the true risk of the distribution.

Downside deviation is a popular hedge fund risk measure, as it measures only the dispersion of returns below some specified threshold return. The most common formula for downside deviation is:

$$\text{downside deviation} = \sqrt{\frac{\sum_{1}^{n}\left[\min\left(\text{return}_t - \text{threshold}, 0\right)^2\right]}{n-1}}$$

The threshold return in the formula is usually either zero or the risk-free rate of return. Annual hedge fund Sharpe ratios are calculated using annualized measures as:

$$\text{Sharpe}_{HF} = \frac{\text{annualized return} - \text{annualized risk-free rate}}{\text{annualized standard deviation}}$$

The Sharpe ratio has the following limitations with respect to hedge fund evaluation:
* *Time dependency.* Annualized Sharpe ratios are biased upwards by a factor of the square of time.
* *Assumes normality.* Measures that incorporate standard deviation are inappropriate for skewed return distributions.

- *Assumes liquidity.* Illiquid holdings have upward-biased Sharpe ratios (i.e., downward-biased standard deviations).
- *Assumes uncorrelated returns.* Returns correlated across time will artificially lower the standard deviation.
- *Stand-alone measure.* Does not automatically consider diversification effects.

LOS 26.s

CTAs that specialize in systematic trading strategies typically apply sets of rules to trade according to or contrary to short-, intermediate-, and/or long-term trends. A discretionary CTA trading strategy generates returns on the managers' trading expertise, much like any active portfolio manager. CTAs can also be classified according to whether they trade in financial markets, currency markets, or diversified markets.

The primary benefit to managed futures is increased risk-adjusted performance and diversification, although the performance seems to be related to specific strategies and time periods. Private funds seem to add value; publicly traded funds have performed poorly both stand-alone and in portfolios. Even though CTAs often exhibit negative correlations with equities, correlations among CTAs themselves can range from significantly to modestly positive. The CTA beta (relative to other CTAs) can be a good indicator of future risk-adjusted performance.

LOS 26.t

- Long-only value investing attempts to find opportunities where the prospects will improve tries to find them before other investors do. *High-yield investing* is buying publicly traded, below-investment grade debt. *Orphan equities investing* is the purchase of the equities of firms emerging from reorganization.
- Distressed debt arbitrage is the purchasing of a company's distressed debt while short selling the company's equity. The investment can earn a return in two ways:
  - If the firm's condition declines, the debt and equity will both fall in value, but equity should decline more in value.
  - If the company's prospects improve, the returns to bondholders should be greater than that of equity holders.
- Private equity is an "active" approach where the investor acquires positions in the distressed company, and the investment gives some measure of control. The investor can then influence the company as well as acquire more ownership in the process of any reorganization.

LOS 26.u

Distressed securities can have several types of risk:
- Event risk refers to the fact that the return on a particular investment within this class typically depends on an event for the particular company. Because these events are usually unrelated to the economy, they can provide diversification benefits.
- Market liquidity risk refers to low liquidity and the fact that there can be cyclical supply and demand for these investments.
- Market risk from macroeconomic changes is usually less important than the first two types mentioned.
- J-factor risk refers to the unpredictable nature of bankruptcy court judges' rulings.

1. All of the following are special issues for the private wealth client when investing in alternative investments except:
   A. tax issues.
   B. decision risk.
   C. return enhancement.

2. Which of the following represent private equity subgroups where the company invested in has not typically started generating revenues?
   A. Start-up companies only.
   B. Start-up companies and middle-market private companies only.
   C. Start-up companies, middle-market private companies, and private investment in public entities only.

3. The hedge fund structure and private equity fund structure are subgroups of which alternative investment class?
   A. Real estate.
   B. Commodities.
   C. Distressed debt.

4. The strategies of convertible arbitrage, emerging markets, equity market neutral, and fixed-income arbitrage are categories of which alternative investment class?
   A. Real estate.
   B. Hedge funds.
   C. Commodities.

5. For use in evaluating hedge funds, the Sharpe ratio may not be appropriate because the Sharpe ratio assumes the returns:
   A. are positive only.
   B. reflect diversification.
   C. are serially uncorrelated.

6. Based on historical data, when compared to a 50/50 stock/bond portfolio, a 45/45/10 portfolio of bonds, stocks, and which of the following had a higher average return-to-volatility ratio?
   A. Real estate only.
   B. Commodities only.
   C. Hedge funds.

7. When comparing the returns of various types of hedge funds to the returns on stocks and bonds for the period 1996–2015:
   A. none outperformed stocks and bonds by any measure.
   B. some outperformed stocks and bonds and some did not.
   C. all outperformed stocks and bonds on a risk-adjusted basis.

8. Compared to an indirect investment in real estate, a direct investment in real estate has which one of following advantages?
    A. Lower commissions.
    B. Lower information cost.
    C. Potential for more leverage.

9. The buyers of venture capital who are the first investors after the entrepreneur's family and friends would *most likely* be:
    A. vultures.
    B. angel investors.
    C. corporate venture capitalists.

10. Purchasing of a company's distressed debt while selling the company's equity short is called:
    A. market neutral.
    B. preferred arbitrage.
    C. distressed debt arbitrage.

For more questions related to this topic review, log in to your Schweser online account and launch SchweserPro™ QBank; and for video instruction covering each LOS in this topic review, log in to your Schweser online account and launch the OnDemand video lectures, if you have purchased these products.

©2017 Kaplan, Inc.

ANSWERS – CONCEPT CHECKERS

1. **C** Return enhancement is certainly not a special issue. All the other choices are issues of concern for the private wealth client but generally not issues for the institutional client.

2. **A** Start-up companies, middle-market private companies, and private investment in public entities represent three subgroups of private equity. Middle-market private companies typically have revenues, as do public entities. The start-up companies are usually in a pre-revenue phase.

3. **C** Investments in distressed debt can have either of these structures; that is why distressed debt is often considered as a subclass of other alternative investment asset classes.

4. **B** Hedge funds have many strategies that include the following: convertible arbitrage, distressed securities, emerging markets, equity market neutral, fixed-income arbitrage, fund-of-funds, global macro strategies, hedged equity strategies, and merger arbitrage.

5. **C** The Sharpe ratio is probably not applicable to hedge funds because it assumes the returns are normally distributed and not serially correlated. Another problem is that the Sharpe ratio is a stand-alone measure and does not consider the diversification that the hedge fund can add to a portfolio.

6. **C** During 1996–2015 adding hedge funds to a portfolio of stocks and bonds would have increased the return both on an absolute and risk adjusted basis. Adding either real estate or commodities to a bond and stock portfolio would have decreased the average return-to-volatility ratio for the period 1996–2015.

7. **B** The performance of the various classes varied widely, from an average return-to-volatility ratio of 1.19 for the CISDM Equity Long/Short strategies to 3.35 on CISDM Equity Market Neutral strategies.

8. **C** Higher information costs, higher commissions, and political risk are disadvantages of direct investment in real estate. Direct investment allows more leverage, however.

9. **B** Angel investors are usually accredited investors and the first outside investors after the family and friends of the company founders.

10. **C** This is the definition of distressed debt arbitrage.

Use the following information for Questions 1 through 6.

Suzanne Harlan has a large, well-diversified stock and bond portfolio. She wants to try some alternative investments and has contracted with Laurence Philips, principal of Philips Finance, to help assemble a new portfolio.

Before agreeing to make recommendations for Harlan, Philips wants to determine whether she is a good candidate for alternative investments. He gives her a standard questionnaire that asks open-ended questions of all potential clients. Here are some of Harlan's comments:

- "I'm interested in higher returns. I'm not afraid of risk, and I'm investing this money for the benefit of my eventual heirs."
- "I pay several million dollars in taxes every year, and I want any additional investments to be tax-friendly."
- "While I expect risk on an individual-investment basis, I'd like to further diversify my portfolio and reduce overall risk."
- "I pay a lot of attention to expense and return data from my investments and track their performance closely."
- "I'm 65 years old and in excellent health."

After reading Harlan's responses and learning that she is a fairly sophisticated investor, Philips agrees to take her on as a client. Harlan has a lot of experience with investments and has some ideas what she'd like to do. She brings Philips the following ideas:

- "I have a colleague in the lumber business who says the furniture market is booming, and demand should increase in the year ahead. I'd like to purchase some lumber futures in the hopes that the price will rise."
- "Hedge funds are earning excellent returns, and I expect them to continue doing so. However, other investors have told me that the difficulty lies in assessing the quality of the funds, because they are not well regulated. So I'm interested in purchasing a fund-of-funds, so I can diversify my risk while potentially sharing in some outsized returns."
- "I already own a couple of REITs, but they represent a very small portion of my assets, and I'd like to increase my exposure to real estate. I've heard about pooled real estate funds, and I'm interested in one of those funds."
- "My neighbors founded Kelly Tool and Die, a machine-tool business, 20 years ago and have not managed the company well. They have told me they are considering filing for bankruptcy. I have contacts in the manufacturing business overseas who would be interested in acquiring Kelly's assets. My Asian colleagues are willing to pay about 60% of book value for the assets, and my neighbors are willing to sell me the company for about 50% of the book value of its assets."

Harlan then tells Philips that it is imperative that the returns of any investments he recommends must be in some way comparable to a benchmark.

Philips is not excited about the commodity idea and does not like funds- of- funds. However, he does know of several managers of individual hedge funds that might interest Harlan. He talks her out of the fund- of- funds idea and suggests she put her money in the Stillman Fund, which is run by one of his college friends. Fund manager Mark Stillman concentrates on spin-offs, generally buying the spun-off company and shorting the parent company.

1. Harlan seeks alternative investments that will both boost returns and diversify her portfolio. Which pair of her proposed investments represents the worst choices for each goal?

   <u>Net Returns</u>   <u>Diversification</u>
   A. Lumber   Hedge funds
   B. Lumber   Kelly Tool and Die
   C. Real estate funds   Hedge funds

2. Based on her investment suggestions and survey answers, Harlan is least concerned with:
   A. inflation.
   B. liquidity.
   C. volatility.

3. In his attempt to talk Harlan out of investing in a fund-of-funds, Philips addressed the advantages of investing in individual funds. Which of the following is his most compelling argument?
   A. The lower expenses of individual funds.
   B. The lack of benchmarks for a fund-of-funds.
   C. The likelihood of style drift in a fund-of-funds.

4. The Stillman Fund uses which strategy?
   A. Hedged equity.
   B. Relative value.
   C. Merger arbitrage.

5. Which of Harlan's responses is *most likely* to make Philips consider her a bad candidate for alternative investments?
   A. "I'm interested in higher returns. I'm not afraid of risk, and I'm investing this money for the benefit of my eventual heirs."
   B. "I pay several million dollars in taxes every year, and I want any additional investments to be tax-friendly."
   C. "I pay a lot of attention to expense and return data from my investments and track their performance closely."

6. If Harlan is truly concerned about benchmarks, she should avoid which of her suggested investments?
   A. Hedge funds.
   B. Kelly Tool and Die.
   C. None of them; benchmarks are available for all asset classes.

SELF-TEST ANSWERS: ALTERNATIVE INVESTMENTS PORTFOLIO MANAGEMENT

1. **B**   Commodity investments are primarily diversification tools, having little correlation with traditional stocks and bonds. The Kelly Tool and Die investment is private equity, which is more of a return enhancer than a diversifier. Real estate funds can boost both diversification and returns, while hedge funds can boost returns, diversify, or both, depending on the nature of the fund.

2. **B**   While Harlan's comment about being willing to accept risk may suggest she is not concerned about volatility, she is most definitely concerned on a portfolio level, as evidenced by her desire to use alternative assets for diversification purposes. Nothing in the information presented above offers any hint about Harlan's concerns about inflation. However, Harlan's stated desire to build wealth for her heirs suggests liquidity is not a concern.

3. **A**   The biggest disadvantage of the fund-of-funds is the extra layer of fees. Style drift could be an issue for both an individual hedge fund and a fund-of-funds, much as it is with traditional mutual funds. The issue with benchmarks is probably more troubling for individual funds than for funds-of-funds.

4. **C**   Merger arbitrage funds usually focus on mergers, spin-offs, or takeovers, buying one company in the transaction and shorting the other.

5. **C**   Alternative assets can provide high returns, and a high risk tolerance and low need for liquidity are positives for investors in alternative asset classes. And while many alternative assets are risky, they can provide a substantial diversification benefit when combined with mainstream investments. Many alternative investments are tax-friendly. However, most of the investments considered for this exam are not easy to value, and difficult to track closely over short periods of time.

6. **C**   Benchmarks are available for commodities, real estate, private equity, and hedge funds, though not all of them are easy to interpret.

©2017 Kaplan, Inc.

RISK MANAGEMENT

EXAM FOCUS

Risk management is a key component of investment management. Without risk, reward is unlikely; too much risk, failure looms. Be able to compare an enterprise risk management (ERM) system to a decentralized system of risk management as well as evaluate an existing ERM system. Value at risk (VaR) is an important topic. Be able to calculate VaR using different methods, know the pros and cons of various methods, and discuss other tools to measure or manage risk (including credit risk).

The focus of this material is on an overall organization. How does an investment firm or other organization manage risk?

MANAGING RISK

LOS 27.a: Discuss features of the risk management process, risk governance, risk reduction, and an enterprise risk management system.

CFA® Program Curriculum, Volume 5, page 134

Investment managers should take necessary risks and those where they have information or another advantage in order to generate return. Other risks should be reduced, avoided, or completely hedged. **Risk reduction** refers to recognizing and reducing, eliminating, or avoiding those unnecessary risks.

The **risk management** process requires:

1. Top level management of the organization setting policies and procedures for managing risk.

2. Defining risk tolerance to various risks in terms of what the organization is willing and able to bear. For some risks tolerance will be high, for others it will be low.

3. Identifying risks faced by the organization. Those risks can be grouped as *financial* and *non-financial risks*. This will require building and maintaining investment databases for both types of risk.

4. Measuring the current levels of risk.

5. Adjusting the levels of risk—upward where the firm has an advantage and seeks to generate return to exploit an advantage, downward in other cases. As part of adjusting risk levels the firm must:
   - Execute transactions to change the level of risk using derivatives or other instruments.
   - Identify the most appropriate transaction for any given objective.
   - Consider the cost of any transaction.
   - Execute each transaction.

The risk management process is ongoing, data and analysis must be continuously updated. Once a risk to the firm has been identified, it may be necessary to determine appropriate models to quantify the risk and or evaluate possible ways to adjust the risk. If a firm faces risk in the value of option positions, the firm must select appropriate option pricing models, quantify needed inputs, and consider various approaches to modifying the option position used. For example, the firm could use dynamic hedging or take offsetting option positions in exchange traded or OTC options. The appropriate transactions must be executed and the risk measurement and management process must begin again.

Risk governance is a part of the overall *corporate governance system* and refers to the overall process of developing and putting a risk management system into use. The system must specify between centralized and decentralized approaches, reporting methods, methodologies to be used, and infrastructure needs. High quality risk governance will be 1) transparent, 2) establish clear accountability, 3) cost efficient in the use of resources, 4) and effective in achieving desired outcomes.

Senior management is responsible for the overall system and must determine whether the system will be **decentralized** or **centralized**.

- A *decentralized* risk governance system places responsibility for execution within each unit of the organization. It has the benefit of putting risk management in the hands of those closest to each part of the organization.
- The *centralized* system [also called an **enterprise risk management** (ERM) system] places execution within one central unit of the organization. It provides a better view of how the risk of each unit affects the overall risk borne by the firm (i.e., individual risks are less than perfectly correlated, so the risk of the firm is less than the sum of the individual unit risks). For example, individual units might take offsetting positions in global equity markets, and the offsetting effects of the trades can only be seen from the perspective of upper management. In addition, a centralized system locates responsibility closer to senior management who bear ultimate responsibility. Management must consider each risk in isolation but also the overall impact on the firm. The centralized system will offer economies of scale.

©2017 Kaplan, Inc.

LOS 27.b: Evaluate strengths and weaknesses of a company's risk management process.

CFA® Program Curriculum, Volume 5, page 138

LOS 27.c: Describe steps in an effective enterprise risk management system.

CFA® Program Curriculum, Volume 5, page 140

In either the decentralized or centralized approach, senior management must find a way to assess the overall impact of risk on the organization. Those who measure and report on risk levels must be independent of those who trade and take risk in the organization. The **back office**, which is responsible for processing transactions, record keeping, and compliance, must be independent from the **front office**, which generates transactions and sales in order to provide a check on the activities of the front office. The back office must also interact with third parties, such as custodians and trading partners, to verify all transactions are accounted for and reported correctly.

An effective system will:

- Identify each risk factor to which the company has exposure.
- Quantify the factor in measurable terms.
- Include each risk in a single aggregate measure of firm-wide risk. VaR will be the most commonly used tool.
- Identify how each risk contributes to the overall risk of the firm. This is an advantage of VaR.
- Systematically report the risks and support an allocation of capital and risk to the various business units of the firm.
- Monitor compliance with the allocated limits of capital and risk.

Risk management will involve costs but is essential. Regardless of whether the approach is centralized or decentralized, the system must centralize the data collection and storage used in the process in order to be technologically efficient.

EVALUATING RISK

LOS 27.d: Evaluate a company's or a portfolio's exposures to financial and nonfinancial risk factors.

CFA® Program Curriculum, Volume 5, page 140

A company faces both **financial** and **non-financial risks**. Financial risks arise from events external to the company and in the financial markets. Financial risks include:

- **Market risk** is related to changes in interest rates, exchange rates, equity prices, commodity prices, and so on. Each of these risks can be tied to changes in supply and demand in particular markets. Market risk is frequently the largest component of risk.

It may be appropriate to measure market risk in terms of changing market value. In the case of defined benefit pension plans and other entities with definable liabilities, an asset liability approach (ALM) to measuring surplus may be required.

- **Credit risk** is frequently the second largest financial risk. It is defined here as the risk of loss caused by a counterparty's or debtor's failure to make a promised payment. Traditionally, credit risk was seen as binary—a payment is made or not. The evolution of trading in credit derivatives has allowed for more refined measurement of credit risk and for the ability to hedge credit risk.

- **Liquidity risk** is the possibility of sustaining significant losses due to the inability to take or liquidate a position quickly at a fair price. It can be difficult to measure because liquidity can appear adequate until adverse events occur. A narrow **bid-ask spread** is usually taken as an indicator of good liquidity for traded securities but this spread normally applies only to small transactions. Another problem is that the valuation models used to value non-traded securities generally do not incorporate liquidity risk in estimating value. **Average** or **typical trading volume** may provide a better indication of liquidity. It is often assumed that derivatives can provide an alternative to transactions in the actual item, but in reality, derivative liquidity is generally linked to liquidity of the underlying item.

Non-financial risks are defined as all other risks and include:

- **Operational** or **operations risk** is a loss due to failure of the company's systems and procedures or from external events outside the company's control. Examples and solutions to operational risk include: computer failure which can be mitigated with backup systems and procedures, human failure which can be reduced by developing procedures to monitor actions, and terrorism or weather events for which insurance may be available.

- **Settlement risk** is present when funds are being exchanged to settle a translation. One party could be making a payment while the other side of the exchange could be in the process of defaulting and fail to deliver on the transaction. This is also known as **Herstatt risk** after a bank that received swap payments and then defaulted without making payments. This level of risk varies. It is minimal for exchange trades when a clearinghouse assumes responsibility for the transaction. OTC transactions will have considerably more risk. On a swap where cash flows are exchanged, netting can be used to reduce the risk. Instead of each side making a payment and being at risk the other side will not pay, the smaller net difference in payments is computed and only that difference is sent. Many foreign exchange trades are now done through *continuously linked settlements* (*CLS*), which provide for settlement within a defined time window to reduce settlement risk.

- **Model risk** is present for many derivatives and non-traded instruments. Models are only as good as their construction and inputs (e.g., the assumptions regarding the sensitivity of the firm's assets to changes in risk factors, the correlations of the risk factors, or the likelihood of an event).

- **Sovereign risk** is a form of credit risk (financial risk) but has other elements as well. The analyst must consider financial issues (the ability of the government to pay) in addition to non-financial issues (the willingness of a sovereign government to repay its obligations). It can be difficult to collect if a sovereign government does not want to pay.

©2017 Kaplan, Inc.

Professor's Note: While the CFA text notes that sovereign risk has both financial and non-financial elements, it is discussed under non-financial, so if forced to choose, I'd put it there.

- **Regulatory risk** arises when it is not clear how a transaction will be regulated or if the regulations can change. Even if a transaction is unregulated, the parties to the transaction may be regulated, making the transaction indirectly regulated.
- **Tax, Accounting**, and **Legal/Contract risk** are similar to regulatory risk in that they refer to situations where the rules are unclear or can change. Such situations can also lead to costly litigation. **Political risk** refers to a change in government which could then lead to any of these types of changes and risks.

  Clearly derivatives are prime candidates for these risks. Many derivatives are new and subject to uncertain or changing rules. They can at times be politically unpopular.

Other risks include:

- **ESG (environmental, social, governance) risk** exists if company decisions result in environmental damage, human resource issues, or poor corporate governance polices and these decisions cause harm that results in a decline in the company's value.
- **Performance netting risk** can exist among multiple counterparties. Consider a case where A must pay B, B must pay C, and C must pay D. Default by A could trigger a chain of defaults.
- **Settlement netting risk** is different. It refers specifically to the liquidator of a counterparty in default changing the terms of expected netting agreements, such that the non-defaulting party now has to make payments (a payment that was expected to have been netted and therefore reduced) to the defaulting party.

Measuring Risks

Risk measurement is focused primarily on measuring market and credit risk. Traditionally, market risk has been measured with tools such as:

1. Standard deviation to measure price or surplus volatility.

2. Standard deviation of excess return. Excess return is the return minus the relevant benchmark return. The standard deviation of excess returns is also called **active risk** or **tracking risk**.

Tools exist to make simple, linear, first-order projections of the change in price for many securities: beta for stock, duration for bonds, and delta for options. Second-order techniques to measure change from straight line price projections exist for bonds (convexity) and options (gamma). Option price analysis can also incorporate the change in the option price for a change in time to expiration (theta) and the change in volatility (vega).

 Professor's Note: While the above items are discussed in the reading, VaR is considered a superior tool to aggregate and measure risk in an organization.

VALUE AT RISK (VaR)

LOS 27.e: Calculate and interpret value at risk (VaR) and explain its role in measuring overall and individual position market risk.

CFA® Program Curriculum, Volume 5, page 153

VaR gained prominence in the 1990s as a single aggregate risk measure applicable to many situations. VaR states at some probability (often 1% or 5%) the expected loss during a specified time period. The loss can be stated as a percentage of value or as a nominal amount. VaR always has a dual interpretation.

Example: Interpreting VaR

A $100 million portfolio has a 1.37% VaR at the 5% probability over one week. Calculate what could be lost and explain what the loss means.

Answer:

Over one week, the portfolio could lose 1.37% of $100 million or $1.37 million. There is a 5% chance that more than this will be lost and a 95% chance that less than this will be lost.

Analysis should consider some additional issues with VaR:

- The VaR time period should relate to the nature of the situation. A traditional stock and bond portfolio would likely focus on a longer monthly or quarterly VaR while a highly leveraged derivatives portfolio might focus on a shorter daily VaR.
- The percentage selected will affect the VaR. A 1% VaR would be expected to show greater risk than a 5% VaR.
- The left-tail should be examined. *Left-tail* refers to a traditional probability distribution graph of returns. The left side displays the low or negative returns, which is what VaR measures at some probability. But suppose the 5% VaR is losing $1.37 million, what happens at 4%, 1%, and so on? In other words, how much worse can it get?

METHODS FOR COMPUTING VaR

LOS 27.f: Compare the analytical (variance–covariance), historical, and Monte Carlo methods for estimating VaR and discuss the advantages and disadvantages of each.

CFA® Program Curriculum, Volume 5, page 155

Three approaches are used in calculating VaR.

The Analytical VaR Method

The **analytical method** (or variance-covariance method) is based on the normal distribution and the concept of one-tailed confidence intervals.

Example: Analytical VaR

The expected annual return for a $100,000,000 portfolio is 6.0% and the historical standard deviation is 12%. Calculate VaR at 5% probability.

Answer:

A CFA candidate would know that 5% in a single tail is associated with 1.645, or approximately 1.65, standard deviations from the mean expected return. Therefore, the 5% annual VaR is:

$$VAR = \left[\hat{R}_p - (z)(\sigma)\right]V_p$$
$$= \left[6.0\% - 1.65(12.0\%)\right](\$100,000,000)$$
$$= -13.8\%(\$100,000,000)$$
$$= -\$13,800,000$$

where:
$\hat{R}_p$ = expected return on the portfolio
V_p = value of the portfolio
z = z-value corresponding with the desired level of significance
σ = standard deviation of returns

The interpretation is that there is 5% probability that the annual loss will exceed $13.8 million and a 95% probability the annual loss will be less.

For the Exam: Be sure to know:

- 5% VaR is 1.65 standard deviations below the mean.
- 1% VaR is 2.33 standard deviations below the mean.
- VaR for periods less than a year are computed with return and standard deviations expressed for the desired period of time. For monthly VaR, divide the annual return by 12 and the standard deviation by the square root of 12. Then, compute monthly VaR. For weekly VaR, divide the annual return by 52 and the standard deviation by the square root of 52. Then, compute weekly VaR.
- For a very short period (1-day) VaR can be approximated by ignoring the return component (i.e., enter the return as zero). This will make the VaR estimate worse as no return is considered, but over one day the expected return should be small.

Example: Computing weekly VaR

For the previous example compute the weekly VaR at 1%.

Answer:

The number of standard deviations for a 1% VaR will be 2.33 below the mean return. The weekly return will be 6% / 52 = 0.1154%. The weekly standard deviation will be $12\% / 52^{1/2} = 1.6641\%$

$$VaR = 0.1154\% - 2.33(1.6641\%) = -3.7620\%$$

Advantages of the analytical method include:

- Easy to calculate and easily understood as a single number.
- Allows modeling the correlations of risks.
- Can be applied to shorter or longer time periods as relevant.

Disadvantages of the analytical method are mostly related to its assumption that returns are normally distributed. Specific issues include:

- Securities may have skewed returns. Long option positions have positive skew with frequent small losses (lose the premium paid) and occasional large gains if the option moves deep in-the-money. Short option positions will have the opposite payoff and negative skew.
- Many securities exhibit a greater number of extreme return events than are consistent with the normal distribution. This is called leptokurtosis or more commonly "fat tails" and means the amount and frequency of losses is underestimated by the method.

One approach to dealing with the skewed return distribution of options is the **delta-normal method**. This mathematical trick continues to assume the returns of the underlying are normally distributed and then applies option delta to change in the underlying to estimate change in the option. Delta is a straight line projection of how the option changes. The limitation is that delta is not stable and the greater the change in the underlying the more the actual change in the option will diverge from its delta projection. Adding the second order gamma effect improves the projection but further complicates the analysis.

The Historical VaR Method

The historical method for estimating VaR is sometimes referred to as the **historical simulation** method. One way to calculate the 5% daily VaR using the historical method is to accumulate a number of past daily returns, rank the returns from highest to lowest, and identify the lowest 5% of returns. The highest of these lowest 5% of returns is the 1-day, 5% VaR.

Example: Historical VaR

You have accumulated 100 daily returns for your $100,000,000 portfolio. After ranking the returns from highest to lowest, you identify the lowest five returns:

$$-0.0019, -0.0025, -0.0034, -0.0096, -0.0101$$

Calculate daily VaR at 5% significance using the historical method.

Answer:

Because these are the lowest five returns, they represent the 5% lower tail of the "distribution" of 100 historical returns. The fifth lowest return (−0.0019) is the 5% daily VaR. We would say there is a 5% chance of a daily loss exceeding 0.19%, or $190,000.

Advantages of the historical method include:

- Very easy to calculate and understand.
- Does not assume a returns distribution.
- Can be applied to different time periods according to industry custom.

The primary *disadvantage* of the historical method is the assumption that the pattern of historical returns will repeat in the future (i.e., it is indicative of future returns). This becomes particularly troublesome the more the manager trades. Also keep in mind that many securities (e.g., options, bonds) change characteristics with the passage of time.

The Monte Carlo VaR Method

The **Monte Carlo method** uses computer software to generate hundreds or thousands of possible outcomes from the distributions of inputs *specified by the user*. The user might specify normal distributions for some assets, skewed for others, leptokurtic for others, and complex shifting correlations over time. The runs of possible outcomes can be ranked from highest to lowest (just like historical outcomes) to determine the result at any given probability. The data could be shown graphically to provide a visual display of all outcomes and frequency.

Example: Monte Carlo VaR

A Monte Carlo model has generated 100 runs of possible output over 1-week periods. The average return and standard deviation are 5.7% and 2.1% respectively. The worst six outcomes are +0.5%, +1.5%, +1.6%, +0.3%, +0.7% and +0.5%. The portfolio is known to include extensive option positions.

Calculate the 1-week VaR at 5% significance for a beginning portfolio value of GBP 100 million.

Answer:

Option positions make the use of standard deviation inappropriate for calculating VaR. Based on the Monte Carlo simulations, the 5th percentile worst result is the 5th worst return of +1.5% for a GBP 1,500,000 gain in portfolio value over one week. 5% of the time the gain would be worse.

It appears this is a very conservative portfolio because the VaR is a gain. Typically VaR is a loss but not in this case.

The primary *advantage* of the Monte Carlo method is also its primary disadvantage. It can incorporate any assumptions regarding return patterns, correlations, and other factors the analyst believes are relevant. For some portfolios it may be the only reasonable approach to use.

That leads to its downside: the output is only as good as the input assumptions. This complexity can lead to a false sense of overconfidence in the output among the less informed. It is data and computer intensive which can make it costly to use in complex situations (where it may also be the only reasonable method to use).

Professor's Note: Both historical and Monte Carlo simulation (MCS) are similar in that they are based on selecting from a set of possible outcomes. You can use historical outcomes or, if that is unavailable or considered no longer appropriate, MCS essentially generates a "simulated history."

©2017 Kaplan, Inc.

GENERAL ADVANTAGES AND LIMITATIONS OF VaR

LOS 27.g: Discuss advantages and limitations of VaR and its extensions, including cash flow at risk, earnings at risk, and tail value at risk.

CFA® Program Curriculum, Volume 5, page 168

VaR, whatever the method of computation, has several advantages over other risk measures:

- It has become the industry standard for risk measurement and is required by many regulators.
- It aggregates all risk into one single, easy to understand number.
- It can be used in capital allocation. For example, a firm willing to accept a maximum of $1,000,000 VaR is essentially saying it is willing to lose $1,000,000 of equity capital (at some probability level). Senior management could further allocate a maximum VaR to each business unit in the firm and evaluate each unit on the return generated for the VaR allowed. Generally, the total VaR by unit will be more than the $1,000,000 firm-wide VaR. When the correlation between units is less than 1.0, the firm-wide VaR will be less than their simple summation. This is known as **risk budgeting**, how much risk can each unit take?

VaR also has clearly acknowledged limitations:

- Some of the methods (Monte Carlo) are difficult and expensive.
- The different computation methods can generate different estimates of VaR.
- It can generate a false sense of security. It is only as good as the inputs and estimation process. Even when done correctly it is probabilistic; things can always be worse.
- It is one-sided, focusing on the left tail in the return distribution, and ignores any upside potential.

VaR should not be used in isolation but in combination with other tools and actions:

- VaR projections should be continually **back-tested** to compare actual results across multiple time periods with projections. Does the pattern of results fit the probability and outcomes projected by VaR?
- **Incremental VaR** (IVaR) is the effect of an individual item on the overall risk of the portfolio. IVaR is calculated by measuring the difference between the portfolio VaR before and after an additional asset, asset class, or other aspect of the portfolio is changed.
- **Cash flow at risk** (CFAR) measures the risk of the company's cash flows. Some companies cannot be valued directly, which makes calculating VaR difficult or even meaningless. Even when VaR can be calculated, CFAR may offer additional information. CFAR is interpreted much the same as VaR, but substitutes cash flow for value. In other words, CFAR is the minimum cash flow loss at a given probability over a given time period.
- **Earnings at risk** (EAR) is analogous to CFAR only from an *accounting earnings* standpoint. Both CFAR and EAR are often used to add validity to VaR calculations.

- **Tail value at risk** (TVaR) is intended to give additional insight into what happens if VaR is exceeded. It is VaR plus the average of the outcomes in the tail. For example if the 5%, 1-day VaR is $1 million and TVaR is $2.7 million, then 5% of the time losses exceed $1 million and the average lost is another $1.7 million beyond $1 million for a total average loss of $2.7 million.
- **Credit VaR** projects risk due to credit events. It will be discussed shortly.
- **Stress testing** is a complement to VaR.

STRESS TESTING

LOS 27.h: Compare alternative types of stress testing and discuss advantages and disadvantages of each.

CFA® Program Curriculum, Volume 5, page 171

Stress testing is often employed as a complement to VaR. It may reveal outcomes not reflected in the typical VaR calculation. For example, the manager might use the historical standard deviation in estimating VaR, and if nothing unusual occurred during the measurement period, the estimated VaR will reflect only "normal" circumstances. Stress testing is just an extreme scenario.

Scenario Analysis

In a scenario analysis the user defines the events, such as interest rate movements, changes in currencies, changes in volatilities, changes in asset liquidity, and so on, and compares the value of the portfolio before and after the specified events. Multiple scenarios might consider both favorable and unfavorable scenarios.

Any scenario analysis is only as good as the accuracy of the assumptions made. Another problem is the sequence of events. Altering the sequence or having all events occur simultaneously can produce different results.

There are various forms of scenario analysis. With **stylized scenarios**, the analyst changes one or more risk factors to measure the effect on the portfolio. Rather than having the manager select risk factors, some stylized scenarios are more like industry standards. For example, in *Framework for Voluntary Oversight,*[1] the Derivatives Policy Group (DPG) identifies nine specific risk factors to include in stress testing.

---

1. *Framework for Voluntary Oversight*, Derivatives Policy Group, March 1995.

©2017 Kaplan, Inc.

For the Exam: The following lists risk factors that might be modeled in a scenario analysis.

1. Parallel yield curve shifts.

2. Changes in steepness of yield curves.

3. Parallel yield curve shifts combined with changes in steepness of yield curves.

4. Changes in yield volatilities.

5. Changes in the value of equity indices.

6. Changes in equity index volatilities.

7. Changes in the value of key currencies (relative to the U.S. dollar).

8. Changes in foreign exchange rate volatilities.

9. Changes in swap spreads in at least the G-7 countries plus Switzerland.

By providing guidelines, these stylized scenarios help managers avoid the "Oh no" syndrome, as in, "Oh, no! Why didn't we think of that?"

Other forms of scenario analysis include **actual extreme events** and **hypothetical events**, which are quite similar. With the former, the analyst measures the impact of major past events, such as the market crash of 1987 or the 1990s technology bubble, on the portfolio value. Hypothetical events are extreme events that might occur but have not previously occurred. These tests are subject to the same weaknesses as other scenario analyses (e.g., incorrect assumptions and correlations, user bias).

Stressing Models

Stress testing and stressing models are just an extension of scenario analysis focusing on adverse outcomes. Stressing can be done as:

- **Factor push analysis** is a simple stress test where the analyst pushes factors to the most disadvantageous combination of possible circumstances and measures the resulting impact on the portfolio.
- **Maximum loss optimization** uses more sophisticated mathematical and computer modeling to find this worst combination of factors.
- **Worst-case scenario** is the worst case the analyst thinks is likely to occur.

For the Exam: Scenario analysis is discussed in multiple sections of the CFA material. Understand the concept, vocabulary, and be prepared to answer questions.

EVALUATING CREDIT RISK

LOS 27.i: Evaluate the credit risk of an investment position, including forward contract, swap, and option positions.

CFA® Program Curriculum, Volume 5, page 173

Credit risk exists when there is a possibility a counterparty to a transaction will not fulfill its responsibility. Credit risk is complicated to measure. Complicating the analysis is the fact that defaults are rare so there is little data available to assist in making estimates. Projecting credit losses is a function of:

1. The probability of a default event.

2. The amount of value lost if the default event occurs, which requires estimating the loss and any recovery after the initial loss.

Credit risk can be both immediate and potential. **Current credit risk** (also called **jump-to-default risk**) is the amount of a payment currently due. Because payments are only due on specific dates, current credit risk is zero on all other dates. **Potential credit risk** is associated with payments due in the future and exists even if there is no current credit risk. It will change over time. A firm can be currently solvent and able to make payment but that does not guarantee future payments will be made. Likewise, a firm could be in short-term financial difficulty but expected to recover if given time.

Credit risk can also be affected by **cross-default-provisions**. In most lending agreements, a debtor is considered in default of all obligations if it defaults on any one of its obligations. In addition to potential credit risk associated with their own receipts, therefore, creditors are exposed to potential credit risk from a debtor defaulting on an obligation to another creditor.

Credit VaR

Credit VaR (also called **credit at risk** or **default VaR**) is defined much like VaR as an expected loss (due to default) at a given probability during a given time period. However, it is more difficult to calculate and interpret than market VaR.

*   It cannot be separated from VaR. If a security has little market value (for example, a bond with little value due to high interest rates) then there can be little credit VaR because there is little value to be lost if default occurs. While market VaR is called left-tail risk because it occurs when returns on the asset are low and market value is lost, credit VaR is right-tail risk as credit risk is greatest when returns and market value are highest.
*   Even if the probability of default can be estimated, there is still the issue of estimating recovery rates.
*   The pricing data of credit derivatives has provided additional insight into the market opinion of potential loss on securities. Option pricing models have also been applied to gain some insight. Like options, credit risk is one-sided, on a reasonable quality security upside is limited but default leads to substantial loss of value.

©2017 Kaplan, Inc.

- Credit risk across multiple exposures is difficult to aggregate and would depend on the correlation of default between each pair of exposures.

Despite the difficulty of modeling and aggregating credit risk, at any one moment the potential credit risk of an investment is its current market value. That market value will be determined by 1) the remaining cash flows to be exchanged (and at risk) and 2) the degree to which market conditions have changed to create a gain or loss in value. The credit risk is one-sided, meaning the party with positive market value is at risk if the counterparty does not perform. The counterparty with negative market value has no potential credit risk. Under current conditions they are at a loss and would actually benefit if the transaction could somehow cease to exist. However, this does not mean potential credit risk will remain stable. As payments are made, the remaining cash flows at risk decrease which leads to a tendency for VaR to decrease. Additionally, market conditions can change, causing VaR to increase, decrease, or even reverse between the party with the gain and the party with the loss.

Forward Contracts

At the initiation of a standard forward contract, there is no exchange of cash and initial value is zero. As time passes, interest rates or prices have probably changed so that one of the counterparties will have a gain, putting that party at risk if the counterparty defaults. At any one point the potential credit risk is with the party who has a gain. At settlement of the contract the counterparty entitled to receive the payment faces *current credit risk*, as the payment is due immediately and the counterparty could default.

While at any future point in time the potential credit risk will be the current market value for the party with a gain, it can be anticipated that the potential credit risk will be highest in the middle to later part of the contract's life. All cash flow occurs at expiration so all cash flow remains at risk until expiration; the more time that passes from initiation of the contract, the greater the opportunity for conditions to change and create significant gain and credit risk for one counterparty.

Example: Credit risk in a forward contract

Suppose a forward contract that expires in one year is available on an asset that is currently worth $100 and the risk-free rate is 4%; therefore, the forward price would be $100 × 1.04 = $104. It is now nine months later, and the asset is worth $101.50. **Determine** who bears the credit risk in the forward contract and **calculate** the amount of the credit risk.

Answer:

The holder of the long position in the contract is obligated to buy the asset for $104 in one year. The value to the long is:

$$\$101.50 - \frac{\$104}{1.04^{3/12}} = -\$1.4852$$

Because the value is negative, this means the long position would owe the short position this amount if the contract was settled today. The value to the short position is positive, representing a claim on the asset in this amount from the long; thus, the short bears the *potential* credit risk, and because the contract is not settled for another three months, there is no *current* credit risk.

Example: Valuing the credit risk of a foreign exchange forward contract

As part of a foreign exchange hedging strategy, a U.S. portfolio manager has shorted a forward contract on 1,000,000 euros denominated in U.S. dollars with a forward price of $1.8095/€. With three months remaining on the contract, the spot rate is now $1.8038/€, the U.S. interest rate is 5.5%, and the foreign interest rate is 5.0%. **Determine** the value and direction of any credit risk.

Answer:

The value of the contract on the base currency (B) to the long position is:

$$\text{value to long} = \frac{S_t}{(1+B)^t} - \frac{F_0}{(1+P)^t}$$

©2017 Kaplan, Inc.

In this case the exchange rates are given as direct quotes for the EUR (i.e., as USD/EUR). The USD is P (the pricing currency), and the EUR is B (the base currency). The contract position is short B, the EUR. The remaining contract term is three months or 0.25 of a year.

$$\frac{\$1.8038/€}{1.05^{0.25}} - \frac{\$1.8095/€}{1.055^{0.25}} = -\$0.003509/€$$

This is negative value to the long EUR position and positive value to our 1,000,000 short EUR position of €1,000,000 × ($0.003509/€) = $3,509. At this moment in time, the potential credit risk to the short position is its positive value of $3,509. Think of this as the value immediately lost if the counterparty immediately ceases to exist.

 Professor's Note: It is common to see this value formula shown with f for the B base currency and d for the P pricing currency. That works in this case because the contract is on the foreign currency from the investor's perspective and it is the base currency in the quotes.

Swaps

A swap should be thought of as a series of forward contracts. Following this analysis, the swap will have actual credit risk on each payment exchange date as well as potential credit risk throughout its life. So unlike the forward there is actual credit risk on multiple dates and on each of these dates, as cash flows are exchanged, subsequent cash flows to be exchanged in the future decrease. At any future point, potential credit risk is the value of the swap for the counterparty with a gain.

Unlike a forward, the credit risk of most swaps (such as *interest rate* and *equity swaps*) is expected to be highest somewhere around the middle of their life. Assuming the swap is correctly priced, the initial value and credit risk are zero. Then as some time passes and conditions change, one or both parties will have credit risk. If both parties are required to make payments both will be at risk the other counterparty is unable to pay. In the more common netting of payment situation, the credit risk will be one–sided and to the party with the gain. As the swap nears its maturity and the number of remaining settlement payments decreases, the credit risk also decreases.

The exception to this is a *currency swap*. Because payments are in different currencies, netting of settlement payments is inappropriate and both parties can be simultaneously exposed to current credit risk on settlement dates. Also, due to the exchange of principals at inception and the return of principals on the maturity date, the credit risk of a currency swap is highest between the middle and final maturity of the agreement. The notional principal is very large in relation to the periodic cash flows and remains at risk until the last exchange.

Options

With an option, unlike a forward or swap contract, only the long position (the buyer) faces credit risk. The buyer decides whether to exercise the option and will only do so when there is positive value. Only the buyer is at risk the seller will be unable to perform.

For both American and European options, the buyer will have potential credit risk equal to the current market value of the option. Theoretically the American-style option value can be somewhat higher because it is never worth less than a European-style option. Neither style can have actual credit risk until it is exercised. With the American, that actual risk could occur prior to expiration if the owner chooses to exercise early (a rare event). The European-style option can only have actual credit risk on the expiration date.

Liquidity and Non-financial Risks

Liquidity is not considered in measuring VaR. Implicit in VaR is the assumption that positions can be sold at their trading or estimated market value. Thus, VaR can give an inaccurate estimate of the true potential for loss. Estimating liquidity is difficult. For example, due to a statistical anomaly and in spite of large bid-ask spreads, some infrequently traded securities have low historical volatility. Even if historical volatility is accurate, the inability to quickly adjust a position can lead to increased losses not caught in the VaR measure. The manager should take this into account and consider how large their position is in relation to past and likely future trading volume.

Non-financial risks are difficult to measure. Many are outlier events for which the insurance industry may offer insurance and have a data base from which estimates of loss, recovery, and probability could be made.

©2017 Kaplan, Inc.

MANAGING MARKET RISK

LOS 27.j: Demonstrate the use of risk budgeting, position limits, and other methods for managing market risk.

CFA® Program Curriculum, Volume 5, page 182

Risk budgeting is the process of determining which risks are acceptable and how total enterprise risk is allocated across business units or portfolio managers. Through an enterprise risk management (ERM) system, upper management allocates different amounts of capital across portfolio managers. In this fashion, the amount of capital (and the associated VaR) allocated to portfolio managers (e.g., foreign currency, domestic and international bonds, equities) is based upon management's prior determination of the desired exposure to each sector.

An ERM system affords the ability to continuously monitor the risk budget so that any deviations are immediately reported to upper management. Another benefit of a risk budgeting system is the ability to compare manager performance in relationship to the amount of capital and risk allocated (i.e., measure risk-adjusted performance with **return on VaR**).

Example: Return on VaR

Assume Manager A and B work for the same firm. Manager A has been allocated $100 million of capital and a weekly VaR of $5 million. Manager B has been allocated $500 million and a weekly VaR of $10 million. Over a given period, A earns a profit of $1 million, and B earns a profit of $3 million. Their combined capital and VaR are $600 million and $13.7 million

Compare their results using *return on capital* and *return on VaR*. **Discuss** their combined capital and VaR.

Answer:

	A	B
Capital (funds that can be invested)	$100,000,000	$500,000,000
VaR	$5,000,000	$10,000,000
Profit	$1,000,000	$3,000,000
Return on capital	1%	0.6%
Return on VaR	20%	30%

By comparing the managers on return on capital, it appears that A outperformed B. When we measure return on VaR, however, Manager B outperformed Manager A on a risk-adjusted basis.

The capital position of each manager is a simple summation of capital positions. VaR is a more complex aggregation and will be less than a simple addition when correlation is less than 1.0

In addition to VaR, methods for managing market risk include:

- **Position limits** that place a nominal dollar cap on a given position.
- **Liquidity limits** are related to position limits. In an effort to minimize liquidity risk, risk managers may set nominal position limits as some portion of typical trading volumes.
- A **performance stopout** sets an absolute dollar limit for losses to the position over a certain period. If the stopout level is hit, the position must be closed to limit further loss.
- In addition to a VaR allocation, the portfolio manager may be subject to individual **risk factor limits**. As the name implies, the manager must limit exposure to individual risk factors as prescribed by upper management.

Other measures include **scenario analysis limits**, which require the manager to structure the portfolio so as to limit the impact of given scenarios, and **leverage limits**, which limit the amount of leverage the manager can employ.

MANAGING CREDIT RISK

LOS 27.k: Demonstrate the use of exposure limits, marking to market, collateral, netting arrangements, credit standards, and credit derivatives to manage credit risk.

CFA® Program Curriculum, Volume 5, page 186

Credit VaR based on standard deviation is inherently difficult to apply to one-sided credit risk. Credit change for most traditional securities is on the downside with limited upside. While credit VaR may be considered, other methods to limit credit risk are extensively employed:

- **Limiting exposure** is a rational first line of defense against credit risk. It means limiting the amount of loans to any individual debtor or the amount of derivative transactions with any individual counterparty.
- **Marking to market** is employed with many derivative contracts in which the value to one party will be positive while the value to the other will be negative. The party whose value is negative pays this amount to the other party, and the contract is repriced.

Example: Marking to market of a forward contract

Assume there is a 1-year forward contract at $106 with the risk-free rate of 5%, and it is three months into the life of the contract. If the current spot price is $104, **determine** the cash flows, assuming the parties have agreed to mark to market every three months.

©2017 Kaplan, Inc.

Answer:

The market value to the long is as follows:

$$\$104 - \frac{\$106}{1.05^{9/12}} = \$1.8087$$

Therefore, the short owes the long this amount. The contract will be repriced at $\$104(1.05)^{9/12} = \$107.876$, and the two parties will mark to market again at the 6-month point.

- **Collateral** is often required in transactions that generate credit risk. For example, consider the typical home purchase where the homeowner must provide equity of 5% to 20% of the total value of the home. In business transactions, collateral can be business assets or liquid marketable securities.

  In derivatives markets, both parties are often required to post *margin*, and if the contract is marked to market, either side may be required to post additional margin (collateral).

- **Payment netting** is frequently employed in derivatives contracts that can generate credit exposure to both sides. When each side has credit risk, we value and *net* the two to determine which side has the greater obligation. If the contract has a mark-to-market clause, one side pays the other, and the contract is repriced at the new forward rate.

- **Closeout netting** is employed in *bankruptcy* proceedings. In this case, all the transactions between the bankrupt company and a single counterparty are netted to determine the overall exposure. When this is done, the bankrupt firm cannot claim assets equaling payments it is due while at the same time defaulting on its obligations.

- It is always wise to impose **minimum credit standards** on a debtor. The quality of the debtor—the debtor's creditworthiness—is sometimes hard to evaluate with any confidence. For example, commercial banks, the largest derivatives dealers, make loans to many types of debtors at the same time they are in countless derivatives contracts. Any time the dealer, or any counterparty for that matter, is simultaneously in numerous contracts, creditworthiness is difficult to ascertain.

  A lower credit quality entity can meet minimum credit standards by creating subsidiaries with the special purpose of entering into derivatives (or other) contracts. These **special purpose vehicles** (SPVs) and **enhanced derivatives products companies** (EDPCs) are completely separate from the parent companies and established with sufficient capital to ensure high credit ratings. By restructuring them this way, problems with the parent, such as credit downgrades, are not reflected in the ratings of the SPV or EDPC.

- Risk can be transferred to somebody else through **credit derivatives**, such as credit default swaps, credit forwards, credit spread options, and total return swaps.
  - In a **credit default swap**, the protection buyer (i.e., the asset holder) makes regular payments to the dealer and receives a payment when a specified credit event occurs.

- ◆ A **credit spread forward** is also based upon a credit spread, but as with other forward contracts, there will almost always be a payment by one of the parties. That is, there will be a payment unless the reference spread equals the spread specified in the contract.
- ◆ The holder of a **credit spread option** receives a payment when the rate on an asset exceeds a reference yield (such as LIBOR) by more than the specified spread. The payment partially compensates for the decline in the value of the asset. Note that because this is an option, it has value, and a payment is made only if it is in-the-money.
- ◆ In a **total return swap**, the asset owner agrees to accept a variable return from a dealer in exchange for the total return on an asset. When the asset is subject to capital gains and losses, the dealer accepts both the credit and interest rate risk. That is, if the asset increases in value, the owner passes the capital gain along to the dealer in the form of a cash payment. Likewise, if the asset decreases in value, the dealer makes a payment to the asset owner.

MEASURING RISK-ADJUSTED PERFORMANCE

LOS 27.1: Discuss the Sharpe ratio, risk-adjusted return on capital, return over maximum drawdown, and the Sortino ratio as measures of risk-adjusted performance.

CFA® Program Curriculum, Volume 5, page 189

The **Sharpe ratio** measures excess return (over the risk-free rate) per unit of risk, measured as standard deviation. The principal drawback to applying the Sharpe ratio as a measure of risk-adjusted return is the assumption of normality in the excess return distribution. This is particularly troublesome when the portfolio contains options and other instruments with non-symmetric payoffs. The formula for the Sharpe ratio is:

$$S_P = \frac{\overline{R}_P - \overline{R}_F}{\sigma_P}$$

Risk-adjusted return on invested capital (RAROC). RAROC is the ratio of the portfolio's expected return to some measure of risk, such as VaR (see our earlier discussion of return on VaR). Management can then compare the manager's RAROC to his historical or expected RAROC or to a benchmark RAROC.

Return over maximum drawdown (RoMAD). RoMAD is the annual return divided by the fund or portfolio's largest percentage drawdown. Any single drawdown is the percent drop in valuation from a "high water" mark to a subsequent low. For example, the annual return is 17% with a maximum percentage decline of 25%. The RoMAD is 0.68.

$$RoMAD = \frac{\overline{R}_P}{\text{maximum drawdown}}$$

To demonstrate RoMAD, consider Figure 1.

Figure 1: Monthly Portfolio Values and Maximum Drawdown

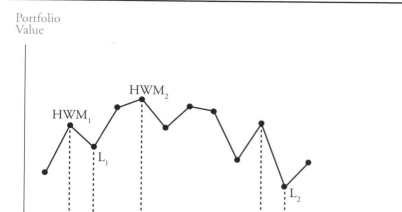

Based only on the information in the chart, the portfolio rises to an initial high water mark at point 2, followed by a subsequent low at point 3. Suppose that is a 2.1% decline. The portfolio then rises to a new HWM at point 5 and declines to a subsequent low at point 11. Suppose this is a 9.7% decline. The maximum drawdown is 9.7%. Each decline starts with a high water mark until the next lowest low. If the portfolio rises above a previous HWM, a new drawdown analysis starts.

The **Sortino ratio** is the ratio of excess return to risk. Excess return for the Sortino ratio (the numerator) is calculated as the portfolio return less the *minimum acceptable portfolio return* (MAR). The denominator of the ratio is the standard deviation of returns calculated using only returns below the MAR. The motivation behind the downside measure of volatility utilized in the Sortino ratio is the sense that very good performance (high returns) can unfairly inflate the volatility measure (the standard deviation used as the risk measure).

$$\text{Sortino} = \frac{\bar{R}_p - MAR}{\text{downside deviation}}$$

SETTING CAPITAL REQUIREMENTS

LOS 27.m: Demonstrate the use of VaR and stress testing in setting capital requirements.

CFA® Program Curriculum, Volume 5, page 191

Firms have limited capital and will allocate that capital across units of the firm to maximize return to the firm at acceptable levels of risk. VaR and stress testing both lend themselves to a systematic process of capital allocation.

VaR measures downside risk and has the benefit of considering correlation and the potential risk reduction through diversification across business units. A firm could project the expected profit to VaR of each unit and allocate more capital to the higher return to risk units. The process would be more complex than simply allocating all capital to the highest return to risk because the capital must be spread across units in order to achieve diversification. Another benefit of using VaR for capital allocation is it can be integrated with a VaR-based risk management process.

Cons:

- VaR is only as good as the assumptions used in its calculation, and it does not consider all worst-case scenarios.
- VaR may not be well understood by the business units.
- Diversification issues can be counterintuitive. It may be appropriate to allocate capital to a very low return unit if the diversification benefit is large enough to allow an increase in allocation to a higher risk and return unit.

Stress testing is the natural complement to VaR as it can consider more extreme outlier events that may not be reflected in the VaR calculation.

Other Methods of Capital Allocation

Nominal, notional, or monetary position limits. These are easy to understand. For example, a firm might set a max capital allocation to two traders of $50,000,000 each. This fails to consider the correlation between the trader's positions and if it is less than +1, the true risk is generally less than $100,000,000. In addition, one or both traders may have large long and short positions that net to less than $50,000,000 of capital each. In other words, simple nominal limits do not consider correlation between and leveraging in the positions.

Max loss limits. VaR can be seen as a kind of max loss at a specified probability but, in addition, a unit could have an assigned max loss for that unit alone (ignoring correlation issues). In theory, adding all the max loss limits would be the most the firm can lose.

Internal and regulatory capital requirements. Either firm management may desire or regulators may require the firm to have a specified minimum amount of capital to minimize the probability of bankruptcy. For example, if the firm has a 1 year 1% VaR of GBP 50M and the capital of the firm is GBP 55M, in a given year, there is a less than 1% chance losses could be large enough to deplete the firm's capital.

Behavioral conflicts. The ERM system must recognize the potential for incentive conflicts between management, which allocates the risk, and those who make the investment decisions, the portfolio managers. For example, once the portfolio is recognized to be headed for a loss for the period, the portfolio manager, whose salary and bonus are typically tied to positive performance, has little incentive to minimize risk. In fact, the manager might well have an incentive to increase risk in hopes of generating a profit. Recognizing this potential, the system and upper management must take steps to avoid it through monitoring or even in the structuring of performance incentives.

©2017 Kaplan, Inc.

KEY CONCEPTS

LOS 27.a

Risk management is a continual process of:
- Identifying and measuring specific risk exposures.
- Setting specific risk tolerance levels.
- Monitoring the process and taking any necessary corrective actions.

Risk governance should originate from senior management, which determine the structure of the system [i.e., whether centralized (a single group) or decentralized (risk management at the business unit level)].

A decentralized risk governance system has the benefit of putting risk management in the hands of the individuals closest to everyday operations. A centralized system (also called an enterprise risk management system or ERM) provides a better view of how the risks of the business units are correlated.

LOS 27.b, c

In evaluating a firm's ERM system, the analyst should ask whether:
- Senior management consistently allocates capital on a risk-adjusted basis.
- The ERM system properly identifies and defines all relevant internal and external risk factors.
- The ERM system utilizes an appropriate model for quantifying the potential impacts of the risk factors.
- Risks are properly managed.
- There is a committee in place to oversee the entire system to enable timely feedback and reactions to problems.
- The ERM system has built in checks and balances.

A risk management problem can be an event associated with a macro or micro factor, or even the ERM system itself. When a problem occurs:
- Identify the problem and assess the damage.
- Determine whether the problem is due to a temporary aberration or a long-term change in capital market structure or pricing fundamentals.
- If the problem is temporary, the best action may be none at all.
- If the problem is deemed a long-run change in fundamentals or comes from within the ERM system itself, corrective action is justified.
- If the problem stems from a risk factor that was previously modeled incorrectly, revisit the risk model.
- If the problem stems from a risk factor that was not originally identified and priced, management must determine whether to manage the risk or hedge it.
- A problem can also arise from reliance on an incorrectly specified risk pricing model (i.e., risk could be modeled using an incorrect metric).

LOS 27.d
- Financial market risks are related to price changes on traded securities or instruments (interest rates, exchange rates, equity prices, and commodity prices).
- Financial, but not market risks are those that have traditionally not had directly observable market pricing:
  - Liquidity risk if positions cannot be quickly changed at close to expected fair prices.
  - Credit risk from losses due to failure to pay by a counterparty. This risk is acquiring more marketlike characteristics with the growth in credit derivatives.
- Non-financial risks:
  - Operations risk from failure of a firm's operating systems; including its ERM system, due to personal, technological, mechanical, or other problems.
  - Settlement risk when one side of a position is paying while the other is defaulting.
  - Model risk when improper models or assumptions are used to value items that lack market pricing.
  - Regulatory, tax, accounting, legal, and political risk have similar elements in that they refer to how rules can change. These risks can be more significant when dealing with new security types and instruments.
  - Sovereign risk has elements of credit risk but requires estimating not only the ability of a foreign government but also its willingness to pay.
  - Other risks include ESG, performance netting, and settlement netting risks.

LOS 27.e
VaR is an estimate of the minimum expected loss (alternatively, the maximum loss):
- Over a set time period.
- At a desired level of significance (alternatively, at a desired level of confidence).

For example, a 5% VaR of $1,000 over the next week means that, given the standard deviation and distribution of returns for the asset, management can say there is a 5% probability that the asset will lose a minimum of (at least) $1,000 over the coming week. Stated differently, management is 95% confident the loss will be no greater than $1,000.

VaR considers only the downside or lower tail of the distribution of returns. Unlike the typical z-score, the level of significance for VaR is the probability in the lower tail only (i.e., a 5% VaR means there is 5% in the lower tail).

LOS 27.f
The analytical method (also known as the variance-covariance method or delta normal method) for estimating VaR requires the assumption of a normal distribution. This is because the method utilizes the expected return and standard deviation of returns.

$$\text{VaR} = \left[\hat{R}_p - (z)(\sigma) \right] V_p$$

where:
$\hat{R}_p$ = expected return on the portfolio
V_p = value of the portfolio
z = z-value corresponding with the desired level of significance
σ = standard deviation of returns

Advantages of the analytical method include:
- Easy to calculate and easily understood.
- Allows modeling the correlations of risks.
- Can be applied to different time periods according to industry custom.

Disadvantages of the analytical method include:
- The need to assume a normal distribution.
- The difficulty in estimating the correlations between individual assets in very large portfolios.

The historical method for estimating VaR is sometimes referred to as the historical simulation method. The easiest way to calculate the 5% daily VaR using the historical method is to accumulate a number of past daily returns, rank the returns from highest to lowest, and identify the lowest 5% of returns. The highest of these lowest 5% of returns is the 1-day, 5% VaR.

Advantages of the historical method include:
- Easy to calculate and easily understood.
- No need to assume a returns distribution.
- Can be applied to different time periods according to industry custom.

The primary disadvantage of the historical method is the assumption that the pattern of historical returns will repeat in the future (i.e., is indicative of future returns).

The Monte Carlo method refers to computer software that generates hundreds, thousands, or more possible outcomes from the distributions of inputs specified by the user. After the output is generated it can be ranked from best to worst, just as in the historical method, to determine VaR at any desired probability.

The primary advantage of the Monte Carlo method is the ability to incorporate any returns distribution or asset correlation. This is also its primary disadvantage, however. The analyst must make thousands of assumptions about the returns distributions for all inputs as well as their correlations.

LOS 27.g

One primary *advantage* of VaR is the ability to compare the operating performance of different assets with different risk characteristics. A *disadvantage* of all methods for calculating VaR is that they suffer from the constant need to estimate inputs and make assumptions, and thus the problem becomes more and more daunting as the number of assets in the portfolio gets larger.

Cash flow at risk (CFAR) measures the risk of the company's cash flows. CFAR is interpreted much the same as VaR, only substituting cash flow for value.

Earnings at risk (EAR) is analogous to CFAR only from an *accounting earnings* standpoint. Both CFAR and EAR are often used to add validity to VaR calculations.

Tail value at risk (TVaR) is VaR plus the expected value in the tail of the distribution, which could be estimated by averaging the possible losses in the tail.

Extensions of VaR: VaR can also be used to measure credit at risk, and efforts have been made to estimate a variation of VaR for assets with non-normal distributions.

LOS 27.h

Stress testing, which is typically employed as a complement to VaR, measures the impacts of unusual events that might not be reflected in the typical VaR calculation. Stress testing can take two forms: scenario analysis and stressing models.

Scenario analysis is used to measure the effect on the portfolio of simultaneous movements in several factors or to measure the effects of unusually large movements in individual factors.

Potential weaknesses in any scenario analysis include the inability to accurately measure by-products of major factor movements (i.e., the impact a major movement in one factor has on other factors) or include the effects of simultaneous adverse movements in risk factors.

Stressing models are extensions to the scenario analysis models and include factor push models, maximum loss optimization, and worst-case scenarios.

In factor push analysis, the analyst deliberately pushes a factor or factors to the extreme and measures the impact on the portfolio. Maximum loss optimization involves identifying risk factors that have the greatest potential for impacting the value of the portfolio and moving to protect against those factors. Worst-case scenario is exactly that the analyst simultaneously pushes all risk factors to their worst cases to measure the absolute worst case for the portfolio.

Because stressing models are just another version of scenario analysis, they suffer from the same potential problems; specifically, incorrect inputs and assumptions as well as the possibility of user bias.

LOS 27.i

Credit risk is the possibility of default by the counterparty to a financial transaction. The monetary exposure to credit risk is a function of the probability of a default event and the amount of money lost if the default event occurs.

At the settlement date for a forward contract, one or both parties will have to pay the other. The value of the forward contract (the associated credit risk) is the present value of any net payoff.

A swap should be thought of as a series of forward contracts, so the credit risk associated with a swap is *potential* until each settlement date. Likewise, the value of a swap is the present value of future settlement payments.

Unlike forward and swap contracts, the credit risk to an option is only borne by the long position. The credit risk to a *European* option, even if it is in-the-money, can only be potential until the date it matures. The credit risk of an American option will be at least as great as a similar European option.

LOS 27.j

Risk budgeting is the process of determining which risks are acceptable and how total enterprise risk is allocated across business units or portfolio managers. In addition to VaR, methods for managing market risk include:

- A position limit places a nominal dollar cap on a given position. Position limits are generally used by upper management to help maintain the desired level of firm wide diversification.
- Liquidity limits are related to position limits. In an effort to minimize liquidity risk, risk managers will set dollar position limits according to the frequency of trading volumes.
- A performance stopout goes beyond the VaR measure by setting an absolute dollar limit for losses to the position over a certain period.
- In addition to a VaR allocation, the portfolio manager may be subject to individual risk factor limits. As the name implies, the manager must limit exposure to individual risk factors as prescribed by upper management.

LOS 27.k

Due to the lack of historical data, measures such as VaR (which assumes a normal distribution) are very difficult, if not inappropriate, to use in managing credit risk. Several non-VaR measures have been developed to help control credit risk.

- Limiting exposure means limiting the amount of loans to any individual debtor or the amount of derivative transactions with any individual counterparty.
- Marking to market is employed with many derivative contracts.
- Collateral is often required in transactions that generate credit risk.
- Payment netting is frequently employed in derivatives contracts that can generate credit exposure to both sides. When each side has credit risk, we value and net the two to determine which side has the greater obligation.
- It is always wise to impose minimum credit standards on a debtor.
- Risk can be transferred to someone else through credit derivatives such as credit default swaps, credit forwards, credit spread options, and total return swaps.

LOS 27.l

The Sharpe ratio measures excess return (over the risk-free rate) per unit of risk, measured as standard deviation. The principal drawback to applying the Sharpe ratio as a measure of risk-adjusted return is the assumption of normality in the excess return distribution. This is particularly troublesome when the portfolio contains options and other instruments with non-symmetric payoffs.

$$S_P = \frac{\bar{R}_P - \bar{R}_F}{\sigma_P}$$

Risk-adjusted return on invested capital (RAROC). RAROC is the ratio of the portfolio's expected return to some measure of risk, such as VaR. Management can then compare the manager's RAROC to his historical or expected RAROC or to a benchmark RAROC.

Return over maximum drawdown (RoMAD). Drawdown is the difference between a portfolio's high water marks and subsequent lows during a measurement period. The maximum drawdown is the largest drawdown over the total period.

$$RoMAD = \frac{\overline{R}_p}{\text{maximum drawdown}}$$

The Sortino ratio is the ratio of excess return to risk. Excess return for the Sortino ratio (the numerator) is calculated as the portfolio return less the minimum acceptable portfolio return (MAR). The denominator of the ratio is the standard deviation of returns calculated using only returns below the MAR.

$$\text{Sortino} = \frac{\overline{R}_p - MAR}{\text{downside deviation}}$$

LOS 27.m

Firms naturally want to allocate capital across business units to maximize total return on total capital. VaR and stress testing are useful tools in this process. VaR can be interpreted as a maximum loss at a given probability. It has the benefits of capturing the diversification benefits between business units and can be integrated with the firm's risk management process.

Stress testing is a natural complement to VaR by allowing the firm to consider even more extreme events.

Other methods of allocating capital include:
- Nominal, notional, or monetary position limits.
- Max loss limits.
- Internal and regulatory capital requirements.

©2017 Kaplan, Inc.

CONCEPT CHECKERS

1. As risk manager for ABC Enterprises, J.Q. Smith is assessing the firm's various risk exposures to include in a regular semiannual report to upper management. ABC is a medium-size import/export firm located in Charleston, South Carolina. Its primary sources for imports, which it sells in the United States, are located in China and Mexico. It has customers throughout the world, but more than half of its exports go to the Eurozone.[2] ABC customarily borrows to cover funds tied up in exports. **Discuss** risk exposures Smith should report.

2. In her first semiannual review of the firm's ERM system, B. Jones, the new risk manager, comes across the following two statements in the risk management policies and procedures manual:
   - The performance of each of the firm's portfolio managers will be assessed annually, and managers will be ranked from highest to lowest total return. Managers who have added the most value to their portfolios will receive increased capital allocations for the following year.
   - It is the responsibility of each portfolio manager to monitor and maintain the risk of the portfolio within normal, acceptable levels as described in the IPS.

   State and **explain** whether the actions described in each of the statements is appropriate for an effective ERM system. In addition to your discussion on these two statements, **state** at least two other characteristics of a good ERM system.

3. A portfolio contains two assets, A and B. The expected returns are 9% and 13%, respectively, and their standard deviations are 18% and 21%, respectively. The correlation between the returns on A and B is estimated at 0.50. **Calculate** the 5% (analytical) VaR of a $100,000 portfolio invested 75% in A and 25% in B. **List** a total of two advantages and/or disadvantages of analytical VaR.

---

2. Eurozone is the name given to the countries that have adopted the euro as currency. They include Austria, Belgium, Cyprus, Estonia, Finland, France, Germany, Greece, Ireland, Italy, Luxembourg, Malta, the Netherlands, Portugal, Slovakia, Slovenia, and Spain.

4. Below are 40 monthly returns (in percent) for LMN Portfolio, ranked from highest to lowest. **Calculate** the 5% historical VaR for the $1,500,000 portfolio. **List** a total of two advantages and/or disadvantages of historical VaR.

6.147	2.377	1.594	0.993	–0.672	–1.523
5.875	2.232	1.320	0.989	–0.749	–1.726
3.660	2.064	1.189	0.962	–0.851	–2.024
3.432	2.059	1.148	0.901	–1.112	–2.250
3.376	1.839	1.128	0.353	–1.182	–3.359
2.510	1.652	1.054	–0.231	–1.313	
2.388	1.609	0.996	–0.550	–1.367	

5. **List** and **describe** three types of financial risk, and **offer** mitigating strategies.

6. **List** and **describe** five types of nonfinancial risk, and **offer** mitigating strategies.

7. Because VaR has certain limitations, managers will often back test their VaR models (i.e., check the accuracy of their VaR predictions after the fact). In addition, there are measures that can be used as supplements to the regular VaR measure (i.e., supplement the information provided by VaR). **List** and **describe** two measures that can be used as supplements to VaR.

©2017 Kaplan, Inc.

8.   **List** and **discuss** three methods for managing credit risk.

9.   One of your portfolio managers, Mort Van Sleet, has recently complained that by measuring risk-adjusted returns using the Sharpe ratio, he is placed at an unfair disadvantage. He has stated flatly that the standard deviation of his portfolio returns is artificially inflated. **Explain** how this can be true, and **offer** and **explain** a potential solution to the problem.

10.   While reading and entering return data into a performance evaluation model, the programmer transposed the number 0.10 to 0.01. As a result, the average return and maximum drawdown for the period were calculated incorrectly for that manager. The mistake was discovered only immediately before paying out bonuses and allocating capital for the coming year. **Discuss** the failure in the ERM system and possible remedies.

11.   A German portfolio manager entered a 3-month forward contract with a U.S. bank to deliver $10,000,000 for euros at a forward rate of €0.8135/$. One month into the contract, the spot rate is €0.8170/$, the euro rate is 3.5%, and the U.S. rate is 4.0%. **Determine** the value and direction of any credit risk.

For more questions related to this topic review, log in to your Schweser online account and launch SchweserPro™ QBank; and for video instruction covering each LOS in this topic review, log in to your Schweser online account and launch the OnDemand video lectures, if you have purchased these products.

ANSWERS – CONCEPT CHECKERS

1. In determining the risks to report, the credit manager should consider market, credit, liquidity, operational, model, settlement, regulatory, legal, tax, accounting, sovereign, and political risks.

    *   Market risk pertains to interest rates, exchange rates, and stock and commodity prices. The manager should report ABC's exposures to interest rates (because it borrows to cover short-term cash needs) and exchange rates (because of exposures to international foreign currencies).
    *   The manager should report exposure to credit risk because the firm's customers no doubt buy on credit.
    *   Liquidity risk, which pertains to the ability to buy/sell securities quickly at a fair price, is probably not a concern for ABC, unless it utilizes forward contracts on foreign currencies.
    *   The firm will face operational risk to the extent that its business activities are sensitive to operational difficulties (e.g., interruptions in the transportation of products).
    *   The firm faces model risk if it values its exposures to foreign currencies and attempts to take offsetting positions. Some exposures may be very difficult to determine accurately because they deal with customers all over the globe, and small currencies may be difficult to model.
    *   Settlement risk applies to transactions that include payments due to and receipts due from counterparties. There is not enough information to make a determination on whether the firm faces settlement risk.
    *   They are exposed to regulatory risk in that foreign countries can change regulations on imports and exports.
    *   Legal risk pertains to the enforcement of contracts. Different international laws can make enforcement of contracts somewhat challenging if a foreign counterparty disputes the terms of a contract.
    *   Any business is subject to the possibility of changing tax laws. Global trade exacerbates this problem, also.
    *   The company may be exposed to accounting risk if it deals with less-developed nations that follow different and possibly changing accounting rules. Changing accounting rules can affect the profitability (business risk) of those customers.
    *   Sovereign risk generally pertains to governments, so unless the company deals with a foreign government, sovereign risk is probably not a concern. If it does sell to foreign governments, payment of bills is always subject to the government's willingness and ability to pay.
    *   Political risks pertain to changing political climate. Even if the firm faces little domestic political risk, it is definitely exposed to the risks associated with the political climate of its trading partners.

2. "The performance of each of the firm's portfolio managers will be assessed annually, and managers will be ranked from highest to lowest total return. Managers who have added the most value to their portfolios will receive increased capital allocations for the following year."

    Inappropriate. Senior management should allocate capital (consistently) on a risk-adjusted basis.

    "It is the responsibility of each portfolio manager to monitor and maintain the risk of the portfolio within normal, acceptable levels as described in the IPS."

Inappropriate. A functional ERM system should provide for performance monitoring by a risk management committee that reports directly to upper management.

Other characteristics of an ERM system:
- The ERM system properly identifies and defines all relevant internal and external risk factors.
- The ERM system utilizes an appropriate model for quantifying the potential impacts of the risk factors.
  - Does the model include correlations of the risk factors to enable management to evaluate the firm's overall risk position from a portfolio perspective?
  - Does the model allow for potential combinations of risk factors simultaneously impacting the firm?
  - Does the model allow for changing factor sensitivities?
- Risks are properly managed.
  - Has management identified risks for which it has sufficient experience, information, and tools to provide effective management?
  - Has management identified risks it is uncomfortable with and that should be reduced or eliminated (hedged)?
  - There is a committee in place to oversee the entire system to enable timely feedback and reactions to problems.
- The ERM system has built-in checks and balances.
  - Does it provide for continual monitoring and feedback on the risk factors?
  - Does it provide for continual monitoring and feedback on the risk management system itself?
  - Does it evaluate the ability of the risk model to accurately estimate and quantify the risks?
  - Does it have a mechanism for incorporating newly identified risks?

3. To calculate VaR, we need the portfolio expected return and standard deviation:

$$\hat{R}_P = 0.75(0.09) + 0.25(0.13) = 0.0675 + 0.0325 = 0.10$$
$$\sigma_P^2 = (0.75)^2(0.18)^2 + (0.25)^2(0.21)^2 + 2(0.75)(0.25)(0.18)(0.21)(0.50) = 0.02807$$
$$\sigma_P = \sqrt{\sigma_P^2} = 0.1675$$

then:
$$VAR = V_P\left[\hat{R}_P - Z(\sigma_P)\right], \text{where } Z = 1.65$$
$$VAR = \$100,000\left[0.10 - 1.65(0.1675)\right] = -\$17,637$$

The manager is 95% confident the maximum loss over the coming year will not be greater than $17,637. Alternatively, the manager can say there is a 5% probability of a loss greater than $17,637 (i.e., that $17,637 is the minimum loss).

Advantages of the analytical method include:
- It is easy to calculate and easily understood.
- It allows modeling the correlations of risks.
- It can be applied to different time periods according to industry custom.

Disadvantages of the analytical method include:
- The need to assume a normal distribution.
- The difficulty in estimating the correlations of very large portfolios.
- No indication of the size of potential losses in the tail.

4.

6.147	2.377	1.594	0.993	−0.672	−1.523
5.875	2.232	1.320	0.989	−0.749	−1.726
3.660	2.064	1.189	0.962	−0.851	−2.024
3.432	2.059	1.148	0.901	−1.112	−2.250
3.376	1.839	1.128	0.353	−1.182	−3.359
2.510	1.652	1.054	−0.231	−1.313	
2.388	1.609	0.996	−0.550	−1.367	

Using the historical method, 5% VaR is determined using the highest return of the lowest 5% of historical returns. With 40 returns, the bottom 5% would be the 0.05(40) = 2 lowest returns (highlighted in the table above). Because −2.25% is the higher of the two, the 5% historical VaR is (−2.25%)(1,500,000) = −$33,750.

The manager could say she is 95% confident that the portfolio will not experience a loss greater than $33,750. Alternatively, the manager could say with 5% significance that the minimum loss will be $33,750 (5% probability of a loss greater than $33,750).

Advantages of the historical method include:
- It is easy to calculate and easily understood.
- There is no need to assume a returns distribution.
- It can be applied to different time periods according to industry custom.

The primary disadvantage of the historical method is the assumption that the pattern of historical returns will repeat in the future (i.e., is indicative of future returns).

5. Financial risks:
- Market risk: Factors that directly affect firm or portfolio values (e.g., interest rates, exchange rates, equity prices, commodity prices, etc.).
- Liquidity risk: The possibility of sustaining significant losses due to the inability to take or liquidate a position quickly at a fair price.
- Credit risk: Default of a counterparty. This risk can be mitigated through the use of derivative products, such as credit default options.

Mitigating strategies for financial risks will typically include the use of financial and credit derivatives including options, futures and/or forward contracts, futures options, and swaps.

6. Nonfinancial risks:
- Operations risk (non-financial risk). The potential for failures in the firm's operating systems, including its ERM system, due to personal, technological, mechanical, or other problems.
- Model risk (non-financial risk). Models are only as good as their construction and inputs (e.g., the assumptions regarding the sensitivity of the firm's assets to changes in risk factors, the correlations of the risk factors, or the likelihood of an event).
- Sovereign risk: There are elements of credit risk here, as changes in spread will affect bond prices, but the underlying issues are political. The country must choose economically viable policies to be able to repay and be willing to repay.

- Regulatory risk (non-financial). Different securities in the portfolio can fall under different regulatory bodies. Also, synthetic positions (combinations of two or more securities to create the effect of a totally different asset) can be quite confusing.
- Some other risks (all non-financial) include political risk, settlement risk, tax risk, and legal risk, which relate directly or indirectly to changes in the political climate.

Due to the difficulties in predicting the occurrence and size of a loss due to nonfinancial risks, managers will often simply purchase insurance protection.

7. Supplements (additions) to VaR used to provide more confidence in the accuracy of the VaR calculation include:
    - Incremental VaR (IVaR). IVaR is the effect of an individual asset on the overall risk of the portfolio. IVaR is calculated by measuring the difference between the portfolio VaR with and without the asset.
    - Cash flow at risk (CFAR). Some companies cannot be valued directly, which makes calculating VaR difficult or even meaningless. Instead of using VaR, CFAR measures the risk of the company's cash flows.
    - Earnings at risk (EAR) is analogous to CFAR only from an *accounting earnings* standpoint.
    - Tail value at risk (TVaR). TVaR is VaR plus the expected value in the tail of the distribution, which could be estimated by averaging the possible losses in the tail.

8. Methods used to limit credit risk include:
    - Limiting exposure, which means limiting the amount of loans to any individual debtor or the amount of derivative transactions with any individual counterparty.
    - Marking to market is employed with many derivative contracts. Contracts are settled on a regular basis, which means that profits and losses are settled.
    - Collateral is often required in transactions that generate credit risk. In derivatives markets, both parties are often required to post *margin*, and if the contract is marked to market, either side may be required to post addition margin (collateral).
    - Payment netting is frequently employed in derivatives contracts that can generate credit exposure to either side. The party with the net payment due is the only party at risk. Netting is also employed in *bankruptcy* proceedings. In this case, all the transactions between the bankrupt company and a single counterparty are netted to determine the overall exposure.

9. In calculating the traditional standard deviation, all returns for the measurement period are used (e.g., all the positive and negative alphas). This is like looking at the entire normal distribution, with the benchmark return as the center of the distribution. Negative alphas would fall to the left of the benchmark return, and positive alphas would fall to the right.

The manager is arguing that only negative alphas are relevant for measuring risk. This would be analogous to using only the left half of that normal distribution. Using the Sortino ratio compensates for this by only using returns below a designated level.

Excess return for the Sortino ratio (the numerator) is calculated as the portfolio return less the minimum acceptable portfolio return (MAR). The denominator of the ratio is the standard deviation of returns calculated using only returns below the MAR. The motivation behind the downside measure of volatility utilized in the Sortino ratio is the sense that very good performance (high returns) can unfairly inflate the volatility measure (the standard deviation used as the risk measure).

10. This "failure" in the ERM system is part of the operational risk associated with implementing the performance evaluation model (risk-adjusted performance compared to some benchmark), not a problem with the model itself. The first step in reacting to any risk management problem is determining the value of any damage and whether the problem is transient or permanent. In this case, the occurrence in question is not permanent in nature, and any monetary damage can be quickly and easily rectified. The likelihood of a similar occurrence in the future is high, however, so management should be sure a process is in place to help reduce the likelihood of future incorrect data entries.

11. The German manager (short position) has contracted with a U.S. bank to sell dollars at €0.8135, and the dollar has strengthened to €0.8170. The value of the contract to the long position is:

$$V_{bank\ (long)} = \frac{€8,170,000}{(1.04)^{2/12}} - \frac{€8,135,000}{(1.035)^{2/12}} = €28,278$$

The U.S. bank has the long position and credit risk of EUR 28,278. The German manager has no credit risk at this point. Credit risk is the value of the contract to the party with a gain. This is sometimes denoted as potential credit risk.

©2017 Kaplan, Inc.

Use the following information for Questions 1 through 6.

Mark Stober, William Robertson, and James McGuire are consultants for a regional pension consultancy. One of their clients, Richard Smitherspoon, chief investment officer of Quality Car Part Manufacturing, recently attended a conference on risk management topics for pension plans. Smitherspoon is a conservative manager who prefers to follow a long-term investment strategy with little portfolio turnover. Smitherspoon has substantial experience in managing a defined benefit plan but has little experience with risk management issues. Smitherspoon decides to discuss how Quality can begin implementing risk management techniques with Stober, Robertson, and McGuire. Quality's risk exposure is evaluated on a quarterly basis.

Smitherspoon is curious about risk management techniques, and in particular the concept of VAR. He asks, "What does a daily 5% VAR of $5 million mean? I just get so confused with whether VAR is a measure of maximum or minimum loss. Just last month, the consultant from MinRisk, a competing consulting firm, told me it was 'a measure of maximum loss, which in your case means we are 95% confident that the maximum one-day loss is $5 million.'" McGuire states that his definition of VAR is that "VAR is a measure that combines probabilities over a certain time horizon with dollar amounts, which in your case means that one expects to lose a minimum $5 million five trading days out of every 100."

Smitherspoon expresses bewilderment at the different methods for determining VAR. "Can't you risk management types formulate a method that works like calculating a beta? It would be so easy if there were a method that allowed one to just use mean and standard deviation. I need a VAR that I can get my arms around."

Smitherspoon asks Stober if it would be possible to calculate the VAR for each individual portfolio manager as well as the overall Quality fund. Stober replies with three responses:

1. "VAR is a universally accepted risk measure because it can be applied to practically any investment and is interpreted effectively the same way in each case; it is either the minimum or maximum loss at a given level of significance or confidence. For me to calculate the delta-normal VAR, you will need to provide me with each manager's historical returns distribution and expected return, the time frame you wish to use, and the desired level of significance. I can then calculate VAR for each manager using historical standard deviations and expected returns."

2. "We can calculate VAR using: the delta-normal method (also known as the mean variance approach), the historical method, or the Monte Carlo method. To calculate each manager's 95% VAR, all we would have to do is use standard deviations and expected returns to calculate 90% confidence intervals."

3. "Because of the way it is calculated, individual mean-variance VARs can probably be calculated for each of our portfolio managers, regardless of their style or assets under management. The overall fund VAR is then the sum of the individual VARs. To calculate the fund VAR directly, we would have to measure the fund's overall expected return and standard deviation. The problem with calculating it directly like this, however, is that to calculate the fund standard deviation we must consider the correlations of the managers' returns."

The next week, Stober visits the headquarters of TopTech, a communications firm. Their CFO is Ralph Long, who prefers to manage the firm's pension himself because he believes he can time the market and spot upcoming trends before analysts can. Long also believes that risk measurement for TopTech can be evaluated annually because of his close attention to the portfolio. Stober calculates TopTech's 95% surplus at risk to be $500 million for an annual horizon. The expected return on TopTech's asset base (currently at $2 billion) is 5%. The plan has a surplus of $100 million. Stober uses a 5% probability level to calculate the minimum amount by which the plan will be underfunded next year.

Before implementing risk management techniques, Smitherspoon expresses confusion regarding some other measures of risk management. "I know beta and standard deviation, but what is all this stuff about convexity, delta, gamma, and vega?" Stober informs Smitherspoon that delta is the first derivative of the call-stock price curve, and Robertson adds that gamma is the relationship between how bond prices change with changing time to maturity.

1. Regarding the definitions of VAR, are MinRisk and McGuire correct or incorrect?
    A. One is correct.
    B. Both are correct.
    C. Neither is correct.

2. Of the following VAR calculation methods, the measure that would *most likely* suit Smitherspoon is:
    A. the historical simulation method.
    B. the variance-covariance method.
    C. the Monte Carlo simulation method.

3. Which of Stober's responses regarding VAR is *most correct*?
    A. Response 1.
    B. Response 2.
    C. Response 3.

4. Using Stober's 5% probability level, the minimum amount by which TopTech's plan will be underfunded next year is *closest to*:
    A. $5 million.
    B. $25 million.
    C. $300 million.

5. VAR is a more relevant measure of firm risk for:
    A. Quality, because of its industry type.
    B. TopTech, because of its industry type.
    C. Quality, because of its measurement process.

6. Regarding the statements on delta and gamma, are Stober and Robertson correct or incorrect?
    A. Only Stober is correct.
    B. Only Robertson is correct.
    C. Both are correct *or* both are incorrect.

©2017 Kaplan, Inc.

SELF-TEST ANSWERS: RISK MANAGEMENT

1. **B**   Both MinRisk and McGuire are correct.

   VAR can be considered a minimum loss expected over a time horizon at a given probability. In this particular case, one would expect to exceed the VAR 5% of the time. MinRisk interpretation is also correct. Watch the wording in VAR questions.

   VAR is a measure that combines probabilities over a certain time horizon with dollar amounts, which in the statement means that one expects to lose at least $5 million in five trading days out of 100.

2. **B**   The variance-covariance method is correct.

   The variance-covariance method, also known as the delta-normal method, only requires estimates of mean and standard deviation of returns to estimate VAR. This is the closest method to which Smitherspoon refers.

3. **C**   Response 1 is almost a definition of VAR. Response 2 might appear incorrect at first, because of the reference to the 90% confidence interval. Remember, however, that VAR considers only the lower tail of the distribution. To calculate the 95% VAR we use the z-value corresponding to a 90% confidence interval (1.65), because that isolates the lower 5% of the distribution. Response 3 has an incorrect component. The last statement about calculating the overall VAR directly is correct; you must incorporate the correlations of the managers' returns to calculate the overall fund standard deviation. That is the problem with using individual VARs to calculate a fund VAR; VAR is not additive. Adding individual VARs overstates the fund VAR, because adding them ignores the correlations of individual manager's returns.

4. **C**   The current surplus is $100 million and the asset base is expected to generate $100 million ($2,000 million × 0.05). The 5% SAR of $500 million indicates that the underfunding of the plan at year end will be $300 (= 200 – 500) or more, 5% of the time.

5. **C**   VAR will be a more relevant risk measure for Quality because its portfolio experiences less turnover and because VAR is evaluated more frequently.

   Coupling a high turnover with a long time horizon decreases VAR's usefulness. VAR is calculated for a specific portfolio at a point in time. High turnover will change a portfolio's composition, which will also change the underlying statistical characteristics of the portfolio. These changes in statistical characteristics then decrease the usefulness of VAR calculations, especially in situations with long time horizons.

6. **A**   Stober is correct, and Robertson is incorrect.

   Gamma is the second derivative of the change in the underlying asset price movements. Stober correctly defines delta.

The following is a review of the Risk Management Applications of Derivatives principles designed to address the learning outcome statements set forth by CFA Institute. Cross-Reference to CFA Institute Assigned Reading #28.

RISK MANAGEMENT APPLICATIONS OF FORWARD AND FUTURES STRATEGIES

Study Session 15

EXAM FOCUS

Be able to perform any of the calculations using futures contracts to alter the beta of an equity portfolio, alter the duration of a bond portfolio, change the portfolio allocation among various classes of debt and equity, create synthetic positions, or preinvest an expected cash flow. Understand the basic concepts and risks involved.

WARM-UP: FUTURES AND FORWARDS

The CFA curriculum includes a long section of optional material that has no Learning Outcome Statements and will not be tested directly. It does review how to calculate the number of contracts to modify duration of a fixed income position and you are responsible for those calculations. The formulas are consistent with those covered earlier in the fixed income lesson but are laid out in a different form. We will cover the calculations in this reading assignment and review the formulas needed.

Forward and futures contracts are effective tools for managing both interest rate and equity risks. Although very similar, however, one or the other may be preferred in some cases. The primary differences between the two are that forward contracts can be tailored to meet the specific needs of the counterparties but have higher default risk and less liquidity than futures. In contrast, futures contracts are standardized, so they are less likely to be exactly what the two parties need; however, they trade on an exchange, so the risk of loss from default is minimal.

ADJUSTING THE PORTFOLIO BETA

LOS 28.a: Demonstrate the use of equity futures contracts to achieve a target beta for a stock portfolio and calculate and interpret the number of futures contracts required.

CFA® Program Curriculum, Volume 5, page 227

To modify the beta of an equity portfolio with futures on an equity index, we need to know the beta of the equity portfolio to be hedged or leveraged, as well as the beta of the futures contract. Both betas would be measured with respect to the reference index.

©2017 Kaplan, Inc.

You might ask, "Shouldn't the beta of the index futures contract equal one?" The answer is no, for two reasons. First, for an index like the S&P 500, it will probably be close to one, but for a more precise hedge, a manager should compute the beta. Second, as seen later, we may wish to adjust exposure with respect to a class of equity (e.g., small-cap stocks) where the beta will be very different from one.

Recall the formula for beta:

$$\beta_i = \frac{\text{Cov}(i,m)}{\sigma_m^2}$$

where:

i = an individual stock, equity portfolio, or equity index

$\text{Cov}(i,m)$ = covariance of returns on asset i with the market

σ_m^2 = variance of the market returns

Having computed our betas and selected a *target beta*, we can find the appropriate number of contracts to sell or buy to hedge or leverage the position (reduce or increase beta), respectively:

$$\text{number of contracts} = \left(\frac{\beta_T - \beta_P}{\beta_f}\right)\left(\frac{V_p}{P_f(\text{multiplier})}\right)$$

where:

β_T = desired portfolio beta

β_P = portfolio beta

β_f = equity futures contract beta

V_p = current value of the portfolio

P_f = futures price

 Professor's Note: If you recall the earlier fixed income hedging formula you should recognize this is essentially the same formula but using beta instead of duration as the risk measure. In addition, there is no yield beta for stock.

Example: Adjusting portfolio beta

A manager of a $5,000,000 portfolio wants to increase the beta from the current value of 0.8 to 1.1. The beta on the futures contract is 1.05, and the total futures price is $240,000.

Calculate the required number of futures contracts to achieve a beta of 1.1.

Calculate the required number of futures contracts to achieve a beta of 0.0.

Answer:

target beta = 1.1

$$\text{number of contracts} = \left(\frac{1.1 - 0.8}{1.05}\right)\left(\frac{\$5,000,000}{\$240,000}\right) = 5.95, \text{ buy 6 contracts at } \$240,000$$

Answer:

target beta = 0.0

$$\text{number of contracts} = \left(\frac{0 - 0.8}{1.05}\right)\left(\frac{\$5,000,000}{\$240,000}\right) = -15.87, \text{ sell 16 contracts at } \$240,000$$

HEDGING IS RARELY PERFECT

It is highly unusual for the results of the risk adjustment to be perfect. Generically this is referred to as basis risk. Basis risk occurs whenever the item hedged (in the numerator of the hedge formula calculation) is not a perfect match for the hedging vehicle (in the denominator of the hedge formula) and, as a result, the two change in relationship to each other in unpredictably ways. The typical reasons for basis risk include:

- The numerator and denominator are not based on the same item. For example:
  - A stock portfolio hedged using a contract based on the S&P 500 Index.
  - A bond portfolio hedged with a Treasury bond contract based on a single deliverable Treasury bond.
- The betas and durations used in the hedge calculation do not reflect the actual subsequent market value changes of the portfolio or contract, a very common issue.
- The hedge results are measured prior to contract expiration and/or the hedge is closed prior to contract expiration. Alternatively, the hedge may need to be extended after the expiration of the initial contract position.
  - Note: If a contract is held to expiration, the contract price will converge and be equal to the spot price of the underlying at expiration, a relationship called convergence. This is not basis risk because it is a known change between spot and forward price. Holding contracts to expiration reduces basis risk.
- The number of contracts is rounded.
  - The exam convention is to round 0.5 or greater up to the closest whole number and round less than 0.5 down.
- The future and spot price are not fairly priced based on the cash and carry arbitrage model.

Effective beta of the position can be measured ex post (after the fact) as:

effective beta = % change in value of the portfolio / % change in the index

©2017 Kaplan, Inc.

Example: Ex Post Results Evaluation

Continuing the previous example, assume the unhedged portfolio increased in value 5.1% from $5,000,000 to $5,255,000, and the futures price also increased 5.1% from 240,000 to 252,240. One month remains to contract expiration. The market had a return of 5.2%. For each scenario, **compute** the i) hedged portfolio ending value, ii) the ex post beta, and iii) give two relevant reasons the ex post beta was not as expected.

Answers:

Scenario 1, target beta of 1.1 and 6 (not 5.95) contracts purchased:

i)   hedged portfolio ending value = unhedged ending value + G/L on contracts

The contract price increased $12,240 for a gain on the long position of:

$12,240 × 6 = $73,440

hedged portfolio ending value = $5,255,000 + 73,440 = $ 5,328,440

hedged portfolio return = (5,328,440/5,000,000) − 1 = +6.57%

ii) The effective beta was: 6.57/5.2 = 1.26.

iii)

- The number of contracts was rounded up, which in a rising market, increased the gain and hedged portfolio percent return and effective beta of the hedged portfolio.
- The ex post valuation period was not at contract expiration. The relationship of futures and underlying prices can, therefore, change in unexpected ways.
- The performance of the portfolio and/or index may have been different from their ex ante betas. Given that the portfolio and contract increased by the same percent amount, they acted as if their betas were the same and did not reflect the initial estimates of beta.

Scenario 2, target beta of 0 and 16 (not 15.87) contracts sold:

i)   hedged portfolio ending value = unhedged ending value + G/L on contracts

The contract price increased $12,240 for a loss on the short position of:

$12,240 × 16 = $195,840

hedged portfolio ending value = $5,255,000 – 195,840 = $5,059,160

hedged portfolio return = (5,059,160 / 5,000,000) – 1 = +1.18%

ii) The effective beta was: 1.18 / 5.2 = 0.23.

iii)

- The number of contracts sold was rounded up, which in a rising market, increased the loss on the short position and reduced the percent return on the hedged portfolio and its effective beta.
- The ex post valuation was not at contract expiration. The relationship of futures and underlying prices can, therefore, change in unexpected ways.
- The performance of the portfolio and/or index could have been different from their ex ante betas. Because ex post beta was higher than the target of zero, the portfolio beta must have been higher or futures beta less than expected. The portfolio could have acted as if its beta were more than 0.8 and/or the contract less than 1.05.

SYNTHETIC POSITIONS

LOS 28.b: Construct a synthetic stock index fund using cash and stock index futures (equitizing cash).

CFA® Program Curriculum, Volume 5, page 233

Synthetic positions are based on the same formulas using beta or duration to modify portfolio risk. However, synthetic positions more precisely replicate the same initial investment and ending results that would have occurred if the replicated position had been owned instead. Synthetic equity or bond positions require purchasing contracts and holding sufficient cash equivalents earning the risk-free rate to pay for the contracts at expiration. Alternatively, synthetic cash positions involve holding the underlying and shorting contracts to hedge the position in such a way that the hedged position "earns" the risk-free rate over the hedging period.

In both cases, the number of contracts is computed using the previous risk modification formulas; however, the quantity to hedge (in the numerator of the hedging formula) is the FV of the amount to modify.

- If the objective is to create synthetic equity from cash and the desired β_T is the same as the β_F, then the first term in the calculation becomes $(\beta_T - 0) / \beta_F = 1.0$. Because it has no effect on the calculation, the betas can be "ignored."
- If the objective is to create synthetic cash from equity and the existing β_P is the same as the β_F, then the first term in the calculation becomes $(0 - \beta_P) / \beta_F = -1.0$. Because it has no effect on the calculation, the betas can be "ignored."
- In other cases, the existing or desired betas are not the same as the futures beta and will be given. In such cases, the betas are used and do affect the computation.

The cash equivalents in the synthetic position may be variously referred to as: cash equivalents, a bond or zero coupon bond, a risk-free bond or risk-free zero coupon bond, or any other equivalent terminology.

Example: Synthetic Positions

Manager A holds $25,000,000 market value of 3-month Treasury bills yielding 1% and wishes to create $20,000,000 of synthetic S&P 500 stock exposure for three months. The S&P contract is priced at 1,750, the dollar multiplier is 250, and the underlying stocks have a dividend yield of 2.5%.

Calculate the number of contracts to buy or sell and the zero coupon position to take.

Answer:

Purchase 46 contracts. (Because no betas were given, it is presumed the desired beta is the same as the futures beta. Purely for illustration, assume they are both 1.07. They will have no affect.)

$$N_f = [(1.07 - 0)/1.07] \times [(\$20,000,000 \times 1.01^{3/12}) / (1,750 \times \$250)]$$

$$= (1) \times (20,049,814 / 437,500) = 45.83 \approx 46$$

This is a full "purchase price" at expiration of: $46(1,750)(\$250) = \$20,125,000$

At 1% interest, the amount to invest in T-bills today is $\$20,125,000 / 1.01^{3/12} = \$20,075,000$. This is somewhat higher than the desired $20,000,000 because the number of contracts purchased was rounded up.

Manager B has a large position in U.K. stocks that are similar to a major U.K. stock index. She wishes to create GBP 15,000,000 of synthetic cash earning 2.0% for a six-month period. The futures index contract is priced at 3,700 with a multiplier of 10. The stocks have a dividend yield of 3.0%.

Calculate the number of contracts to buy or sell and the amount of synthetic cash created.

Answer:

Sell 409 contracts. (Because no betas were given, it is presumed the portfolio beta is the same as the futures beta. Purely for illustration, assume they are both 0.95. They will have no affect.)

$$N_f = [(0.0 - 0.95) / 0.95] \times [(15,000,000 \times 1.02^{6/12}) / (3,700 \times 10)]$$

$$= (-1) \times (15,149,257 / 37,000) = -409.44 \approx -409$$

This is a full "price" at expiration of: $409(3,700)(10) = 15,133,000$

At 2% interest, the present value invested today in risk-free assets is $15,133,000 / 1.02^{6/12} = $ GBP 14,983,903. This is somewhat less than the desired GBP 15,000,000 because the amount hedged (number of contracts sold) was rounded down.

Why Future Value (FV) Is Used in the Synthetic Calculations

The use of the risk-free rate and FV would, in a perfect hedge, mean the synthetic position completely replicates the beginning and ending results that would have been obtained if the desired synthetic position had been actually held. This can be seen by evaluating the results achieved with the rounded number of contracts as either a theoretical delivery of the underlying (which may or may not be allowed by the contract) or by comparing the initial investment as well as ending gains or losses in the synthetic position with those from having held an actual position.

- For delivery analysis, it is expedient and acceptable to view the contract price as a price per share and the number of contracts × contract multiplier as the number of shares.
- Recall the contract price is based on the cash and carry arbitrage relationship studied at Level II. F_0 is the FV of S_0 minus the FV of any dividends to occur during contract life on the underlying.
- The dividend yield is, therefore, already "priced" into the contract price. Alternatively, the dividend yield would have been earned if the underlying were owned.
- The analysis must be based on the rounded number of contracts actually used because fractional contracts do not exist.

©2017 Kaplan, Inc.

Performance of a Synthetic Position if Delivery is Allowed

To illustrate, return to the example of Manager A who wishes to create $20,000,000 of synthetic S&P 500 stock exposure for three months when the risk-free rate is 1%. The S&P contract is priced at 1,750, the dollar multiplier is 250, the underlying index has a dividend yield of 2.5%, and it is priced at 1,756.461648 (6 decimals are used only to demonstrate the accuracy of the analysis).

The manager purchased 46 contracts, not the desired fractional number of 45.82.

This is conceptually equivalent to buying $46 \times 250 = 11,500$ shares at a forward price of 1,750.

This is a PV amount invested today of:

$$[46(1,750)(\$250)] \, / \, 1.01^{3/12} \ = \$20,125,000 \, / \, 1.01^{3/12} = \$20,075,000$$

That, of course, also means that if $20,075,000 were invested today at the risk-free rate of 1%, it will be worth $20,125,000 and it will have earned interest of $50,000. The ending amount can be used to pay the contracted price of 1,750 on 11,500 shares. The investor will then own 11,500 shares worth S_T.

Alternatively, the $20,075,000 could have been used to buy shares initially. If they were purchased, the dividends can then be reinvested in the purchase of more shares.

- The shares purchased today will be the contracted number of shares discounted by the dividend yield. This is $(46 \times 250) \, / \, 1.025^{3/12} = 11,429.227$
- A more direct way to calculate this is the initial investment amount divided by today's share price. This is: $\$20,075,000 \, / \, 1,756.461648 = 11,429.228$
- The two approaches are equivalent because the spot and future price relationship reflects the initial dividend yield and risk-free rate. (Ignoring the small rounding discrepancy.)
- Reinvesting the dividends, this will be $11,429.227 \times 1.025^{3/12} = 11,500$ shares worth S_T at the end of the contract period.

The synthetic and actual ownership had the same initial investment, and both result in owning 11,500 shares worth S_T at contract expiration.

Performance of a Synthetic Position Based on G/L

Professor's Note: The analysis of equivalence of synthetic and actual positions based on G/L or examples where both spot and futures price are given is not covered directly in the CFA text. It is included because we get questions from candidates about why the CFA text presumes delivery of the underlying items to settle the contract when this is generally not allowed. You may skip this entire note if you wish.

Assuming, as is done in the CFA text, that dividend yield and risk-free rates are compounded annual rates, then $F_0 = S_0 [(1 + r_f)/(1 + dividend\ yield)]^T$. In the example, this is $1,750 = 1,756.461648(1.01/1.025)^{0.25}$.

For illustration, assume the ending stock and contract price are 1,900. They will be equal based on convergence.

The initial 11,429.227 shares at 1,756.461648 are worth $20,075,000. (Precision requires using infinite decimal places in all calculations). The ending shares (with dividend reinvestment) of 11,500 shares at 1,900 are worth $21,850,000. This is a gain of $1,775,000.

Recall the synthetic position holds cash equivalents and earns interest of $50,000. The futures price increases from the initial purchase price of 1,750 to 1,900 for a gain of $(1,900 − 1,750)(46)(250) = 1,725,000$, making the total gain $1,775,000.

Based on either delivery or G/L analysis, the synthetic and actual ownership produce the same result.

     ©2017 Kaplan, Inc.

Study Session 15

LOS 28.c: Explain the use of stock index futures to convert a long stock position into synthetic cash.

CFA® Program Curriculum, Volume 5, page 237

Example: Synthetic Cash Position

Manager C holds equity positions similar to the Russell 2000 and wishes to synthetically convert $50,000,000 to cash equivalents for five months. He decides to use a contract overlay position rather than sell the stocks and then have to repurchase them. The Russell 2000 futures contract price is 1,135 with a multiplier of 500. The Russell Index dividend yield is 1.7%, and the zero coupon bond rate is 0.9%.

Calculate: i) the number of contracts for the position, ii) the effective beginning investment in cash equivalents, iii) the effective number of shares in the index converted to cash, and iv) assuming the index closes at 1,057, **demonstrate** the strategy is equivalent to having invested at the risk-free rate.

Answers:

i) The betas of the index and portfolio were not given, are assumed to be equal, and, therefore, do not affect the calculation. The number of contracts to sell is:

$$50,000,000(1.009^{5/12}) \, / \, (1,135)(500) = 50,187,010 \, / \, 567,500 = 88.44 \approx 88$$

ii) The effective initial amount of cash equivalents is:

$$[88(\$500)(1,135)] \, / \, 1.009^{5/12} = \$49,940,000 \, / \, 1.0037402 = \$49,753,910$$

iii) The effective number of shares converted to cash is:

$$88(500) \, / \, 1.017^{5/12} = 44,000 \, / \, 1.0070485 = 43,692.04$$

With dividends reinvested, this is ending shares of:

$$43,692.04(1.017^{5/12}) = 44,000$$

iv) At contract expiration, the index and contract price will converge to 1,057. The pay off on the short contract position is a gain because the contract price declined. The gain is:

$$(1,135 - 1,057)(88)(\$500) = \$3,432,000$$

The ending value of the shares is:

$$44,000(1,057) = \$46,508,000$$

This makes the total ending value $49,940,000 versus an initial synthetic cash position of $49,753,910 for an effective annual return:

($49,940,000 / $49,753,910)$^{12/5}$ – 1 = 0.9%

This synthetic position produced a return equivalent to the initial risk-free rate of 0.9%.

ALTERING BOND EXPOSURE USING CONTRACTS

LOS 28.d: Demonstrate the use of equity and bond futures to adjust the allocation of a portfolio between equity and debt.

CFA® Program Curriculum, Volume 5, page 241

The same formula used to adjust equity beta can be used to adjust bond duration by using duration instead of beta in the calculation.

TARGET DURATION

The number of futures contracts needed to combine with a bond to achieve a targeted portfolio duration is:

$$\text{number of contracts} = (\text{yield beta})\left(\frac{MD_T - MD_P}{MD_F}\right)\left(\frac{V_p}{P_f\,(\text{multiplier})}\right)$$

where:
V_p = current value of the portfolio
P_f = futures price
MD_T = target (desired) modified duration
MD_P = modified duration of the portfolio
MD_F = modified duration of the futures

Professor's Note: Superficially the formula looks different than one seen in fixed income. The results are the same.

$$number\ of\ contracts = \frac{(D_T - D_P)P_P}{D_{CTD}P_{CTD}}(CTD\ conversion\ factor)$$

- *If yield beta is not given, it is implicitly assumed to be 1.0 and irrelevant. If it is given, include it as a multiplier.*
- *One formula uses D, and one uses MD. This is just notation difference in the two readings. The duration of the CTD is the duration of the contract.*
- P_f *(multiplier) is the full value of the contract. The fixed income reading assignment gave that number directly and used it. This assignment shows you it is calculated as P_f (multiplier).*
- *This reading assignment uses the price of the futures contract while the fixed income assignment used price of the CTD and its conversion factor. The conversion factor is the link between these two prices, making the two formulas identical mathematically.*

The bottom line is to know both formulas and use the one for which inputs are given.

Example: Altering duration

A) The manager has a bond portfolio with a value of $103,630 and a holding period of one year. The 1-year total futures price is $102,510. The modified duration of the portfolio and futures contracts are 1.793 and 1.62, respectively. The yield beta is 1.2.

Calculate the number of contracts to reduce the portfolio duration to 0.

Answer:

$$number\ of\ contracts = (1.2)\left(\frac{0-1.793}{1.62}\right)\left(\frac{\$103,630}{\$102,510}\right) = -1.34$$

Sell one contract at 102,510. This is going to produce a rather significant rounding error.

B) Suppose the manager wants to change the portfolio duration from 1.793 to 3.0.

Calculate the number of contracts to increase duration to 3.

Answer:

$$number\ of\ contracts = (1.2)\left(\frac{3-1.793}{1.62}\right)\left(\frac{\$103,630}{\$102,510}\right) = 0.9 \rightarrow buy\ one\ contract\ at\ 102,510$$

ADJUSTING PORTFOLIO ASSET ALLOCATION

Adjusting asset allocation uses the same number of contracts formulas but requires multiple steps:

- Adjustments are often stated as percent allocations; however, the calculations require dollar or other nominal amounts (e.g., a 10% shift of a EUR 50M portfolio is a EUR 5M V_p).
- Changing an allocation requires selling contracts to remove one exposure and buying contracts to create a different exposure.

Example: Altering debt and equity allocations

A manager has a $50 million portfolio that consists of 50% stock and 50% bonds (i.e., $25 million each).

- The beta of the stock position is 0.8.
- The modified duration of the bond position is 6.8.

The manager wishes to achieve an effective mix of 60% stock (i.e., $30 million) and 40% bonds (i.e., $20 million). Because the move is only temporary, and rather than having to decide which bonds to sell and which stocks to buy to achieve the desired mix, the manager will use futures contracts.

- The price of the stock index futures contract is $300,000 (including the multiplier), and its beta is 1.1.
- The price, modified duration, and yield beta of the futures contracts are $102,000, 8.1, and 1, respectively.

Determine the appropriate strategy.

Answer:

The desired shift is $5,000,000. Sell bond contracts to reduce duration to 0 on a $5,000,000 position:

$$\text{number of bond futures} = (\text{yield beta})\left(\frac{MD_T - MD_P}{MD_f}\right)\left(\frac{V_p}{P_f\,(\text{multiplier})}\right)$$

$$= (1)\left(\frac{0.0 - 6.8}{8.1}\right)\left(\frac{\$5,000,000}{\$102,000}\right) = -41.2$$

Sell 41 bond contracts at 102,000.

©2017 Kaplan, Inc.

Buy equity contracts targeting the desired beta of 0.8 on $5,000,000:

$$\text{number of equity index futures} = \left(\frac{\beta_t}{\beta_f}\right)\left(\frac{V_p}{P_f\,(\text{multiplier})}\right)$$

$$= \left(\frac{0.8}{1.1}\right)\left(\frac{\$5,000,000}{\$300,000}\right)$$

$$= (0.727)(16.666) = 12.12$$

Buy 12 equity contracts at 300,000.

ADJUSTING THE EQUITY ALLOCATION

LOS 28.e: Demonstrate the use of futures to adjust the allocation of a portfolio across equity sectors and to gain exposure to an asset class in advance of actually committing funds to the asset class.

CFA® Program Curriculum, Volume 5, page 245

The same process can be used to make any portfolio asset allocation, as long as the appropriate contracts to buy and sell are available.

Example: Changing equity allocations

A manager of $20 million of mid-cap equities would like to move half of the position to small-cap equities. The beta of the mid-cap position is 1.1, and the average beta of small-cap stocks is 1.5. The betas of the corresponding mid- and small-cap futures contracts are 1.05 and 1.4, respectively. The mid- and small-cap futures total prices are $244,560 and $210,500, respectively. **Determine** the appropriate strategy.

Answer:

The desired reallocation is $10,000,000. Sell mid-cap contracts and buy small-cap contracts.

$$\text{number of contracts}_{\text{mid cap}} = \left(\frac{0-1.1}{1.05}\right)\left(\frac{\$10,000,000}{\$244,560}\right) = -42.84$$

Sell 43 mid-cap contracts at 244,560.

$$\text{number of contracts}_{\text{small cap}} = \left(\frac{1.5-0}{1.4}\right)\left(\frac{\$10,000,000}{\$210,500}\right) = 50.90$$

Buy 51 small-cap contracts at 210,500.

PREINVESTING

Preinvesting refers to buying contracts in anticipation of cash that will be received. Buying contracts does not require initial cash flow, which makes contracts a natural vehicle for such transactions. It is assumed the account has other assets that can be posted to meet margin requirements. Because this is hedging a future value amount, it is most appropriate to refer to this as a synthetic position.

Example: Preinvesting

A portfolio manager knows that $5 million in cash will be received in a month. The portfolio under management is 70% invested in stock with an average beta of 0.9 and 30% invested in bonds with a duration of 4.8. The most appropriate stock index futures contract has a total price of $244,560 and a beta of 1.05. The most appropriate bond index futures have a yield beta of 1.00, an effective duration of 6.4, and a total price of $99,000. **Determine** the appropriate strategy to synthetically preinvest the $5 million in the same proportions as the current portfolio.

Answer:

The goal is to create a $3.5 million equity position (0.7 × $5 million) with a beta of 0.9 and a $1.5 million bond position (0.3 × $5 million) with a duration of 4.8:

number of stock futures =
$$\left(\frac{0.9-0}{1.05}\right)\left(\frac{\$3,500,000}{\$244,560}\right) = 12.27, \text{ buy 12 contracts at 244,560}$$

number of bond futures =
$$(1.0)\left(\frac{4.8-0}{6.4}\right)\left(\frac{\$1,500,000}{\$99,000}\right) = 11.36, \text{ buy 11 contracts at 99,000}$$

The manager should take a long position in 12 stock index futures and 11 bond index futures.

 Professor's Note: The anticipated $5,000,000 has no duration or beta.

    ©2017 Kaplan, Inc.

EXCHANGE RATE RISK

LOS 28.f: Explain exchange rate risk and demonstrate the use of forward contracts to reduce the risk associated with a future receipt or payment in a foreign currency.

CFA® Program Curriculum, Volume 5, page 250

Three types of foreign exchange risk are:

1. **Transaction exposure:** This is when cash flow of one currency must be exchanged for another at a future date to settle a specific transaction. This risk can be hedged with derivatives. For example:
   - An exporter will receive foreign currency in payment for goods or services at a future date and is at risk if that currency depreciates. For example, a U.S. exporter has contracted to sell EUR 9million to a European trade partner, exchange in three months. The spot exchange rate is USD1.10/EUR and the three-month forward exchange rate is USD1.12/EUR. The spot market is not relevant because the EURs are not yet in hand. Fortuitously, the forward rate of USD1.12 is more attractive and can be locked in by selling the EUR forward at USD1.12.
   - An importer must pay the foreign currency in exchange for goods or services at a future date and is at risk if that currency appreciates. For example, a U.K. company must pay CAD100 million in six months. The spot exchange rate is GBP0.51/CAD and the six-month forward exchange rate is GBP0.53/CAD. The cost of buying the CAD forward is higher than in the spot market but unfortunately the CAD are not yet needed. The forward market does allow the U.K.-based company to lock in the GBP cost of the transaction at GBP0.53.

2. **Translation exposure:** This is when financial statements in one currency must be converted to a different currency. Accounting rules determine the translation method used and the effect on the parent company's financial statements. (Note that the resulting gains or losses do not necessarily reflect real economic gain or loss and the CFA text does not discuss hedging such a risk.)

3. **Economic exposure:** This is less directly observable and occurs when currency volatility or changes in value affect the competitive standing of a business. For example if Disney World in the United States incurs all revenue and expenses in the USD, a decline in the USD may be beneficial if it induces more foreign travelers to visit the United States and Disney World. If this is the only effect on the company, profits and the stock price may increase. (Note that this issue may be discussed elsewhere under the concept of a minimum variance hedge ratio.)

Figure 1: Strategies for Hedging Expected Currency Positions

Contractual Agreement	Position	Action
Receiving foreign currency	Long	Sell forward contract
Paying foreign currency	Short	Buy forward contract

Example: Managing exchange rate risk

Mach, Inc., is a U.S.-based maker of large industrial machines and has just received an order for some of its products. The agreed-upon price is £5 million (British pounds), and the delivery date is 60 days. The current exchange rate is $1.42 per pound, and the 60-day forward rate is $1.43 per pound. **Explain** the best way for Mach, Inc., to hedge the corresponding exchange rate risk.

Answer:

On the day the order comes in, Mach, Inc., effectively has a long position in pounds; therefore, it should take a short position in a forward contract. This contract would obligate Mach, Inc., to deliver the pounds that it will receive for dollars. Ideally, the contract would be to exchange the £5,000,000 for:

$7,150,000 = (5,000,000)($1.43)

According to the contract, in 60 days, Mach will exchange the £5,000,000 for $7,150,000. If it does not hedge and the realized spot rate in 60 days is $1.429, Mach will receive only $7,145,000 = 5,000,000($1.429), or $5,000 less than with the hedged position.

Example: Exchange rate risk

U.S.-based Goblet, Inc., imports wine from France. It has just contracted to pay €8 million for a shipment of wine in 30 days. The current spot rate is €0.8/$, and the 30-day forward rate is €0.799/$. **Explain** the strategy Goblet, Inc., could employ to eliminate the exchange rate risk.

Answer:

Because Goblet, Inc., will have to pay euros, it is short the currency and should go long (buy) the forward contract. Goblet, Inc., should enter a forward contract that will allow it to buy the €8,000,000 it will need for the contract for $10,012,516 = €8,000,000 ($/€0.799).

What if Goblet, Inc., had not hedged, and the exchange rate is €0.7995/$ in 30 days? If this is the case, Goblet, Inc., would get the necessary €8 million from converting $10 million at that spot rate. The dollar cost would be $10,006,254 = €8,000,000($/€0.7995). Thus, without the contract, Goblet, Inc., would have been $6,262 dollars better off in the spot market.

HEDGING LIMITATIONS

LOS 28.g: Explain the limitations to hedging the exchange rate risk of a foreign market portfolio and discuss feasible strategies for managing such risk.

CFA® Program Curriculum, Volume 5, page 254

Professor's Note: You are responsible for any of the calculations in this section, but they are covered elsewhere. It is important you focus on the implications of the math discussed here, not just the plug and do. We are returning to the issue of investing in foreign assets carrying two sources of return and risk. Remember that perfect hedging of the currency risk is unlikely, as that would require knowing the ending value of the asset at the start of the hedging period.

An equity investment in a foreign market has both equity risk and foreign exchange risk. That is, the foreign position will increase or decrease in value according to the activity in the foreign market, and then the domestic investor will face additional return volatility because of the uncertainty caused by fluctuations of the exchange rate. A foreign equity position may increase by 10%, but if the foreign currency depreciates by that much, the net change to the domestic investor is approximately zero.

The two hedging strategies utilized by global portfolio managers to manage the risk of a foreign-denominated portfolio involve selling forward contracts on the foreign market index (to manage market risk) and selling forward contracts on the foreign currency (to manage the currency risk). They can choose to hedge one or the other, both, or neither. Their four choices can be summed up as follows:

1. Hedge the foreign market risk and accept the foreign currency risk.

2. Hedge the foreign currency risk and accept the foreign market risk.

3. Hedge both risks.

4. Hedge neither risk.

Hedging Market Risk

To hedge the market value (i.e., market risk) of a foreign investment, the manager can short (i.e., sell forward) the foreign market index. The degree to which the portfolio is correlated with the market index will determine the effectiveness of the hedge. If the manager shorts the appropriate amount of the index and it is *perfectly correlated* with the portfolio of investments, the return from the hedging strategy must be the **foreign risk-free rate**.

If the same manager then chooses to hedge the currency risk, she knows the exact value of the foreign currency to hedge, and the return to the (double) hedging strategy must be the manager's **domestic risk-free rate**.

Hedging Currency Risk

An obvious problem faced when trying to hedge the foreign currency risk of a foreign investment is its uncertain future value. Managers use various strategies for managing the currency risk of a foreign portfolio, including:

- Hedging a minimum future value below which they feel the portfolio will not fall.
- Hedging the estimated future value of the portfolio.
- Hedging the initial value (i.e., the principal).

None of these strategies can eliminate all the currency risk. For example, even if management has determined a minimum future value below which the portfolio will not fall, they are still exposed to values above that. If they hedge the principal, portfolio gains are unhedged. A loss in portfolio value would represent an over-hedge (i.e., management has agreed to deliver too much of the foreign currency).

Another proposed strategy is doing nothing (i.e., hedging choice #4 noted previously). As long as the market and currency risks are not highly correlated, changes in the two values will tend to offset one another.

Hedging with Futures or Forwards?

Calculating and constructing the hedge treats futures and forwards interchangeably. There could be occasions when one or the other is favored for practical reasons. Some differences to know are:

- Futures are standardized contracts while forwards can be customized as to amount and expiration date.
- Futures are obligations of the exchange clearinghouse while forwards have counterparty risk.
- Futures are more regulated and transparent, and they require margin.

Empirically:

- Most bond and equity hedging is done with futures even though this usually creates some cross-hedge or basis risk because the futures provide ongoing liquidity and are continually priced.
- Hedging of interest payments or receipts is usually done with forwards (FRAs), so exact amounts and dates can be hedged.
- Likewise, currency hedging generally uses forwards to tailor amounts and dates.
- Eurodollar futures are a very large market but are mostly used by dealers and market makers to hedge their own business needs and positions and not used directly by final customers.

KEY CONCEPTS

LOS 28.a

Buy contracts to increase beta or duration. Sell contracts to decrease beta or duration.

$$\text{number of contracts} = \left(\frac{\beta_T - \beta_P}{\beta_f}\right)\left(\frac{V_p}{P_f\,(\text{multiplier})}\right)$$

where:
β_T = desired portfolio beta
β_P = portfolio beta
β_f = equity futures contract beta
V_p = current value of the portfolio
P_f = futures price

The same formula is used to calculate the number of bond contracts by replacing beta with duration. Yield beta is included as a multiplier if it is given, otherwise it is assumed to be 1.0.

LOS 28.b and c

The same formulas used to adjust beta and duration can also be used to create synthetic positions. V_p must be replaced with a future value amount $V_p \times (1 + r_f)^T$.

Often the desired change in beta or duration is equal to the beta or duration of the contract being used (e.g., −1.1/1.1 or 0.97/0.97). This produces an absolute ratio of 1.00 and, as a result, the betas and durations do not affect the number of contracts calculation.

A synthetic equity position requires buying contracts and holding sufficient cash earning r_f to pay for the contracts at contract expiration.

The initial required cash position is:

$$\frac{(\text{number of contracts}_{\text{rounded}})(P_f)(\text{multiplier})}{(1 + R_F)^T}$$

A synthetic cash position requires selling contracts and holding sufficient shares (with dividends reinvested in more shares) to provide the shares to deliver and close the short position.

The initial number of shares required is:

$$\frac{(\text{number of contracts}_{\text{rounded}})(\text{multiplier})}{(1 + \text{dividend yield})^T}$$

LOS 28.d and e

Adjusting asset allocation uses the same number of contracts formulas but requires multiple steps:

- Adjustments are often stated as percent allocations; however, the calculations require dollar or other nominal amounts (e.g., a 10% shift of a EUR 50M portfolio is a EUR 5M V_p).
- Changing an allocation requires selling contracts to remove one exposure and buying contracts to create a different exposure.

LOS 28.f

1. Transaction exposure is the risk that changes in exchange rates will directly affect the value of a contracted payment in or receipt of a foreign currency.

   Derivatives are often used to hedge transaction exposure:

   Strategies for Hedging Expected Currency Positions

Contractual Agreement	Position	Action
Receiving foreign currency	Long	Sell forward contract
Paying foreign currency	Short	Buy forward contract

2. Translation exposure is the risk of converting financial statements in one currency to another currency.

3. Economic exposure is the risk that changes in currency value may affect competitive position, sales, and profits.

LOS 28.g

An equity investment in a foreign market has both equity risk and foreign exchange risk. The investment is exposed to both the change in value of the foreign investment measured in the foreign currency and the change in value of the foreign currency. This leads to four possible hedging strategies: hedge neither risk, hedge one but not the other risk, or hedge both risks. If both risks are perfectly hedged, all risk is removed and the hedged results should equal the investor's (not the foreign asset's) risk-free rate.

©2017 Kaplan, Inc.

CONCEPT CHECKERS

1. The duration of a bond portfolio is 6, and the duration of the most appropriate bond futures contract is 4. The size of the portfolio is 24 times the total futures price. The yield beta of the futures contract is 1. The *most appropriate* strategy to completely hedge the portfolio against changes in interest rates is:
    A. short 1 futures contract.
    B. go long 24 futures contracts.
    C. short 36 contracts.

2. A portfolio manager expects a large cash inflow in the near future and wishes to preinvest the cash flow to earn an equity market return. The *most appropriate* strategy is to:
    A. take a short position in a stock index futures contract today.
    B. take a long position in a stock index futures contract today.
    C. take a short position in a stock index futures contract when the cash is received.

3. A domestic firm experiences a loss of revenue from the loss in sales caused by changes in value of the domestic currency. This type of loss is referred to as:
    A. translation risk.
    B. transaction risk.
    C. economic risk.

4. Sweat Pants, Inc., a U.S.-based firm, has entered into a contract to import £2,000,000 worth of wool from a firm in Scotland, and the spot exchange rate is $1.50/£. Management of Sweat Pants wants to alleviate the risk associated with the foreign currency. The forward exchange rate corresponding with the delivery of the wool is $1.455/£. Which of the following would probably be the *best* tactic to use to alleviate the foreign exchange risk for Sweat Pants?
    A. Sell £2,000,000 forward and agree to receive $2,910,000.
    B. Buy £2,000,000 forward and agree to deliver $2,910,000.
    C. Sell £2,000,000 forward and agree to receive $1,374,570.

5. A French investor has invested in a large, diversified portfolio of Japanese stocks. Which of the following tactics could be used to hedge the investment and target a return equal to the French risk-free rate?
    A. Buy euros forward and sell the foreign equity index.
    B. Sell euros forward and sell the foreign equity index.
    C. Buy euros forward and buy the foreign equity index.

6. Portfolio Management, Inc., (PMI) expects a cash flow of $10,000,000 in two months. The composition of the PMI portfolio is 40% large-cap equities, 40% small-cap equities, and 20% bonds. Using the following information, **determine** the appropriate strategy for PMI managers to synthetically preinvest the $10,000,000, so that it earns returns equivalent to those of their current positions.

- Large-cap beta = 0.9; small-cap beta = 1.35; bond duration = 6.3; yield beta = 1.0.
- Large-cap futures beta = 1.0; small-cap futures beta = 1.30.
- Treasury futures duration = 5.8.
- Large-cap futures price = $1,400, multiplier = $250; (= $350,000).
- Small-cap futures price = $1,100, multiplier = $250; (= $275,000).
- Treasury futures price = $100,000.

7. A manager has a position in Treasury bills worth $100 million with a yield of 2%. For the next three months, the manager wishes to have a synthetic equity position approximately equal to this value. The manager chooses S&P 500 Index futures, and that index has a dividend yield of 1%. The futures price is $1,050, and the multiplier is $250. **Determine** how many contracts this will require and the initial *value* of the synthetic stock position.

8. A manager of a $10,000,000 portfolio wants to decrease the beta from the current value of 1.6 to 1.2. The beta on the futures contract is 1.25, and the total futures price is $250,000. Using the futures contracts, **calculate** the appropriate strategy.

©2017 Kaplan, Inc.

9. A manager has a $100 million portfolio that consists of 70% stock and 30% bonds. The manager wishes to achieve an effective mix of 50% stock and 50% bonds.
   - The beta of the stock position is 1.2.
   - The modified duration of the bond position is 4.0.
   - The price and beta of the stock index futures contracts are $225,000 and 1.0, respectively.
   - The price, modified duration, and yield beta of the futures contracts are $100,500; 5; and 1, respectively.

   Determine the appropriate strategy.

10. A manager of $10 million of large-cap equities would like to shift 25% of the position to mid-cap equities. The beta of the large-cap position is 0.8, and the average beta of mid-cap stocks is 1.2. The betas of the corresponding large and mid-cap futures contracts are 0.75 and 1.25, respectively. The large- and mid-cap total futures prices are $9,800 and $240,000, respectively. **Determine** the appropriate strategy.

For more questions related to this topic review, log in to your Schweser online account and launch SchweserPro™ QBank; and for video instruction covering each LOS in this topic review, log in to your Schweser online account and launch the OnDemand video lectures, if you have purchased these products.

ANSWERS – CONCEPT CHECKERS

1. **C** $\text{number of contracts} = (\text{yield beta})\left(\dfrac{-MD_P}{MD_f}\right)\left(\dfrac{V_P}{P_f\,(\text{multiplier})}\right) = (1)\left(\dfrac{-6}{4}\right)(24) = -36$

    Short 36 contracts to hedge the portfolio.

2. **B**   The number of equity index futures is determined by dividing the expected cash position by the total price of the equity index.

3. **C**   This is economic exchange rate risk.

4. **B**   To alleviate the risk associated with moving foreign exchange values, Sweat Pants will enter a forward contract in which they agree to deliver \$2,910,000 = (\$1.455/£) (£2,000,000) and receive the £2,000,000 needed to pay for the wool.

5. **A**   The French investor is exposed to two sources of risk: change in value of the foreign stock market and change in value of the foreign currency. If both risks are eliminated, the position is risk-free and the investor earns his own domestic (French) risk-free rate.

    To hedge the foreign market, sell Japanese stock index futures forward. To hedge the foreign currency, sell the JPY forward (which is buy the investor's domestic currency, EUR) forward.

6.   Because the portfolio is currently 40/40/20 large cap, small cap, and bonds, management should assume long positions in futures contracts in those proportions:

    40% small cap and large cap = \$4,000,000 each; 20% bonds = \$2,000,000

    Management should buy large-cap equity futures, small-cap equity futures, and Treasury futures:

    # equity futures $= \left(\dfrac{\beta_T - \beta_P}{\beta_f}\right)\left(\dfrac{V_P}{(P_f)(\text{multiplier})}\right)$

    # large-cap contracts $= \left(\dfrac{0.9 - 0}{1.0}\right)\left(\dfrac{\$4,000,000}{\$350,000}\right) = 10.29$, buy 10 at 350,000

    # small-cap contracts $= \left(\dfrac{1.35 - 0}{1.3}\right)\left(\dfrac{\$4,000,000}{\$275,000}\right) = 15.10$, buy 15 at 275,000

    # Treasury futures $= \beta_{\text{Yield}}\left(\dfrac{D_T - D_P}{D_f}\right)\left(\dfrac{V_P}{P_f}\right)$

    # contracts $= (1)\left(\dfrac{6.3 - 0}{5.8}\right)\left(\dfrac{\$2,000,000}{\$100,000}\right) = 21.72$, buy 22 at 100,000

7. $\text{number of contracts} = \dfrac{(\$100,000,000)(1.02)^{0.25}}{(1,050)(\$250)} = 382.84$, buy 383 at 1,050

    This is equivalent to an initial investment of $[(383)(1,050)(250)] / (1.02)^{0.25} =$ \$100,041,003.

Study Session 15

Cross-Reference to CFA Institute Assigned Reading #28 – Risk Management Applications of Forward and Futures Strategies

8. number of contracts $= \dfrac{(1.2-1.6)(\$10,000,000)}{(1.25)(\$250,000)} = -12.8$, sell 13 contracts at 250,000

9. The desired shift in allocation is 20% of $100M = $20M. Sell stock contracts and buy bond contracts to achieve the desired 0 beta and 4.0 duration.

    number of stock futures $= \dfrac{(0-1.2)(\$20,000,000)}{(1.0)(\$225,000)} = -106.67$, sell 107 at 225,000

    number of bond futures $= (1)\dfrac{(4-0.0)(\$20,000,000)}{(5)(\$100,500)} = +159.20$, buy 159 at 100,500

10. The desired allocation shift is 25% of $10M = $2.5M. Sell large-cap and buy mid-cap equity contracts to achieve a large-cap beta of 0 and mid-cap beta of 1.2.

    number of contracts $= \dfrac{(0-0.8)(\$2,500,000)}{(0.75)(\$9,800)} = -272.11$, sell 272 at 9,800

    number of contracts $= \dfrac{(1.2-0)(\$2,500,000)}{(1.25)(\$240,000)} = 10.0$, buy 10 mid-cap at 240,000

RISK MANAGEMENT APPLICATIONS OF OPTION STRATEGIES

EXAM FOCUS

As you read through this topic review, you will notice that almost all the LOS are quantitative, but do not just focus on the calculations. Instead, learn the underlying concepts. For example, you might memorize the equations associated with a bull spread as presented in the CFA text and not realize end of chapter questions presume you would have noticed the same result can be achieved in other ways. Interest rate collars are appealing choices for exam questions because many candidates are more familiar with options based on price, rather than options based directly on interest rates. Be prepared to work with either. For the exam, be sure you know the construction and payoffs for the strategies as well as their similarities. Be prepared for both item set and constructed response questions and for questions that integrate this material into determining the best solution for a given investor for a given set of facts.

WARM-UP: BASICS OF PUT OPTIONS AND CALL OPTIONS

Professor's Note: The next several pages up to Covered Calls and Protective Puts are review and have only one purpose: you must know the four basic payoff patterns of long or short a call or put and how to compute intrinsic value. These items are the starting point of the material assigned at Level III. Be sure you know it or nothing that follows makes much sense.

Option contracts have asymmetric payoffs. The buyer of an option has the right to exercise the option but is not obligated to exercise. Therefore, the maximum loss for the buyer of an option contract is the loss of the price (premium) paid to acquire the position, while the potential gains in some cases are theoretically infinite. Because option contracts are a zero-sum game, the seller of the option contract could incur substantial losses, but the maximum potential gain is the amount of the premium received for writing the option.

To understand the potential returns, we need to introduce the standard symbols used to represent the relevant factors:

X = strike price or exercise price specified in the option contract (a fixed value)

S_t = price of the underlying asset at time t

C_t = market value of a call option at time t

P_t = market value of a put option at time t

t = time subscript, which can take any value between 0 and T, where T is the maturity or expiration date of the option

Call Options

A *call option* gives the *owner* the right, but not the obligation, to buy the stock from the seller of the option. The owner is also called the *buyer* or the holder of the *long position*. The buyer benefits, at the expense of the option *seller*, if the underlying stock price is greater than the exercise price. The option *seller* is also called the *writer* or holder of the *short position*.

At maturity, time T, if the price of the underlying stock is less than or equal to the strike price of a call option (i.e., $S_T \leq X$), the payoff is zero, so the option owner would not exercise the option. On the other hand, if the stock price is higher than the exercise price (i.e., $S_T > X$) at maturity, then the payoff of the call option is equal to the difference between the market price and the strike price ($S_T - X$). The "payoff" (at the option's maturity) to the call option seller, which will be at most zero, is the mirror image (opposite sign) of the payoff to the buyer.

Because of the linear relationships between the value of the option and the price of the underlying asset, simple graphs can clearly illustrate the possible value of option contracts at the expiration date. Figure 1 illustrates the payoff of a call with an exercise price equal to 50.

 Professor's Note: A payoff *graph* ignores the initial cost of the option.

Figure 1: Payoff of Call With Exercise Price Equal to 50

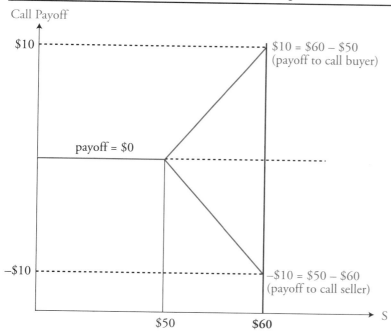

> **Example: Payoff to the writer of a call option**
>
> An investor writes an at-the-money call option on a stock with an exercise price of $50 (X = $50). If the stock price rises to $60, what will be the *payoff* to the owner and seller of the call option?
>
> **Answer:**
>
> The call option may be exercised with the holder of the long position buying the stock from the writer at $50 for a $10 gain. The payoff to the option buyer is $10, and the payoff to the option writer is *negative* $10. This is illustrated in Figure 1, and as mentioned, does not include the premium paid for the option.
>
> This example shows just how easy it is to determine option payoffs. At expiration time T (the option's maturity), the payoff to the option owner, represented by C_T, is:
>
> $$C_T = S_T - X \quad \text{if} \quad S_T > X$$
> $$C_T = 0 \quad \text{if} \quad S_T \leq X$$

Discussion

Another popular way of writing this is with the "max(0, variable)" notation. If the variable in this expression is greater than zero, then max(0, variable) = variable; if the variable's value is less than zero, then max(0, variable) = 0. Thus, letting the variable be the quantity $S_0 - X$, we can write:

$$C_T = \max(0, S_T - X)$$

The payoff to the option seller is the negative value of these numbers. In what follows, we will always talk about payoff in terms of the option owner unless otherwise stated. We should note that $\max(0, S_t - X)$, where $0 < t < T$, is also the payoff if the owner decides to exercise the call option early. In this topic review, we will only consider time T in our analysis. Determining how to compute C_t when $0 < t < T$ is a complex task to be addressed later in this topic review.

Although our focus here is not to calculate C_t, we should clearly define it as the initial cost of the call when the investor purchases at time 0, which is T units of time *before T*. C_0 is the *call premium*. Thus, we can write that the profit to the owner at t = T is:

$$\text{profit} = C_T - C_0$$

This says that at time T, the owner's profit is the option payoff minus the premium paid at time 0. Incorporating C_0 into Figure 1 gives us the profit diagram for a call at expiration, and this is Figure 2.

Study Session 15

Figure 2 illustrates an important point, which is that the profit to the owner is negative when the stock price is less than the exercise price plus the premium. At expiration, we can say that:

if $S_T < X + C_0$ then: call buyer profit $< 0 <$ call seller profit
if $S_T = X + C_0$ then: call buyer profit $= 0 =$ call seller profit
if $S_T > X + C_0$ then: call buyer profit $> 0 >$ call seller profit

The *breakeven price* is a very descriptive term that we use for $X + C_0$, or $X + $ premium.

Figure 2: Profit Diagram for a Call at Expiration

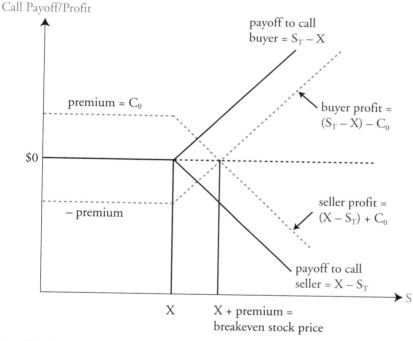

Call Payoff/Profit

payoff to call buyer $= S_T - X$

premium $= C_0$

buyer profit $= (S_T - X) - C_0$

$0

seller profit $= (X - S_T) + C_0$

− premium

payoff to call seller $= X - S_T$

S

X

X + premium = breakeven stock price

Put Options

If you understand the properties of a call, the properties of a put should come to you fairly easily. A *put option* gives the owner the right to sell a stock to the seller of the put at a specific price. At expiration, the buyer benefits if the price of the underlying is less than the exercise price X:

$P_T = X - S_T$ if $S_T < X$
$P_T = 0$ if $X < S_T$

or

$P_T = \max(0, X - S_T)$

For example, an investor writes a put option on a stock with a strike price of $X = 50$. If the stock stays at $50 or above, the payoff of the put option is zero (because the holder may receive the same or better price by selling the underlying asset on the market rather than exercising the option). But if the stock price falls below $50, say to $40, the put option may be exercised with the option holder buying the stock from the market at $40 and selling it to the put writer at $50, for a $10 gain. The writer of the put option must pay the put price of $50, when it can be sold in the market at only $40, resulting in a $10 loss. The gain to the option holder is the same magnitude as the loss to the option writer. Figure 3 illustrates this example, excluding the initial cost of the put and transaction costs. Figure 4 includes the cost of the put (but not transaction costs) and illustrates the profit to the put owner.

Figure 3: Put Payoff to Buyer and Seller

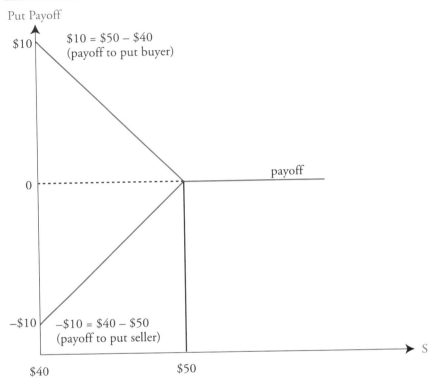

Given the "mirror-image quality" that results from the "zero-sum game" nature of options, we often just draw the profit to the buyer as shown in Figure 4. Then, we can simply remember that each positive (negative) value is a negative (positive) value for the seller.

Figure 4: Put Profit to Buyer

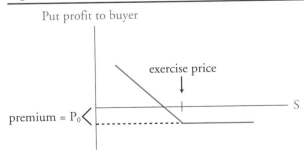

The breakeven price for a put position upon expiration is the exercise price minus the premium paid, $X - P_0$.

Example: Call option

An investor purchases a call option on a stock with an exercise price of $35. The premium is $3.20. **Calculate** the payoffs and profits for the option owner at expiration for each of the following prices of the underlying stock S_T: $25, $30, $35, $40, $45, and $50. **Calculate** the breakeven price (assuming no transaction costs).

 Professor's Note: All examples ignore transactions costs. If by chance you see them on the exam, you can easily include them by just adding any costs onto the option premium in calculating breakeven or profits.

Answer:

The figure below contains the payoffs and profits from a long call with an exercise price of $35.

Payoff and Profit on a Long Call Option

Stock Price	$payoff = max(0, S_T - X)$	$profit = payoff - C_0$	
$25	max($25 – $35, 0) = $0	$0 – $3.20	= –$3.20
$30	max($30 – $35, 0) = $0	$0 – $3.20	= –$3.20
$35	max($35 – $35, 0) = $0	$0 – $3.20	= –$3.20
$40	max($40 – $35, 0) = $5	$5 – $3.20	= $1.80
$45	max($45 – $35, 0) = $10	$10 – $3.20	= $6.80
$50	max($50 – $35, 0) = $15	$15 – $3.20	= $11.80

As for the breakeven price, we clearly see that it is between $35 and $40 because the profit turns positive between these two strike prices. The calculation is simple:

breakeven price = $35.00 + $3.20 = $38.20

Example: Put option

An investor purchases a put option on a stock with an exercise price of $15. The premium is $1.60. **Calculate** the payoffs and profits for the option owner at expiration for each of the following prices of the underlying stock S_T: $0, $5, $10, $15, $20, and $25. What is the breakeven price?

Answer:

The following table contains the payoffs and profits from a long put with an exercise price of $15.

Payoff and Profit on a Long Put Option

Stock Price	payoff = $max(0, X - S_T)$	profit = $payoff - P_0$
$0	$max(0, \$15 - \$0)$ = \$15	$15.00 - \$1.60 = \$13.40
$5	$max(0, \$15 - \$5)$ = \$10	$10.00 - \$1.60 = \$8.40
$10	$max(0, \$15 - \$10)$ = \$5	$5.00 - \$1.60 = \$3.40
$15	$max(0, \$15 - \$15)$ = \$0	$0 - \$1.60 = -\$1.60
$20	$max(0, \$15 - \$20)$ = \$0	$0 - \$1.60 = -\$1.60
$25	$max(0, \$15 - \$25)$ = \$0	$0 - \$1.60 = -\$1.60

We see that the breakeven price is between $15 and $10 because the profit turns positive between these two strike prices. The formula is simple:

breakeven price = $15.00 – $1.60 = $13.40

These examples illustrate the properties that we have mentioned so far.

- In both cases, the payoffs and profits are linear functions of S_T for the regions above and below X.
- The call option has the potential for an infinite payoff and profit because there is no upper limit to $S_T - X$, nor to $S_T - X - C_0$.
- The put has an upper payoff, which is X, and the upper limit to the profit is $X - P_0$.

COVERED CALLS AND PROTECTIVE PUTS

LOS 29.a: Compare the use of covered calls and protective puts to manage risk exposure to individual securities.

CFA® Program Curriculum, Volume 5, page 286

Professor's Note: Covered calls and protective puts are the first of the combined positions. They were taught at Level I and Level II and have been tested at Level III. Know them well.

Covered Call

An investor creates a *covered call* position by buying the underlying security and selling a call option. Covered call writing strategies are used to generate additional portfolio income when the investor believes that the underlying stock price will remain unchanged over the short term. The profit profile for a covered call is given in Figure 5.

©2017 Kaplan, Inc.

Figure 5: Profit Profile for a Covered Call

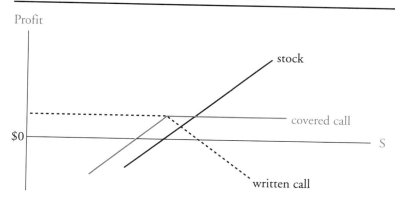

At expiration, the following relationships hold for the investor that both buys the stock and sells the call:

$$\text{profit} = -\max(0, S_T - X) + S_T - S_0 + C_0$$
$$\text{maximum profit} = X + C_0 - S_0$$
$$\text{maximum loss} = S_0 - C_0$$
$$\text{breakeven price} = S_0 - C_0$$
$$S_0 = \text{initial stock price paid}$$

Important Professor's Note: The CFA text has more than 65 formulas relating to value at expiration, profit, max profit, max loss, and breakeven(s) in this and the subsequent option positions material. Candidates who try to memorize these equations report being very frustrated and find the formulas are not sufficient to solve all of the end-of-chapter questions. The CFA material does not number the equations or in any way denote that memorization is expected.

We use a different approach in our videos and classes. It is mathematically identical to the formulas and consists of a few steps that work for all combined positions:

Calculate the initial investment in the strategy. Sales are a receipt of funds and purchases an expenditure. Therefore, the initial investment can be a net receipt or expenditure. If the underlying is part of the combination, its initial value at the start of the combination must also be included.

Max profit and loss are all found by examining the payoff pattern to determine the underlying price where max gain or loss occurs. At that underlying price, compute the intrinsic value of all positions in the combination, compare this to the initial investment, and the difference is the max profit or loss.

To compute profit or loss for any stated price of the underlying, the same process applies, just use the specified price of the underlying.

For breakeven start from the max gain or loss and from the payoff pattern, determine if the underlying must increase or decrease and by how much.

Example: Covered call

An investor purchases a stock for $S_0 = \$43$ and sells a call for $C_0 = \$2.10$ with a strike price, $X = \$45$.

(1) **Compute** the maximum profit and loss and the breakeven price.

(2) **Compute** the profits when the stock price is $0, $35, $40, $45, $50, and $55.

Answer (1):

$$
\begin{aligned}
\text{maximum profit} &= X + C_0 - S_0 \\
&= \$45.00 + \$2.10 - \$43.00 = \$4.10 \\
\text{maximum loss} &= S_0 - C_0 \\
&= \$43.00 - \$2.10 = \$40.90 \\
\text{breakeven price} &= S_0 - C_0 \\
&= \$43.00 - \$2.10 = \$40.90
\end{aligned}
$$

Answer (2):

The figure below shows profit calculations at the various stock prices.

Covered Call Profits

S_T	*Covered Call Profits* $profit = -max(0, S_T - X) + S_T - S_0 + C_0$	
$0	$-max(0, \$0 - \$45) + \$0 - \$43.00 + \$2.10$	$= -\$40.90$
$35	$-max(0, \$35 - \$45) + \$35.00 - \$43.00 + \$2.10$	$= -\$5.90$
$40	$-max(0, \$40 - \$45) + \$40.00 - \$43.00 + \$2.10$	$= -\$0.90$
$45	$-max(0, \$45 - \$45) + \$45.00 - \$43.00 + \$2.10$	$= \$4.10$
$50	$-max(0, \$50 - \$45) + \$50.00 - \$43.00 + \$2.10$	$= \$4.10$
$55	$-max(0, \$55 - \$45) + \$55.00 - \$43.00 + \$2.10$	$= \$4.10$

Protective Put

A *protective put* (also called *portfolio insurance* or a *hedged portfolio*) is constructed by holding a long position in the underlying security and buying a put option. You can use a protective put to limit the downside risk at the cost of the put premium, P_0. You will see by the diagram in Figure 6 that the investor will still be able to benefit from increases in the stock's price, but it will be lower by the amount paid for the put, P_0. The profit profile for a protective put is shown in Figure 6.

©2017 Kaplan, Inc.

Figure 6: Protective Put

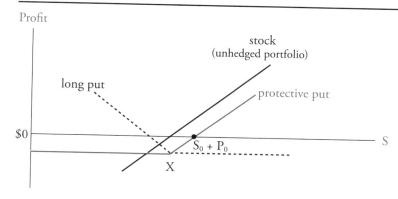

Professor's Note: Economists love these types of graphs because they were forced to spend long hours learning to understand them. Now they like to share that pain. If you like the graphs, use them. **The bottom line is you need to know the net payoff graph shape, the blue line for each combination.** *All the other lines are interim steps used for constructing the graph. You can skip the other lines since they are not covered in the CFA text. Some candidates like seeing the extra lines.*

At expiration, the following relationships hold:

profit $= \max(0, X - S_T) + S_T - S_0 - P_0$

maximum profit $= S_T - S_0 - P_0$ (no upside limit)

maximum loss $= S_0 - X + P_0$

breakeven price $= S_0 + P_0$

Example: Protective put

An investor purchases a stock for $S_0 = \$37.50$ and buys a put for $P_0 = \$1.40$ with a strike price, $X = \$35$.

(1) **Compute** the max profit, max loss, and the breakeven price.

(2) **Compute** the profits for when the price is $0, $30, $35, $40, $45, and $50.

Answer (1):

$$
\begin{aligned}
\text{maximum profit} &= \text{Infinite} \\
\text{maximum loss} &= S_0 - X + P_0 \\
&= \$37.50 - \$35.00 + \$1.40 = \$3.90 \\
\text{breakeven price} &= S_0 + P_0 = \$37.50 + \$1.40 = \$38.90
\end{aligned}
$$

Answer (2):

The figure below shows profit calculations for the protective put.

Protective Put Profits

S_T	Protective Put Profits $\text{profit} = max(0, X - S_T) + S_T - S_0 - P_0$	
$0	max(0, $35 – $0) + $0 – $37.5 – $1.40	= –$3.90
$30	max(0, $35 – $30) + $30.00 – $37.5 – $1.40	= –$3.90
$35	max(0, $35 – $35) + $35.00 – $37.5 – $1.40	= –$3.90
$40	max(0, $35 – $40) + $40.00 – $37.5 – $1.40	= $1.10
$45	max(0, $35 – $45) + $45.00 – $37.5 – $1.40	= $6.10
$50	max(0, $35 – $50) + $50.00 – $37.5 – $1.40	= $11.10

Discussion

The answers here are per one unit of each asset (e.g., one share of stock and one option). The final results can just be multiplied by the number of units involved. For example, in the preceding protective put example, if an investor had 200 shares of the stock and 200 puts, a value of $S_T = 50$ would give a total profit of $200 \times \$11.10$ or $2,220.

©2017 Kaplan, Inc.

OPTION SPREAD STRATEGIES

LOS 29.b: Calculate and interpret the value at expiration, profit, maximum profit, maximum loss, breakeven underlying price at expiration, and general shape of the graph for the following option strategies: bull spread, bear spread, butterfly spread, collar, straddle, box spread.

CFA® Program Curriculum, Volume 5, page 293

Bull Spread

A bull spread provides limited upside if the underlying rises (hence the name bull) with limited downside. It can be constructed when the buyer of the spread purchases a call option with a low exercise price, X_L, and subsidizes the purchase price of that call by selling a call with a higher exercise price, X_H. The prices are C_{L0} and C_{H0}, respectively. At inception, the following relationships hold:

$$X_L < X_H$$
$$C_{L0} > C_{H0}$$

It is usually the case that $S_0 < X_L$ and almost always that $S_0 < X_H$. The investor who buys a bull spread expects the stock price to rise and the purchased call to finish in-the-money such that $X_L < S_T$. However, the investor does not believe that the price of the stock will rise above the exercise price for the out-of-the-money written call. The profit/loss diagram of a bull spread is shown in Figure 7.

Figure 7: Bull Spread Using Calls

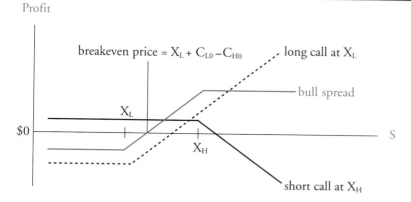

$$\text{profit} = \max(0, S_T - X_L) - \max(0, S_T - X_H) - C_{L0} + C_{H0}$$
$$\text{maximum profit} = X_H - X_L - C_{L0} + C_{H0}$$
$$\text{maximum loss} = C_{L0} - C_{H0}$$
$$\text{breakeven price} = X_L + C_{L0} - C_{H0}$$

Example: Bull spread

An investor purchases a call for C_{L0} = $2.10 with a strike price of X = $45 and sells a call for C_{H0} = $0.50 with a strike price of X = $50.

(1) **Compute** the maximum profit and loss and the breakeven price.

(2) **Compute** the profits for when the price is $0, $35, $45, $48, $50, and $55.

Answer (1):

$$
\begin{aligned}
\text{maximum profit} &= X_H - X_L - C_{L0} + C_{H0} \\
&= \$50.00 - \$45.00 - \$2.10 + \$0.50 \\
&= \$3.40
\end{aligned}
$$

$$
\begin{aligned}
\text{maximum loss} &= C_{L0} - C_{H0} \\
&= \$2.10 - \$0.50 \\
&= \$1.60
\end{aligned}
$$

$$
\begin{aligned}
\text{breakeven price} &= X_L + C_{L0} - C_{H0} \\
&= \$45.00 + \$2.10 - \$0.50 \\
&= \$46.60
\end{aligned}
$$

$$
\begin{aligned}
\text{maximum loss} &= C_{L0} - C_{H0} \\
&= \$2.10 - \$0.50 \\
&= \$1.60
\end{aligned}
$$

$$
\begin{aligned}
\text{breakeven price} &= X_L + C_{L0} - C_{H0} \\
&= \$45.00 + \$2.10 - \$0.50 \\
&= \$46.60
\end{aligned}
$$

Answer (2):

The following figure shows the calculations of the profit on the bull spread.

Bull Spread Profits

S_T	Bull Spread Strategy $profit = max(0, S_T - X_L) - max(0, S_T - X_H) - C_{L0} + C_{H0}$
$0	max(0, $0 − $45) − max(0, $0 − $50) − $2.10 + $0.50 = −$1.60
$35	max(0, $35 − $45) − max(0, $35 −$50) − $2.10 + $0.50 = −$1.60
$45	max(0, $45 − $45) − max(0, $45 − $50) − $2.10 + $0.50 = −$1.60
$48	max(0, $48 − $45) − max(0, $48 − $50) − $2.10 + $0.50 = $1.40
$50	max(0, $50 − $45) − max(0, $50 − $50) − $2.10 + $0.50 = $3.40
$55	max(0, $55 − $45) − max(0, $55 − $50) − $2.10 + $0.50 = $3.40

©2017 Kaplan, Inc.

Bear Spread

A bear spread provides limited upside if the underlying declines (hence the name bear) with limited downside. It is most commonly constructed by selling a call with a low strike price and purchasing a call with a high strike price. As stock prices fall, you keep the premium from the written call, net of the long call premium. The purpose of the long call is to protect you from sharp increases in stock prices. The payoff/profits, shown in Figure 8, are the opposite (inverted image) of the bull spread.

Figure 8: Bear Spread Using Calls

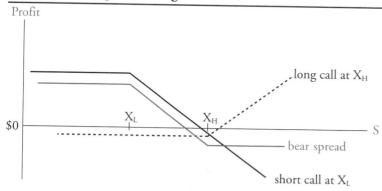

Bear Spread Using Puts

Virtually any payoff pattern can be constructed in more than one way. For example, the bear spread can also be constructed using puts. The investor buys a put with the higher exercise price and sells a put with a lower exercise price. The important relationships are:

$$\text{profit} = \max(0, X_H - S_T) - \max(0, X_L - S_T) - P_{H0} + P_{L0}$$
$$\text{maximum profit} = X_H - X_L - P_{H0} + P_{L0}$$
$$\text{maximum loss} = P_{H0} - P_{L0}$$
$$\text{breakeven price} = X_H + P_{L0} - P_{H0}$$

Example: Bear spread using puts

An investor purchases a put for $P_{H0} = \$4.00$ with a strike price of $X_H = \$25.00$ and sells a put for $P_{L0} = \$1.80$ with a strike price of $X_L = \$20.00$.

(1) **Compute** the maximum profit and loss and the breakeven price.

(2) **Calculate** the profits when the price is $0, $15, $20, $22, $25, and $30.

Answer (1):

$$\text{maximum profit} = X_H - X_L - P_{H0} + P_{L0}$$
$$= \$25.00 - \$20.00 - \$4.00 + \$1.80$$
$$= \$2.80$$

$$\text{maximum loss} = P_{H0} - P_{L0}$$
$$= \$4.00 - \$1.80 = \$2.20$$

$$\text{breakeven price} = X_H + P_{L0} - P_{H0}$$
$$= \$25.00 + \$1.80 - \$4.00$$
$$= \$22.80$$

Answer (2):

The following figure shows the calculations of the profits on the bear spread.

Bear Spread Profits

S_T	Bear Spread $profit = max(0, X_H - S_T) - max(0, X_L - S_T) - P_{H0} + P_{L0}$	
$0	max(0, \$25 - \$0) - max(0, \$20 - \$0) - \$4.00 + \$1.80 =	\$2.80
$15	max(0, \$25 - \$15) - max(0, \$20 - \$15) - \$4.00 + \$1.80 =	\$2.80
$20	max(0, \$25 - \$20) - max(0, \$20 - \$20) - \$4.00 + \$1.80 =	\$2.80
$22	max(0, \$25 - \$22) - max(0, \$20 - \$22) - \$4.00 + \$1.80 =	\$0.80
$25	max(0, \$25 - \$25) - max(0, \$20 - \$25) - \$4.00 + \$1.80 =	–\$2.20
$30	max(0, \$25 - \$30) - max(0, \$20 - \$30) - \$4.00 + \$1.80 =	–\$2.20

Butterfly Spread With Calls

A butterfly spread with calls involves the purchase or sale of four call options of three different types:

- Buy one call with a low exercise price (X_L).
- Buy another call with a high exercise price (X_H).
- Write *two* calls with an exercise price in between (X_M).

Typically the strike prices are equidistant apart, for example 10, 15, and 20.

The buyer of a butterfly spread is essentially betting that the stock price will stay near the strike price of the written calls. However, the loss that the butterfly spread buyer

Study Session 15

sustains if the stock price strays from this level is not large. The two graphs in Figure 9 illustrate the construction and behavior of a butterfly spread. The top graph shows the profits of the components, and the bottom graph illustrates the spread itself.

Figure 9: Butterfly Spread Construction and Behavior

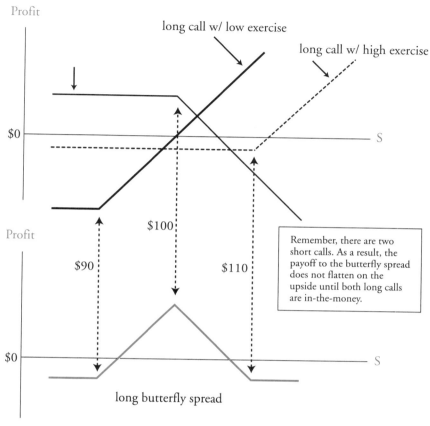

$$\text{profit} = \max(0, S_T - X_L) - 2\max(0, S_T - X_M) + \max(0, S_T - X_H) - C_{L0} + 2C_{M0} - C_{H0}$$

$$\text{maximum profit} = X_M - X_L - C_{L0} + 2C_{M0} - C_{H0}$$

$$\text{maximum loss} = C_{L0} - 2C_{M0} + C_{H0}$$

$$\text{breakeven prices} = X_L + C_{L0} - 2C_{M0} + C_{H0} \text{ and } 2X_M - X_L - C_{L0} + 2C_{M0} - C_{H0}$$

Example: Butterfly spread with calls

An investor makes the following transactions in calls on a stock:

- Buys one call defined by $C_{L0} = \$7$ and $X_L = \$55$.
- Buys one call defined by $C_{H0} = \$2$ and $X_H = \$65$.
- Sells two calls defined by $C_{M0} = \$4$ and $X_M = \$60$.

(1) **Compute** the max profit, max loss, and the breakeven price.

(2) **Calculate** the profits for when the price is $50, $55, $58, $60, $62, and $65.

Answer (1):

$$
\begin{aligned}
\text{maximum profit} &= X_M - X_L - C_{L0} + 2C_{M0} - C_{H0} \\
&= \$60 - \$55 - \$7 + 2(\$4) - \$2 \\
&= \$4
\end{aligned}
$$

$$
\begin{aligned}
\text{maximum loss} &= C_{L0} - 2C_{M0} + C_{H0} \\
&= \$7 - 2(\$4) + \$2 = \$1
\end{aligned}
$$

$$
\begin{aligned}
\text{breakeven prices} &= \$55 + \$7 - 2(\$4) + \$2 \text{ and } 2(60) - \$55 - \$7 + 2(\$4) - \$2 \\
&= \$56 \text{ and } \$64
\end{aligned}
$$

Answer (2):

The figure shows the calculations of the profits on the butterfly spread.

Butterfly Spread Profits

S_T	Butterfly Spread $profit = max(0, S_T - X_L) - 2max(0, S_T - X_M) + max(0, S_T - X_H) - C_{L0} + 2C_{M0} - C_{H0}$
$50	$max(0, \$50 - \$55) - 2max(0, \$50 - \$60) + max(0, \$50 - \$65) - \$1 = -\$1$
$55	$max(0, \$55 - \$55) - 2max(0, \$55 - \$60) + max(0, \$55 - \$65) - \$1 = -\$1$
$58	$max(0, \$58 - \$55) - 2max(0, \$58 - \$60) + max(0, \$58 - \$65) - \$1 = \$2$
$60	$max(0, \$60 - \$55) - 2max(0, \$60 - \$60) + max(0, \$60 - \$65) - \$1 = \$4$
$62	$max(0, \$62 - \$55) - 2max(0, \$62 - \$60) + max(0, \$62 - \$65) - \$1 = \$2$
$65	$max(0, \$65 - \$55) - 2max(0, \$65 - \$60) + max(0, \$65 - \$65) - \$1 = -\$1$

©2017 Kaplan, Inc.

Butterfly Spread With Puts

A butterfly spread with puts is constructed by buying one put with a low exercise price, buying a second put with a higher exercise price, and selling two puts with an intermediate exercise price. The profit function is very similar to that of the butterfly spread with calls. You will notice that in each of the max( ) functions, the S_T and X_i have switched, but otherwise it is basically the same format:

$$\text{profit} = \max(0, X_L - S_T) - 2\max(0, X_M - S_T) + \max(0, X_H - S_T) - P_{L0} + 2P_{M0} - P_{H0}$$

As with the butterfly spread with calls, the long butterfly spread with puts will have its highest terminal value if the stock finishes at the exercise price for the written puts.

Example: Butterfly spread with puts

An investor composes a butterfly spread by buying puts with premiums of $0.80 and $5.50 and exercise prices of $40 and $50, respectively. The investor sells two puts with a premium of $3 and an exercise price of $45. **Calculate** the profit if the value of the underlying stock at expiration is $46.30.

Answer:

$$\text{profit} = \max(0, \$40.00 - \$46.30) - 2\max(0, \$45.00 - \$46.30) + \max(0, \$50.00 - \$46.30) - \$0.80 + 2(\$3.00) - \$5.50$$
$$\text{profit} = 0 - 0 + \$3.70 - \$0.30 = \$3.40$$

The obvious motivation for the butterfly spread is to earn a profit if the underlying asset does not move very much over the lives of the options used to create the spread. If there is a big movement, then the loss is limited to a lower bound (e.g., –$1 in the first example and –$0.30 in the butterfly put example—try it and see). Of course, an investor who thinks there will be a big move will take the other side or short the butterfly spread. The butterfly spread's appeal is that it limits the loss to the long side of the strategy.

Straddle

A *straddle* consists of the purchase of both a put option and a call option on the same asset. The put and call are purchased with the same exercise price and expiration. In a straddle, you expect a large stock price move, but you are unsure of the direction. You lose if the stock price remains unchanged. The profit/loss diagram for a straddle is shown in Figure 10.

Figure 10: Straddle

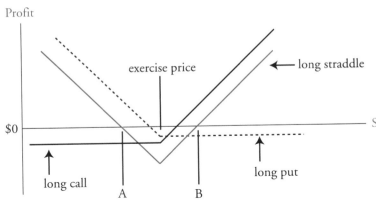

Note that to break even on a straddle, the stock price must move enough to recoup the premiums paid for the options. The breakeven price is equal to the exercise price ± (put + call premium), denoted by points A and B in Figure 10.

For the *straddle*, the important relationships are:

$$\text{profit} = \max(0, S_T - X) + \max(0, X - S_T) - C_0 - P_0$$
$$\text{maximum profit} = S_T - X - C_0 - P_0 \text{ (unlimited upside as } S_T \text{ increases)}$$
$$\text{maximum loss} = C_0 + P_0$$
$$\text{breakeven price} = X - C_0 - P_0 \text{ and } X + C_0 + P_0$$

Example: Straddle

An investor purchases a call on a stock, with an exercise price of $45 and premium of $3, and a put option with the same maturity that has an exercise price of $45 and premium of $2.

(1) Compute the max profit, max loss, and the breakeven price.

(2) Compute the profits when the price is $0, $35, $40, $45, $50, $55, and $100.

Answer (1):

$$\text{maximum profit} = \text{Infinite, as the underlying increases}$$

$$\text{maximum loss} = C_0 + P_0 = \$5$$

$$
\begin{aligned}
\text{breakeven price} &= X - C_0 - P_0 \text{ and } X + C_0 + P_0 \\
&= \$45 - \$5 \text{ and } \$45 + \$5 \\
&= \$40 \text{ and } \$50
\end{aligned}
$$

Answer (2):

The figure below shows the calculation for the profit on a straddle.

Profits on a Long Straddle

S_T	Straddle profit = $max(0, S_T - X) + max(0, X - S_T) - C_0 - P_0$
$0	$max(0, \$0 - \$45) + max(0, \$45 - \$0) - \$3 - \$2 = \$40$
$35	$max(0, \$35 - \$45) + max(0, \$45 - \$35) - \$5 \quad = \$5$
$40	$max(0, \$40 - \$45) + max(0, \$45 - \$40) - \$5 \quad = \$0$
$45	$max(0, \$45 - \$45) + max(0, \$45 - \$45) - \$5 \quad = -\$5$
$50	$max(0, \$50 - \$45) + max(0, \$45 - \$50) - \$5 \quad = \$0$
$55	$max(0, \$55 - \$45) + max(0, \$45 - \$55) - \$5 \quad = \$5$
$100	$max(0, \$100 - \$45) + max(0, \$45 - \$100) - \$5 = \$50$

The values $S_T = \$0$ and $\$100$ were included in the previous example to illustrate the fact that the upside potential for a long straddle is unlimited, and the downside risk is only the sum of the premiums of the call and put.

Professor's Note: It is entirely possible you will get an exam question that "extends the basics." For example, if a straddle is long the call and put (with the same strike price), a reverse straddle is short the call and put. You initially receive the premiums and profit if the underlying does not move from the strike price. The graph flips on the horizontal axis and looks like a broad, flattened A, instead of a V.

Collar

A collar is the combination of a protective put and covered call. The usual goal is for the owner of the underlying asset to buy a protective put and then sell a call to pay for the put. If the premiums of the two are equal, it is called a *zero-cost collar*. The usual practice is to select strike prices such that put strike < call strike. Because this is the case, we can continue to use our X_L and X_H notation where X_L is the put strike price and X_H is the call strike price.

As Figure 11 illustrates, this effectively puts a band or *collar* around the possible returns. Both the upside and downside are limited, the downside by the long put and the upside by the short call. Many possibilities exist. By lowering X_L, for example, the put premium will fall, so the investor could sell a call with a higher X_H to offset the lower put premium. With a lower X_L and higher X_H, the upside and downside potential both increase.

Figure 11: Collar

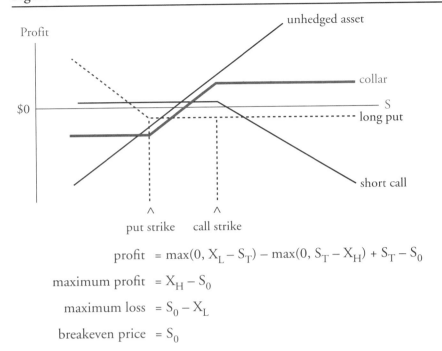

$$\text{profit} = \max(0, X_L - S_T) - \max(0, S_T - X_H) + S_T - S_0$$

$$\text{maximum profit} = X_H - S_0$$

$$\text{maximum loss} = S_0 - X_L$$

$$\text{breakeven price} = S_0$$

Professor's Note: The CFA text only covers zero cost collars where the initial net option premium is zero.

Example: Zero-cost collar

An investor purchases a stock for $29 and a put for $P_0 = \$0.20$ with a strike price of $X_L = \$27.50$. The investor sells a call for $C_0 = \$0.20$ with a strike price of $X_H = \$30$. The two option premiums are equal.

(1) **Calculate** the maximum profit and loss and the breakeven price.

(2) **Calculate** the profits when the price is $0, $20.00, $25.00, $28.50, $30.00, and $100.00.

Answer (1): This is a zero-cost collar because the premiums on the call and put are equal.

$$\begin{aligned} \text{maximum profit} &= X_H - S_0 \\ &= \$30 - \$29 \\ &= \$1 \end{aligned}$$

$$\begin{aligned} \text{maximum loss} &= S_0 - X_L \\ &= \$29.00 - \$27.50 \\ &= \$1.50 \end{aligned}$$

$$\text{breakeven price} = S_0 = \$29$$

Answer (2):

The table on the following page shows the calculations for profits on this zero-cost collar.

Profits on a Zero-Cost Collar

S_T	Zero-Cost Collar profit = $max(0, X_L - S_T) - max(0, S_T - X_H) + S_T - S_0$	
$0.00	$max(0, \$27.50 - \$0) - max(0, \$0 - \$30.00) + \$0 - \$29.00$	= –$1.50
$20.00	$max(0, \$27.50 - \$20.00) - max(0, \$20.00 - \$30.00) + \$20.00 - \$29.00$	= –$1.50
$25.00	$max(0, \$27.50 - \$25.00) - max(0, \$25.00 - \$30.00) + \$25.00 - \$29.00$	= –$1.50
$28.50	$max(0, \$27.50 - \$28.50) - max(0, \$28.50 - \$30.00) + \$28.50 - \$29.00$	= –$0.50
$30.00	$max(0, \$27.50 - \$30.00) - max(0, \$30.00 - \$30.00) + \$30.00 - \$29.00$	= $1.00
$100.00	$max(0, \$27.50 - \$100.00) - max(0, \$100.00 - \$30.00) + \$100.00 - \$29.00$ =	$1.00

We see how the lower limit of dollar return is –$1.50, even when the underlying asset's price is zero. The upper limit on return or profit is $1, even when the underlying asset's price is $100. For a price of the underlying asset between the strike prices, such as S_T = $28.50 in this example, the profit is between –$1.50 and $1.00. The collar is a good strategy for locking in the value of a portfolio at a minimal cost. The cost is zero if the appropriate put and call have the same premium.

Box Spread Strategy

The *box spread* is a combination of a bull spread and a bear spread on the same asset, using only two strike prices. For example, a bull spread is the combination of two calls: a short call with a higher strike price (X_H) and a long call with a lower strike price (X_L).

Figure 12: Bull Spread

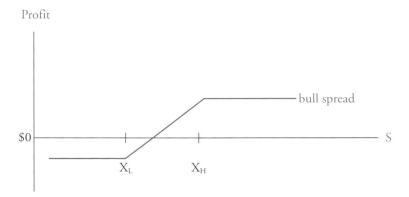

The bear spread is a short put with a lower strike price (X_L) and long put with a higher strike price (X_H).

Figure 13: Bear Spread

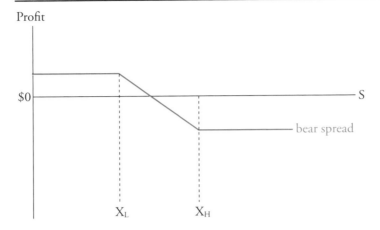

Combining the two produces the box spread with an interesting result. The ending value of the box spread is the same no matter what the ending value of the underlying. The initial investment (net option premium) is the same, so if the options are priced correctly, the difference in ending and beginning value of the box spread must reflect the risk-free rate. If the options are not priced correctly and the box spread return is not the risk-free rate, the box spread has identified an arbitrage opportunity.

Figure 14: Payoff to the Box Spread

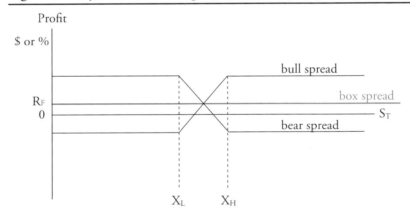

Example: Box spread

An investor buys a call and sells a put with a strike price of $X_L = \$25$. The call and put premiums are $C_{L0} = \$1.75$ and $P_{L0} = \$0.50$. The investor then sells a call and buys a put with a strike price of $X_H = \$30$. For the second pair of options, the call and put premiums are $C_{H0} = \$0.20$ and $P_{H0} = \$3.90$. The options all expire in two months.

Compute the profit and the annualized return on the investment and **determine** whether this a worthwhile investment, if the risk-free rate is 5%.

©2017 Kaplan, Inc.

Answer:

$$profit = X_H - X_L + P_{L0} - C_{L0} + C_{H0} - P_{H0}$$

$$profit = \$30.00 - \$25.00 + \$0.50 - \$1.75 + \$0.20 - \$3.90$$

$$profit = \$0.05$$

The initial cost was $4.95 = + \$0.50 - \$1.75 + \$0.20 - \$3.90$. This means the holding period return is $0.05 / 4.95 = 0.0101$. This is a 2-month return, so the annualized return is 0.06216 (= $1.0101^{12/2} - 1$). Because this return is greater than the risk-free rate of 5%, this would be a worthwhile strategy. If the investor can borrow for less than 0.06216 (6.2%), an arbitrage profit is possible.

INTEREST RATE OPTIONS

LOS 29.c: Calculate the effective annual rate for a given interest rate outcome when a borrower (lender) manages the risk of an anticipated loan using an interest rate call (put) option.

CFA® Program Curriculum, Volume 5, page 312

Professor's Note: The general rule for interest rate options (such as caps and floors) is the interest rate for the payout is set at the expiration of the option but paid at the end of the interest rate period, not when the option expires.

Hopefully, you are already familiar with the basic mechanics of an interest rate call option that makes a payment to the owner when the reference rate (a.k.a. the *underlying*) exceeds the strike rate (i.e., the exercise rate). Because LIBOR is the usual reference rate, we will put that in the formula. The formula for the payment is:

$$payoff = (NP)[max(0, LIBOR - strike\ rate)](D / 360)$$

where *NP* stands for notional principal and *D* stands for *days in underlying rate* (i.e., the number of days the notional principal would be theoretically borrowed). NOTE: Do not confuse this with the maturity of the call! *Maturity* is the time between today and when the payoff is determined.

As an example, we will say that the notional principal of the contract is $20 million, the option expires in 49 days, the strike rate is 6%, and D = 90 days. If at option maturity in 49 days LIBOR is 6.2%, the payoff would be:

$$payoff = (\$20,000,000)(0.002)(90 / 360) = \$10,000$$

The payoff will occur 139 days after the purchase of the option. If the underlying rate (LIBOR) had been less than 6%, then the payoff would have been zero. Because the call has a positive payoff when interest rates rise above a certain level, they can hedge a floating-rate loan.

Example: Interest rate call option

On March 1, a firm plans to borrow $10 million for 90 days beginning on April 1 (31 days in the future, which is the maturity of the *call*). It can currently borrow at LIBOR plus 200 basis points, and LIBOR is currently 4.5%. The firm buys an interest rate call option where LIBOR is the underlying, and the strike rate is 4%. The notional principal is $10 million, and D = 90 days, which is also the length of the loan. The premium of the call is $5,000. **Calculate** the effective borrowing rates of the loan when LIBOR is 2.0%, 3.5%, 4.0%, 4.5%, and 6%.

Answer:

If the manager chooses to purchase the call, that is a cost today. To accurately measure its effect on the borrowing costs, we need to compute its (future) value at the date of the loan, using the firm's cost of borrowing (LIBOR + 0.02):

FV(premium) = premium[1 + (current LIBOR + spread)(maturity / 360)]
FV(premium) = $5,000[1 + (0.045 + 0.02)(31 / 360)]
FV(premium) = $5,028

Hence, when the firm actually borrows on April 1 (31 days in the future), it is effectively receiving:

net amount = loan − FV(premium)
net amount = $10,000,000 − $5,028
net amount = $9,994,972

With the call premium now reflected in the net proceeds of the loan, the interest cost will be LIBOR plus the 200 basis point spread at that time less any payoff from the call:

effective dollar interest cost =
$10,000,000(LIBOR$_{\text{April 1}}$+ 0.02)(90 / 360) − (call payoff)

The call payoff is:

payoff = (NP)[max(0, LIBOR − strike rate)(D / 360)]
payoff = ($10,000,000)[max(0, LIBOR$_{\text{April 1}}$ − 0.04)(90 / 360)]

The effective annual rate (EAR) of borrowing for the 90 days is:

EAR = [($10,000,000 + effective dollar interest cost) / ($9,994,972)]$^{(365/90)}$ − 1

©2017 Kaplan, Inc.

Let's look at the two extremes first: 2% and 6%. If LIBOR is less than 4%, the call payoff is zero. If LIBOR is 2% on April 1, for example, the effective dollar interest cost is:

$$\$100,000 = \$10,000,000(0.02 + 0.02)(90 / 360)$$

If the firm did not hedge, the effective annual rate would be:

EAR without hedge = $(\$10,100,000 / \$10,000,000)^{(365/90)} - 1$
EAR without hedge = 0.04118

Including the cost of the call will increase the rate to:

EAR with hedge   = $(\$10,100,000 / \$9,994,972)^{(365/90)} - 1$
EAR with hedge   = 0.04331

Thus, the cost of the call is incorporated into the effective rate of the loan. Just like a purchased call on a stock, if the underlying is below the strike at expiration, the buyer loses (i.e., the option is worthless and the buyer has paid a premium for it).

Where the borrowing firm benefits is when LIBOR is higher than the strike rate. If $\text{LIBOR}_{\text{April 1}} = 6\%$, the option payoff is:

payoff = $(\$10,000,000)(0.06 - 0.04)(90 / 360)$
payoff = $50,000
effective dollar interest cost = $\$10,000,000(0.06 + 0.02)(90 / 360) - \$50,000$
effective dollar interest cost = $150,000

Comparing the EAR with and without the hedge:

EAR without hedge = $(\$10,200,000 / \$10,000,000)^{(365/90)} - 1$
EAR without hedge = 0.08362

Including the cost of the call will decrease the effective rate to:

EAR with hedge   = $(\$10,150,000 / \$9,994,972)^{(365/90)} - 1$
(call payoff = $50,000)
EAR with hedge   = 0.06441

In fact, this effective rate of 0.06441 is the highest rate the firm can expect to pay with the call.

Let's look at what happens for the cases in between, where $0.02 < \text{LIBOR}_{\text{April 1}} < 0.06$. If $\text{LIBOR}_{\text{April 1}} = 0.035$, the firm will incur dollar interest costs equal to:

effective dollar interest cost = $\$10,000,000(0.055)(90 / 360) = \$137,500$

because the call expires worthless. The effective rate on the net inflow from the borrowing is:

EAR with hedge = $(\$10,137,500 / \$9,994,972)^{(365/90)} - 1 = 0.05910$

If LIBOR$_{\text{April 1}}$ = 0.04, the firm will incur dollar interest costs equal to:

effective dollar interest cost = $10,000,000 × 0.06 × (90 / 360) = $150,000

because the call expires worthless. The effective rate on the net inflow from the borrowing is:

EAR with hedge = ($10,150,000 / $9,994,972)$^{(365/90)}$ − 1 = 0.06441

If LIBOR$_{\text{April 1}}$ = 0.045, the firm will earn a payoff on the call:

payoff = ($10,000,000) × max(0, 0.045 − 0.04) × (90 / 360) = $12,500

The effective dollar interest cost will be:

effective dollar interest cost = $10,000,000(0.065)(90 / 360) − $12,500
effective dollar interest cost = $162,500 − $12,500 = $150,000

The effective rate on the net inflow from the borrowing is:

EAR with hedge = ($10,150,000 / $9,994,972)$^{(365/90)}$ − 1 = 0.06441

This is the same effective cost for when LIBOR$_{\text{April 1}}$ = 0.06.

Let's try another example with less explanation in the answer.

Example: Interest rate option

In 40 days, a firm wishes to borrow $5 million for 180 days. The borrowing rate is LIBOR plus 300 basis points. The current LIBOR is 5%. The firm buys a call that matures in 40 days with a notional principal of $5 million, 180 days in underlying (D = 180), and a strike rate of 4.5%. The call premium is $8,000.

Calculate the effective annual rate of the loan if at expiration LIBOR = 4%, and **calculate** if LIBOR = 5%.

Answer:

First we compute the implied net amount to be borrowed after the cost of the call:

$5,000,000 − $8,000[1 + (0.05+0.03)(40 / 360)] = $4,991,929

For LIBOR = 0.04 at expiration, the dollar cost is (the option is out-of-the-money):

$5,000,000(0.07)(180 / 360) = $175,000

The effective annual rate is:

$$(\$5{,}175{,}000 \,/\, \$4{,}991{,}929)^{(365/180)} - 1 = 0.0758$$

For LIBOR = 0.05, the call option is in-the-money:

$$\text{payoff} = (\$5{,}000{,}000)[\max(0,\ 0.05 - 0.045)(180 \,/\, 360)] = \$12{,}500$$

The dollar interest cost is effectively:

$$\$5{,}000{,}000(0.08)(180 \,/\, 360) - \$12{,}500 = \$187{,}500$$

The effective annual rate is:

$$(\$5{,}187{,}500 \,/\, \$4{,}991{,}929)^{(365/180)} - 1 = 0.0810$$

You should verify that the rate of 0.0810 is the highest possible rate by trying other values higher than LIBOR = 4.5%.

Interest Rate Put

An interest rate put has a payoff to the owner when the reference rate, usually LIBOR, is *below* a certain strike rate at the maturity of the option:

$$\text{payoff} = (NP)[\max(0,\ \text{strike rate} - \text{LIBOR})(D \,/\, 360)]$$

A lender can combine a long position in an interest rate put with a specific floating-rate loan to place a lower limit on the income to be earned on the position. The combination has many of the same basic mechanics as borrowing with an interest rate call. As in the case of the interest rate call, we compute the future value of the put premium, but we *add* it to the loan made by the lender because that represents the total outflow of cash from the lender at the time of the loan.

As in the case of the interest rate call, the payoff of the put places a limit on the effective dollar interest. In this case, the payoff is added to the interest received to ensure a *minimum* amount of revenue to the lender. To make our example easier to follow, we will look at the same loan examined in our last example, which was the second example of an interest rate call. Now we will look at it from the lender's point of view.

> **Example: Interest rate put**
>
> In 40 days, a bank plans to lend $5 million for 180 days. The lending rate is LIBOR plus 300 basis points. The current LIBOR is 5%. The bank buys a put that matures in 40 days with a notional principal of $5 million, 180 days in the underlying, and a strike rate of 4.5%. The put premium is $5,000. **Calculate** the effective annual rate of the loan if at expiration LIBOR = 4%, and then **calculate** the rate if LIBOR = 5%.

Answer:

First we compute the total amount the bank pays out (lends) at time of the loan. This means computing the future value of the premium and adding it to the loan amount.

Loan amount plus future value of premium paid:

$$\$5,000,000 + \$5,000[1 + (0.05 + 0.03)(40 / 360)] = \$5,005,044$$

This amount is used for computing the effective interest rate earned on the outflow of cash at the beginning of the loan. The dollar interest earned by the bank will be based upon the prevailing rate applied to the loan and the payoff of the put. In this case, the expression is:

$$\text{effective interest earned} = \$5,000,000(\text{LIBOR}_{maturity} + 0.03)(180 / 360) + (\text{put payoff})$$

The effective annualized rate on the loan is:

$$\text{EAR} = [(\$5,000,000 + \text{effective dollar interest earned}) / (\$5,005,044)]^{(365/180)} - 1$$

You can see where the lender gets hurt because both the principal returned and the interest earned are based upon the $5 million, but the effective loan is $5,005,044.

If $\text{LIBOR}_{maturity}$ equals 4%, the payoff of the put would be:

$$\text{payoff} = (\$5,000,000)[\max(0, 0.045 - 0.04)(180 / 360)] = \$12,500$$

The dollar interest earned is:

$$\$5,000,000(0.04 + 0.03)(180 / 360) = \$175,000$$

The effective interest rate is:

$$\text{EAR} = [(\$5,000,000 + \$175,000 + \$12,500) / (\$5,005,044)]^{(365/180)} - 1$$
$$\text{EAR} = [(\$5,187,500) / (\$5,005,044)]^{(365/180)} - 1$$
$$\text{EAR} = 0.07531 \text{ or } 7.531\%$$

While not asked, you might notice that in this case the put turned out to be desirable. Without the put the bank would have earned LIBOR + 300 bp or 7%.

If $\text{LIBOR}_{maturity} = 0.05$, the dollar interest earned is:

$$\$5,000,000[0.05 + 0.03](180 / 360) = \$200,000$$
$$\text{EAR} = [(\$5,200,000) / (\$5,005,044)]^{(365/180)} - 1$$
$$\text{EAR} = 0.08057 \text{ or } 8.057\%$$

Without the hedge, and LIBOR = 5% + 300 bp, the lender would have earned $200,000 on only $5 million for an effective rate of $0.08278 = [(\$5,200,000) / (\$5,000,000)]^{(365/180)} - 1$.

©2017 Kaplan, Inc.

INTEREST RATE CAPS, FLOORS, AND COLLARS

LOS 29.d: Calculate the payoffs for a series of interest rate outcomes when a floating rate loan is combined with 1) an interest rate cap, 2) an interest rate floor, or 3) an interest rate collar.

CFA® Program Curriculum, Volume 5, page 323

An interest rate cap is an agreement in which the cap seller agrees to make a payment to the cap buyer when the reference rate exceeds a predetermined level called the *cap strike* or *cap rate*. The cap is a series of interest rate call options. Each individual option can be called a caplet. An interest rate floor is an agreement in which the seller agrees to pay the buyer when the reference rate falls below a predetermined interest rate called the *floor strike* or *floor rate*. The floor is a series of interest rate put options. Each individual option can be called a floorlet.

Caps and floors are over-the-counter contracts, so the two parties involved can tailor the agreement to suit their specific needs. Generally, the terms of a cap or floor agreement will include the:

- Reference rate (typically LIBOR).
- Cap or floor strike that sets the ceiling or floor.
- Length of the agreement.
- Reset frequency, which determines days in each settlement period, D_t.
- Notional principal (*NP*).

For the Exam:

- The CFA text follows the convention that the payoff on the individual caplets and floorlets in interest rate caps and floors based on LIBOR is for the actual number of days in the interest rate period divided by 360. For example, suppose the annual rate is 8% for a quarterly payment and the actual days in the quarter are 92 days; the periodic rate is $8\% \times (92 / 360) = 2.04444\%$. If the actual day count had not been given, this could be approximated as $8\% / 4 = 2.00\%$.
- Like individual interest rate calls and puts, the payments are in arrears with the rate at the expiration of each caplet or floorlet determining the payoff at the end of the next interest rate period.
- Floating rate loan interest payments are also set in arrears. At the origination of the loan, the first interest payment is known and no caplet covers the first loan period. Instead, the first caplet expires at the end of the first loan interest period to be paid at the end of the second loan interest period. Think of the first "floating rate" as in fact a fixed rate known at initiation of the loan, only the subsequent payments are unknown and floating.

These conventions are illustrated in the following examples.

Interest Rate Caps

An interest rate cap is a series of call options on interest rates. The buyer receives the interest rate difference if rates are above the strike rate. Each potential payoff is called a caplet. The natural user of a cap is the payer on a floating rate loan.

Example: Interest rate cap

On April 15, KS, Inc., takes out a one-year floating rate loan for $10 million. Interest payments are quarterly at LIBOR plus 200 basis points based on actual days in the period over 360. The payments are due July 15, October 15, January 15, and April 15. KS purchases a nine-month, quarterly pay cap for $15,000 with a strike rate of 8.5%. The first caplet expires July 15.

Assuming LIBOR rates on April 15, July 15, October 15, and January 15 are 8.0%, 8.4%, 8.65%, and 8.4% respectively, **determine** the four payoff dates on the loan, the loan interest paid, any option payment received, and the effective net interest paid.

Day counts:

> April 15 to July 15: 91 days
> July 15 to October 15: 92 days
> October 15 to January 15: 92 days
> January 15 to April 15: 90 days

Answer:

The payment dates on the loan as stated in the question are July 15, October 15, January 15, and April 15.

Loan interest due:

> July 15: $10,000,000 × (0.08 + 0.02) × (91 / 360) = $252,778
> October 15: $10,000,000 × (0.084 + 0.02) × (92 / 360) = $265,778
> January 15: $10,000,000 × (0.0865 + 0.02) × (92 / 360) = $272,167
> April 15: $10,000,000 × (0.084 + 0.02) × (90 / 360) = $260,000

Cap payoffs:

July 15: N/A. The loan originates April 15 with first loan payment due July 15 based on LIBOR as of April 15. Because the first loan interest payment is known at initiation of the analysis, the first caplet expires July 15 with payoff (if in the money) on October 15.

October 15: July 15 start of period LIBOR is 8.4%, below the strike rate of 8.5%, caplet is out of the money.

January 15: October 15 start of period LIBOR is 8.65%, above the strike rate of 8.5%, caplet is in the money: $10,000,000 × (0.0865 − 0.085) × (92 / 360) = $3,833.

April 15: January 15 start of period LIBOR is 8.4%, below the strike rate of 8.5%, caplet is out of the money.

Effective net interest due:

July 15: $252,778
October 15: $265,778 − 0 = $265,778
January 15: $272,167 − 3,833 = $268,334
April 15: $260,000 − 0 = $260,000

When a long position in a cap is combined with a floating-rate loan, the payoffs can offset interest costs when the floating rate increases. Because caps trade over the counter, the terms of the cap are very flexible, so the cap buyer/borrower can align the settlements of the cap with the interest rate payments.

Interest Rate Floors

An interest rate floor is in essence the opposite of a cap. The buyer receives the interest rate difference if rates are below the strike rate. Each potential payoff is called a floorlet. The natural user of a floor is the receiver on a floating rate loan.

Example: Interest rate floor

The facts in the question are the same as in the previous example, except the example is a lender who purchases a floor.

On April 15, DHBank makes a one-year floating rate loan for $10 million. Interest payments are quarterly at LIBOR plus 200 basis points based on actual days in the period over 360. The payments are due July 15, October 15, January 15, and April 15. DHBank purchases a nine-month, quarterly pay floor for $85,000 with a strike rate of 8.5%.

Assuming LIBOR rates on April 15, July 15, October 15, and January 15 are 8.0%, 8.4%, 8.65%, and 8.4%, respectively, **determine** the four payoff dates on the loan, the loan interest received, any option payment received, and the effective net interest earned by DHBank.

Day counts:

April 15 to July 15: 91 days
July 15 to October 15: 92 days
October 15 to January 15: 92 days
January 15 to April 15: 90 days

Answer:

The payment dates on the loan as stated in the question are July 15, October 15, January 15, and April 15.

Loan interest due:

> July 15: $10,000,000 × (0.08 + 0.02) × (91 / 360) = $252,778
> October 15: $10,000,000 × (0.084 + 0.02) × (92 / 360) = $265,778
> January 15: $10,000,000 × (0.0865 + 0.02) × (92 / 360) = $272,167
> April 15: $10,000,000 × (0.084 + 0.02) × (90 / 360) = $260,000

Floor payoffs:

> July 15: N/A. The loan originates April 15 with first loan payment due July 15 based on LIBOR as of April 15. Because the first loan interest payment is known at initiation of the analysis, the first floorlet expires July 15 with payoff (if in the money) on October 15.

> October 15: July 15 start of period LIBOR is 8.4%, below the strike rate of 8.5%, floorlet is in the money: $10,000,000 × (0.085 − 0.084) × (92 / 360) = $2,556.

> January 15: October 15 start of period LIBOR is 8.65%, above the strike rate of 8.5%, floorlet is out of the money.

> April 15: January 15 start of period LIBOR is 8.4%, below the strike rate of 8.5%, floorlet is in the money: $10,000,000 × (0.085 − 0.084) × (90 / 360) = $2,500

Effective net interest due:

> July 15: $252,778
> October 15: $265,778 + 2,556 = $268,334
> January 15: $272,167 + 0 = $272,167
> April 15: $260,000 + 2,500 = $262,500

Interest Rate Collar

An interest rate collar is a combination of a cap and a floor where the agent is long in one position and short in the other. If the agent buys a 6% cap on LIBOR and sells a 3% floor on LIBOR, the agent will receive cash payments when LIBOR exceeds 6%, and the agent will make payments when LIBOR is below 3%. If LIBOR is between 3% and 6%, the agent neither receives nor pays.

This would be attractive to a bank that has among its liabilities large deposits with floating interest rates. When the rates start to rise, the bank's increasing costs can be offset by the payments from the collar. By selling the floor, the bank may have to make payments if the interest rates on the deposits fall too much, but the bank earned a premium for exposing itself to this risk. That premium offsets the cost of the cap. The overall position provides some certainty to the bank, because it essentially provides a predetermined range for the cost of funds.

A special interest rate collar occurs when the initial premiums on the cap and the floor are equal and offset each other. Suppose that the premium on a 4-year, 3% floor is equal to the premium on the 6% cap. The combination of the two would be called a *zero-cost collar* (a.k.a. a *zero-premium collar*). The motivation for zero-cost collars is that they are a way of providing interest rate protection without the cost of the premiums. Calling the collar zero cost is misleading in some regards. There is no initial cost but there is a back end cost if rates move in such a way that payments must be made.

Example: Interest rate collar

On December 15, the DHBank issues a $50 million "two-year" floating rate liability. The four interest payments are based on 180-day LIBOR plus 150 basis points. The first interest rate is set today with payment 180 days thereafter. Each loan payment is 180 days after the preceding payment. To hedge against rising interest rates, the bank buys an appropriate interest rate cap with a strike rate of 4.75%. To fully offset the initial cost of the cap, the bank sells a floor with a strike rate of 2.25%.

Initial LIBOR is 3.40%. Assuming that in 180, 360, 540, and 720 days LIBOR rates are 4.00%, 5.10%, 2.00%, and 1.75%, respectively, **calculate** the net interest paid by the bank on each payment date and **show** all the cash flows leading to that net payment. **Explain** the cost of the collar.

Answer:

Payment in 180 days:

Paid on floating rate liability: $50,000,000 \times (0.034 + 0.015) \times (180/360) =$ $1,225,000

No payments on the cap or floor. The first of three caplets and floorlets will expire and possible payments will be determined for the next loan payment date.

Net paid on loan: $1,225,000

Payment in 360 days:

Paid on floating rate liability: $50,000,000 \times (0.040 + 0.015) \times (180 / 360) =$ $1,375,000

The cap is out of the money with beginning of period LIBOR at 4.00% versus a cap strike rate of 4.75%

The floor is out of the money with beginning of period LIBOR at 4.00% versus a floor strike rate of 2.25%

Net paid on loan: $1,375,000 − 0 + 0 = $1,375,000

Payment in 540 days:

Paid on floating rate liability: $50,000,000 × (0.051 + 0.015) × (180 / 360) = $1,650,000

The cap is in the money with beginning of period LIBOR at 5.10% versus a cap strike rate of 4.75%: Receive $50,000,000 × (0.051 − 0.0475) × (180 / 360) = $87,500

The floor is out of the money with beginning of period LIBOR at 5.10% versus a floor strike rate of 2.25%

Net paid on loan: $1,650,000 − 87,500 + 0 = $1,562,500

Payment in 720 days:

Paid on floating rate liability: $50,000,000 × (0.020 + 0.015) × (180 / 360) = $875,000

The cap is out of the money with beginning of period LIBOR at 2.00% versus a cap strike rate of 4.75%

The floor is in the money with beginning of period LIBOR at 2.00% versus a floor strike rate of 2.25%: Pay $50,000,000 × (0.0225 − 0.0200) × (180 / 360) = $62,500

Net paid on loan: $875,000 − 0 + 62,500 = $937,500

For a properly structured collar, there will be no additional caplet or floorlet expirations on or after the liability due date. The LIBOR rate at day 720 is irrelevant.

The true cost of the collar is not zero even though the net initial premium was zero. Any time the floor is in the money the bank incurs an obligation to pay on the floor that was sold. For example, on day 720, the bank must make a payment on the floor of $62,500. This increases the bank's cost of funds.

Discussion

Caps and floors are the most common way to modify interest payments or receipts because they can be tailored for exact dates, amounts, and day count conventions. All else the same, the selection of strike rates determines the degree of protection that can be obtained and also affects the premium paid. Like any option, the more in the money the option is at initial purchase, the higher the premium paid and the more likely there will be subsequent payoffs; the more out of the money the option is at initial purchase, the lower the premium paid and the less likely there will be subsequent payoffs. Interest payments can also be modified with FRAs, interest rate swaps, and interest rate futures. These have no initial premium but generally modify upside and downside symmetrically while caps and floors (options) allow for tailored, asymmetric payoff patterns.

©2017 Kaplan, Inc.

DELTA HEDGING

LOS 29.e: Explain why and how a dealer delta hedges an option position, why delta changes, and how the dealer adjusts to maintain the delta hedge.

CFA® Program Curriculum, Volume 5, page 333

The purchase of options has inherent appeal. The option buyer has the potential for a payoff that may far exceed the initial cost of the options. This frequently leads to a natural imbalance, with more demand to buy options than there are sellers. This imbalance provides a business opportunity for dealers. Dealers provide liquidity by being willing to buy or sell options. As compensation they earn the bid/asked spread as the option buyer must buy at the higher or sell at the lower price. Dealers can also serve as a source of supply by being willing to risk capital with a net short position in options. But this exposes the dealer to the potential large downside of short option positions.

Delta hedging allows dealers to hedge the downside risk of short option positions. Recall that a short call decreases in value (has greater negative value) as the underlying increases. If the dealer has a long position in the underlying, that will produce an offsetting gain to hedge the short call position. A short put decreases in value (has greater negative value) as the underlying decreases. If the dealer has a short position in the underlying, that will produce an offsetting gain to hedge the short put position. However, the price moves of the underlying and option are not one for one. Delta determines the ratio of movement.

Delta = change in price of the option/change in price of the underlying

Delta ranges between zero for options that are deep out of the money (OTM) where the price of the option is largely unaffected by the underlying, to one for options that are deep in-the-money (ITM) where the price of the option moves nearly one for one with change in the underlying. An at the money (ATM) option with the price of the underlying equal to the option strike price has a delta of approximately 0.5. For ATM call options, it is generally somewhat higher than 0.5. In reality, deltas can be positive or negative and it is the absolute value of the delta that shifts between zero and one. It is normal to refer to delta in positive terms and the user must interpret if it is + or − in a given situation. A graphic depiction of the delta relationships are shown in Exhibit 15.

Figure 15: Delta for Long and Short Call and Put Options

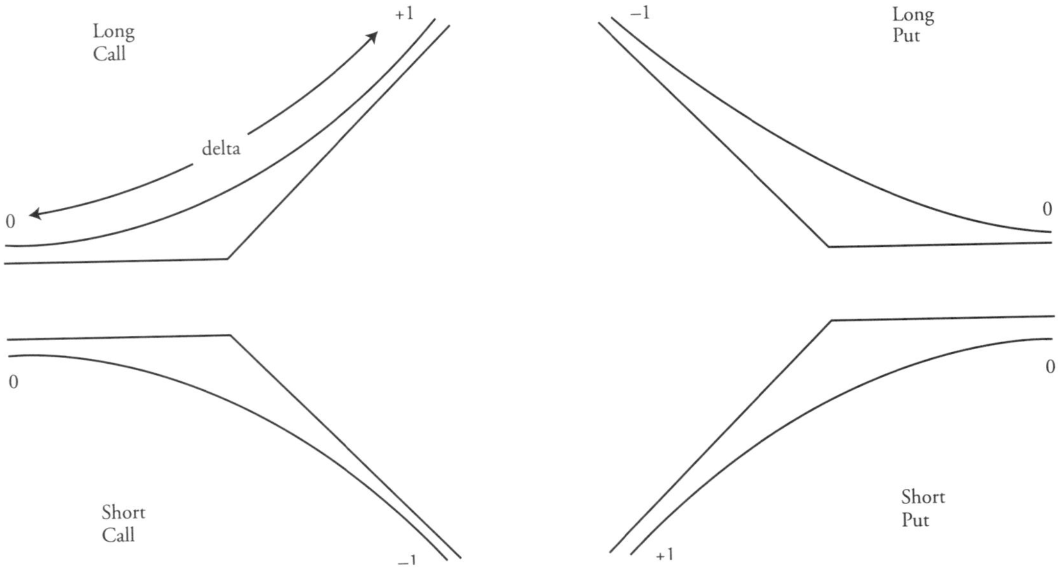

Establishing the delta neutral hedge follows from an understanding of delta:

Suppose a dealer is short calls on 1,000 shares of XYZ and the call delta is 0.40. The dealer would lose approximately USD 400 if the stock price increases USD 1 (1,000 × 0.40). Therefore if the dealer owned 400 shares, the dealer would be hedged as the long 400 shares produce a gain of USD 400 for a USD 1 increase in the stock price. The issue of approximately will be discussed shortly.

Suppose the dealer is also short puts on 10,000 shares of ZZY and the put delta is 0.67. The dealer would lose approximately GBP 6,700 if the stock price decreases GBP 1 (10,000 × 0.67). Therefore if the dealer shorted 6,700 shares, the dealer would be hedged as the 6,700 short position produces a gain of GBP 6,700 for a GBP 1 decrease in the stock price.

Technically, the hedge position in the stock will be:

–delta x number of options

For the 1,000 XYZ short calls: – (–0.40)(1,000) = + 400, (i.e., buy 400 shares).

For the 10,000 ZZY short puts: – (0.67)(10,000) = –6,700, (i.e., short 6,700 shares).

Using the above formula is tricky as you must use the correct + or – sign for the call or put delta, along with the – sign from the formula. Short calls have – delta so in the formula this becomes – –, to indicate buy shares. Short puts have + delta so in the formula this becomes –, to indicate short shares. It is more straightforward to work in two steps:

Step 1: Establish whether to buy or sell the underlying shares:

- Short calls decline as the underlying increases, buy shares to hedge.
- Short puts decline as the underlying decreases, short shares to hedge.

Step 2: Compute the number of shares needed as:

|delta × number of options|

The Reality of Delta Hedging: Rebalancing

Delta hedging is not perfect as delta changes over time and with changing market conditions. Delta is a straight line projection of option price change as the price of the underlying changes. This issue is addressed by continually rebalancing the hedge. Recompute the number of shares required for the hedge. If more shares are required, buy them and borrow the needed funds for the purchase (which can be referred to as a short bond position). If fewer shares are required, sell them and invest the excess funds from the sale (which can be referred to as a long bond position or lending). The required borrowing or lending of funds is for the remaining term of the option and is typically assumed to be at r_f. Theoretically, the expected return of the delta hedged position will be to earn the risk-free rate on the capital invested in the hedged position.

Professor's Note: The ultimate actual return of the delta hedge cannot be known in advance because the hedge must be continually rebalanced and is subject to other risks. If you ran multiple simulations of the hedge and varied the underlying in a way consistent with the initial implied volatility in the option's price, then the risk-free rate would be the average result. Fortunately, that demonstration is well beyond the scope of the CFA material. Just remember the intent of delta hedging is to lock in a fully hedged position, (i.e., no upside or downside).

Example: Initiating and maintaining a delta hedge on calls

A dealer is net short six month calls on 50,000 shares of ACC. The dealer plans to hedge the position and uses an option pricing model to generate the following information:

strike price	46		rf	1.30%
expiration	6 months		volatility	15%

stock price	45.9	46.0	46.1	46.2
option price	2.0469	2.1011	2.1560	2.2118
option delta	0.5376	0.5457	0.5538	0.5618
gamma	0.0812	0.0809	0.0805	0.0801

Answer the following question parts in order.

1. The stock is trading at 46. **Determine** the dealer's initial hedge position for the December calls.

2. **Determine** what to do if the stock then declines from $46 to $45.90. **Calculate** the net gain or loss on the hedged position.

3. **Determine** what to do if the stock then increases from $45.90 to $46.20. **Calculate** the net gain or loss on the hedged position.

Answer:

1. The short call position is at risk if the stock price increases, buy shares of the stock. Buy $50,000 \times 0.5457 = 27,285$ shares at $46.

2. The new required hedge is long: $50,000 \times 0.5376 = 26,880$; therefore sell 405 shares and invest the proceeds of $405 \times \$45.90 = \$18,589.50$. The dealer is now long 26,880 shares at $45.90.

Gain on short call position as stock and option price declined (caution, be sure to use start of period shares, not end of period):

$$50,000 (2.1011 - 2.0469) = 2,710.00$$

Loss on long stock position as stock price declines:

$$27,285 (46 - 45.90) = 2,728.50$$

Net loss: $18.50

3. The new required hedge is long: $50,000 \times 0.5618 = 28,090$; therefore buy 1,210 shares and borrow the needed funds of $1,210 \times \$46.20 = \$55,902$. The dealer is now long 28,090 shares at $46.20.

Loss on short call position as stock and option price increased:

$$50,000 (2.2118 - 2.0469) = 8,245.00$$

Gain on long stock position as stock price increases:

$$26,880 (46.20 - 45.90) = 8,064.00$$

Net loss: $181

Further discussion: When you look at the graph of a short call, it is evident the hedge will not perform perfectly and should systematically underperform as the down side of the short call position exceeds the upside:

In bonds, more limited upside with greater downside would be called negative convexity. In options this convexity effect is called gamma and will be discussed further. In that discussion we will see the options that are relatively far from expiration have gradual changes in delta and as a result, delta hedging works rather well. The hedge also works better when the rebalancing is done frequently and after relatively small changes in the underlying.

 ©2017 Kaplan, Inc.

Example: Initiating and maintaining the delta hedge on puts

The same dealer who is short call positions is also net short puts on 25,000 shares of BBD. The options expire in five days. The dealer generates the following information using the option pricing model:

strike price	32		rf	1.30%	
expiration	5 days		volatility	15%	

stock price	30	31	32	33	34
option price	1.9943	1.0022	0.2213	0.0089	0.0001
option delta	0.9999	0.9632	0.4925	0.0382	0.0003
gamma	0.0009	0.1478	0.7100	0.1433	0.0016

1. The stock is trading at 32. **Determine** the dealer's initial hedge position for the short put position.

2. **Determine** what to do if the stock then declines from $32 to $31. **Calculate** the net gain or loss on the hedged position.

3. **Determine** what to do if the stock then increases from $31 to $34. **Calculate** the net gain or loss on the hedged position.

Answer:

1. The short put position is at risk if the stock price decreases short shares of the stock. Sell 25,000 × 0.4925 = 12,313 shares at $32.

2. The new required hedge is short: 25,000 × 0.9632 = 24,080, therefore sell 11,767 more shares and invest the proceeds of 11,767 × $31 = $364,777. The dealer is now short 24,080 shares at $31.

Loss on short put position as stock and option price declined:

25,000 (1.0022 − 0.2213) = $19,522.50

Gain on short stock position as stock price declined (caution, be sure to use start of period shares, not end of period):

12,313 (32 − 31) = $12,313

Net loss: $7,209.50

3. The new required hedge is short: 25,000 × 0.0003 = 8, therefore buy 24,072 shares and borrow the needed 24,072 × $34 = $818,448. The dealer is now short 8 shares at $34.

Gain on short put position as stock and option price increased:

25,000 (1.0022 − 0.0001) = $25,052.50

Loss on short stock position as stock price increased:

24,080 (34 − 31) = $72,240.00

Net loss: $47,187.50

Further discussion: The options were very close to expiration and ATM. In addition the hedge was rebalanced after relatively large changes in the underlying. Both factors contributed to the poor performance of the hedge. These issues are discussed further under the Reality of Delta Hedging sections.

THE REALITY OF DELTA HEDGING: DELTA, GAMMA, AND TIME TO EXPIRATION

LOS 29.f: Interpret the gamma of a delta-hedged portfolio and explain how gamma changes as in-the-money and out-of-the-money options move toward expiration.

CFA® Program Curriculum, Volume 5, page 342

Figure 16: As Options Approach Expiration

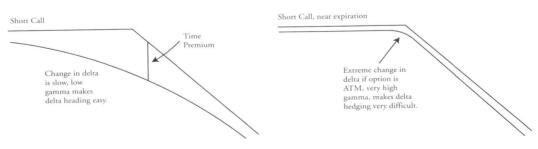

Exhibit 16 depicts what happens as a short call option approaches expiration. Before expiration, options generally trade with a significant time premium (option market value − intrinsic value). That time premium is largest for ATM options and it diminishes as the option moves OTM or ITM. As a result the option's price and delta change smoothly and gradually as the underlying changes. Gamma measures change in delta for change in the underlying (gamma = Δ delta / Δ in underlying), thus the gamma will be small. (In this discussion small means close to zero, no assignment of + or − is being made.) With low gamma and delta being relatively stable, there will be less need to rebalance the hedge. The straight line projection (using delta) of change in value of the option will be relatively accurate and change in value of the shares used for the hedge will closely approximate the change in option value. The delta hedge will work well. The same effects will occur for delta hedging the puts when gamma is low.

However as the time to expiration of the option approaches the time premium will shrink and the option will trade near intrinsic value. This has significant implications for the delta, gamma, and hedge results:

If the option is OTM, the delta will be close to zero and stable (i.e., low gamma). The option will have little value, few shares will be needed for the hedge, the number needed will not change significantly, and the hedge will work well.

If the option is ITM, the delta will be close to one and stable (i.e., low gamma). The option will have more value, approximately one share will be needed for each option, the number need will not change significantly, and the hedge will work well.

But if the option is close to ATM, the delta can fluctuate quickly between zero and one, the gamma is very high, and delta hedging becomes very difficult, as occurred in the put hedging example.

How frequently the hedge is rebalanced also matters. In specific, it matters how much the underlying is allowed to change before rebalancing. In general and all else the same, if the underlying changes more, the delta can have changed more, a larger rebalancing will be needed, and the hedge can suffer more significant losses. Rounding the number of shares used in the hedge to a whole number can also produce a small error.

 Professor's Note: A simple way to think about this is delta neutral hedging is always a bit behind. You do not know if the underlying will increase or decrease, so you do not know if you need to buy or sell shares to rebalance the hedge until after the share price moves. Unfortunately for both short calls and short puts, after the share price moves the delta will have shifted in a way that you must buy shares at a higher price or sell shares at a lower price and the initial hedge position of shares will have undercompensated for how the option position has changed in value. If you rebalance more quickly (as price of the underlying moves), that will minimize the underperformance, though the trade-off is increased transaction costs. The reality is delta hedging basically does not work for ATM options approaching expiration. The dealer would likely think about closing out the positions before expiration or move on to more advance hedging strategies (not part of the CFA material).

Delta is generally obtained from option pricing models. For the exam:
- Delta will most likely be given as in the examples used here.
- Delta could be calculated as change in price of the option divided by change in price of the underlying if given ending and beginning prices of the option and underlying.
- Call delta is the Nd1 term in the Black-Scholes-Merton model.
- The absolute delta of a matched put and call (same expiration and underlying) sum to 1. (e.g., if call delta is 0.7, then put delta is 0.3.)

The correct + or – sign for the delta of each option position are shown in Exhibit 15.

The Reality of Delta Hedging: Vega

The passage of time (approach of expiration) and the price of the underlying are not the only factors that affect the price of options. The most significant additional factor is volatility of the underlying. High volatility makes both call and put options more valuable. (The call benefits from the increased potential upside of the underlying and the put from its potential downside.) Because volatility does not affect the immediate price of shares used in the hedge but does affect the price of the options, it introduces another element in the performance of the hedge:

An increase in volatility makes both calls and puts more valuable. That increase in value is a loss to the dealer's short option position and is not offset by immediate change in value of the shares used for the hedge. There is an immediate loss on the net hedged position.

A decrease in volatility makes both calls and puts less valuable. That decrease in value is a gain to the dealer's short option position and is not offset by immediate change in value of the shares used for the hedge. There is an immediate gain on the net hedged position.

There are some technical details that are not particularly relevant and are therefore not the focus here or in the CFA material:

- Delta is an approximation of option price move because delta is continually changing. Think of delta as the equivalent of duration; both are a good but not perfect projection of price change. (Delta and duration are the first derivative of the price function of the option and bond respectively.)
- Gamma can also be positive or negative. Both short calls and short puts have negative gamma as their potential loss in value (generally) exceeds their gain in value. (Gamma and convexity are the second derivative of the price function of options and bonds respectively.)
- The delta of an ATM call is normally somewhat higher than 0.5. This can be shown with an option pricing model. One way to conceptualize it is that the underlying more upside (unlimited) than downside (to zero), so the delta reflects more weight to the positive side of the intrinsic value graph (and delta of 1) than to the zero side of the intrinsic value graph (and delta of 0).

©2017 Kaplan, Inc.

LOS 29.a

An investor creates a *covered call* position by buying the underlying security and selling a call option. Covered call writing strategies are used to generate additional portfolio income when the investor believes that the underlying stock price will remain unchanged over the short term.

A *protective put* (also called *portfolio insurance* or a *hedged portfolio*) is constructed by holding a long position in the underlying security and buying a put option. You can use a protective put to limit the downside risk at the cost of the put premium, P_0.

The purchase of the put provides a lower limit to the position at a cost of lowering the possible profit (i.e., the gain is reduced by the cost of the *insurance*). It is an ideal strategy for an investor who thinks the stock may go down in the near future, yet the investor wants to preserve upside potential.

LOS 29.b

There are many strategies that combine calls, puts, and the underlying asset.

- A bull spread strategy consists of a long call and a short call. The short call has a higher exercise price, and its premium subsidizes the long call. It offers gains if the underlying asset's price goes up, but the upside is limited.
- A bear spread strategy is the opposite side of a bull spread. It offers a limited upside gain if the underlying asset's price declines.
- A butterfly spread consists of two long and two short call positions. It offers a return, with a limited upside if the underlying asset price does not move very much.
- A collar strategy is simply a covered call and protective put combined to limit the down and upside value of the position.
- A long straddle is a long call and long put with the same exercise price. The greater the move in the stock price, the greater the payoff from a straddle.
- A box spread strategy combines a long put and a short put with a long call and a short call to produce a guaranteed return. That return should be the risk-free rate.

LOS 29.c

The basic approach is simple and consists of steps.

To hedge a future borrowing, purchase a call on interest rates for protecting from increasing rates.

To hedge a future lending, purchase a put on interest rates for protection from declining interest rates.

1. Assume that at time 0 the option to hedge the risk is purchased, and the purchase price is financed by borrowing at a rate reflecting the primary loan spread for a net CF of zero at time 0.

2. At time *t* when the primary loan occurs, net the cash flow of the primary loan with the option premium financing repayment to determine a net CF at time *t*.

3. At time T when the primary loan is repaid, net the repayment of primary loan cash flow and any payoff on the option for a net CF at time T.

4. Calculate the EAR between T_T and T_t net CFs.

LOS 29.d
An interest rate cap is a series of interest rate calls with the same strike rate but different expiration dates. Settlements are at the end of each period but are based on rates at the beginning of each period.

An interest rate floor is a series of interest rate puts with the same strike rate but different expiration dates. As with the cap, settlements are at the end of each period based on rates at the beginning of each period.

An interest rate collar is a combination of cap and floor where the investor is long one and short the other. A short cap and long floor would be of use to a lender of floating-rate loans. The collar will guarantee a range of income for the total position to the lender. A long cap and short floor will guarantee a floating-rate borrower a range of interest costs on the loan.

LOS 29.e
Dealers use delta hedging to hedge the risk of short call or put positions. Short calls are hedged by buying the underlying and short puts by shorting the underlying. The option delta is the number of underlying needed for the hedge. As the underlying, time to expiration, and other conditions change; delta can change and the hedge must be rebalanced. If more (less) units of the underlying are needed, buy them (sell them) and borrow (lend) the needed funds.

LOS 29.f
Gamma measures change in delta as the underlying changes. It is typically a smaller second order effect. But gamma becomes very large, delta changes quickly, and the hedge becomes very difficult to maintain for ATM options approaching expiration.

©2017 Kaplan, Inc.

1. The holder of a long straddle *most likely* will have a net loss if the asset's price:
    A. stays the same.
    B. moves up.
    C. moves down.

2. Which of the following option combinations cannot be used to construct a butterfly?
    A. Two put option contracts.
    B. Four call option contracts.
    C. Two call options and two put options.

3. A stock trades at 51. Calls with strike prices of 47 and 53 are priced at 5.25 and 0.75, respectively. **Compute** the initial investment for a bull spread and the breakeven price or prices of the spread.

4. The EUR is trading at USD 1.035. A trader expects the EUR to become much more volatile than reflected in current option prices. Puts and calls on the EUR are available. Puts with a strike of USD 0.98 are trading at USD 0.005 and with a strike of USD 1.04 are trading at USD 0.017. Calls with a strike of USD 0.98 are trading at USD 0.068 and with a strike of USD 1.04 are trading at USD 0.004. **Compute** the breakeven price or prices of the correct option strategy.

5. For hedging risk, owning an interest rate put would *most likely* be useful for a:
    A. variable-rate borrower.
    B. fixed-rate lender.
    C. variable-rate lender.

6. A cap contract has a notional principle of $5 million, a strike rate of 5%, and an annual frequency of settlement. If the reference rate is 6% for a given settlement date, what is the payoff to the agent long the cap for that period?
    A. $25,000.
    B. $50,000.
    C. $100,000.

Use the following information to answer Questions 7, 8, and 9. Answer the questions in order.

An option dealer sold call options on 1,667 shares of stock. The underlying stock is priced at $70 per share. The options have a delta of 0.60.

7. How many shares of stock must the dealer buy to hedge his price risk with a delta hedge?
    A. 669.
    B. 1,000.
    C. 2,777.

8.   If the delta associated with the call option changes from 0.60 to 0.70, what will the dealer do?
      A. Buy shares and borrow funds.
      B. Buy shares and lend funds.
      C. Sell shares and lend funds.

9.   If the dealer implemented the required hedge from the first question and rebalanced as required in the second question, the excess profit during the time period between initiation and rebalancing is most likely:
      A. zero.
      B. positive.
      C. negative.

10.   In 60 days, a bank plans to lend $10 million for 90 days. The lending rate is LIBOR plus 200 basis points. The current LIBOR is 4%. The bank buys a put that matures in 60 days with a notional principal of $10 million, 90 days in underlying, and a strike rate of 5%. The put premium is $2,000. **Calculate** the effective annual rate of the loan if at expiration the LIBOR = 4.5%, and if the LIBOR = 6.5%.

11.   On August 1, a bank enters a 2-year, zero-cost collar for a $20 million portfolio of floating-rate loans by buying the floor and selling the cap. The floor strike is 2.5%, the cap strike is 4.7%, and the reference rate is LIBOR. The interest payments on the loan assets are LIBOR plus 240 basis points. The collar's semiannual settlement dates exactly match the dates when the floating-rate payments are made: August 1 and February 1 over the next two years. Payments made August 1 cover 181 days and payments made February 1 cover 184 days. Current LIBOR is 4.1%. The values of LIBOR on the next three settlement dates are 2.4%, 5%, and 5%. **Calculate** the actual interest rate payments (to the bank), settlements, and effective interest payments.

For more questions related to this topic review, log in to your Schweser online account and launch SchweserPro™ QBank; and for video instruction covering each LOS in this topic review, log in to your Schweser online account and launch the OnDemand video lectures, if you have purchased these products.

©2017 Kaplan, Inc.

ANSWERS – CONCEPT CHECKERS

1. **A** If the asset's price is between the put and call breakeven points, the long straddle produces a net loss.

2. **A** By examining the payoff pattern of a butterfly, it is clear that there must be three strike prices used. With only two option contracts, there can only be two strike prices. Either of the two other combinations are possible. Starting from the left side of the payoff pattern: a long call with a lower strike price, plus two short calls with a medium strike price, plus a long call with a higher strike price will work. Alternatively, beginning from the middle of the payoff pattern, and utilizing a reverse straddle (sell a medium strike price call and put) plus buy a put with a lower strike price and buy a call with a higher strike price will achieve the same payoff pattern. Be prepared to understand combinations such as this that were not specifically discussed in the reading. It is just combining the four intrinsic value patterns.

3. Buy the 47 call at 5.25 and sell the 53 call at 0.75 for an initial investment of 4.50.

    BE can be computed from either max loss or max gain. Looking at the graph for a bull spread the max loss is at S = 47. Both calls are worthless. The loss is the initial investment of 4.50. Again looking at the graph, the stock must increase 4.50 to 51.50 for BE.

4. Buy ATM puts and calls on the EUR. The 1.04 strike price is the closest to ATM. Buying the call and put will cost: 0.004 + 0.017 = 0.021. Looking at the graph for a straddle, this is the max loss and occurs if the EUR closes at 1.04. For breakeven prices, the EUR must decrease or increase 0.021 to USD 1.019 or 1.061.

5. **C** The put pays the floor holder when interest rates fall, so they would hedge the risk of a variable rate lender (i.e., the owner of a floating rate asset).

6. **B** payoff = $50,000 = ($5,000,000)(0.06 − 0.05)(1)

7. **B** The short call position will lose value if the underlying increases. The loss is 0.6 for each $1 increase in the stock price. To hedge, the dealer will buy 1,667 × 0.6 = 1,000 shares.

8. **A** The hedge is now 1,667 × 0.7 = 1,167 shares. The purchase of another 167 shares is financed by borrowing.

9. **C** Examine the graph of a short call position. As the underlying increases, the loss on the short call accelerates (the delta increases). Any delay in rebalancing the hedge results in the loss on the short calls exceeding the gain on the long shares as the underlying increases.

10. First, we compute the effective amount the bank parts with or lends at time of the loan. This means computing the future value of the premium:

    future value of premium = $2,020 = $2,000[1 + (0.04 + 0.02)(60 / 360)]

    Thus, the cash outflow at the loan's inception is $10,002,020. At the given LIBOR rates of 4.5% and 6.5%, the put's payoffs are:

    LIBOR = 4.5%: payoff = $12,500 = $10,000,000[max(0, 0.050 − 0.045)(90 / 360)]
    LIBOR = 6.5%: payoff = $0 = $10,000,000[max(0, 0.050 − 0.065)(90 / 360)]

The interest income earned is:

LIBOR = 4.5%:   int. income = $162,500 = $10,000,000 × (0.045 + 0.020)(90 / 360)
LIBOR = 6.5%:   int. income = $212,500 = $10,000,000 × (0.065 + 0.020)(90 / 360)

The effective rate earned is:

LIBOR = 4.5%:
EAR = [($10,000,000 + $162,500 + $12,500) / ($10,002,020)]$^{(365/90)}$ − 1
EAR = [($10,175,000) / ($10,002,020)]$^{(365/90)}$ − 1
EAR = 0.0720 = 7.2%

LIBOR = 6.5%:
EAR = [($10,000,000 + $212,500 + $0) / ($10,002,020)]$^{(365/90)}$ − 1
EAR = [($10,212,500) / ($10,002,020)]$^{(365/90)}$ − 1
EAR = 0.0881 = 8.81%

11.   The first collar expiration will occur on February 1 for payment on August 1. There will be no collar payment on the first February 1. The payoffs on the derivatives are:

Floorlets:

Year 1

payoff on Feb. 1 = N/A
payoff on Aug. 1 = $10,056 = $20,000,000[max(0, 0.025 − 0.024)(181 / 360)]

Year 2

payoff on Feb. 1 = $0 = $20,000,000[max(0, 0.025 − 0.050)(184 / 360)]
payoff on Aug. 1 = $0 = $20,000,000[max(0, 0.025 − 0.050)(181 / 360)]

Caplets:

Year 1

payoff on Feb. 1 = N/A
payoff on Aug. 1 = $0 = $20,000,000[max(0, 0.024 − 0.047)(181 / 360)]

Year 2

payoff on Feb. 1 = $30,667 = $20,000,000[max(0, 0.050 − 0.047)(184 / 360)]
payoff on Aug. 1 = $30,167 = $20,000,000[max(0, 0.050 − 0.047)(181 / 360)]

The interest payments are:

pmt. on Feb. 1 = $664,444 = $20,000,000(0.041 + 0.024)(184 / 360)
pmt. on Aug. 1 = $482,667 = $20,000,000(0.024 + 0.024)(181 / 360)
pmt. on Feb. 1 = $756,444 = $20,000,000(0.050 + 0.024)(184 / 360)
pmt. on Aug. 1 = $744,111 = $20,000,000(0.050 + 0.024)(181 / 360)

©2017 Kaplan, Inc.

The following table illustrates how the payments and payoffs combine to give an effective rate for each period.

Settlement	Year	Actual Interest	Floor Payoffs	Cap Payoffs	Effective Interest
Feb. 1	1	$664,444	N/A	N/A	$664,444
Aug. 1	1	$482,667	$10,056	0	$492,723
Feb. 1	2	$756,444	0	−$30,667	$725,777
Aug. 1	2	$744,111	0	−$30,167	$713,944

RISK MANAGEMENT APPLICATIONS OF SWAP STRATEGIES

Study Session 15

EXAM FOCUS

Swaps are commonly used to modify risk in portfolios and on balance sheets. Virtually any swap analysis starts with the swap diagram. The swap diagram begins with the initial situation of the principal involved. Then an appropriate swap can be designed to accomplish the desired objective. From the diagram, the duration of the swap can be inferred. Be prepared for both conceptual as well as calculation questions.

USING SWAPS TO CONVERT LOANS FROM FIXED (FLOATING) TO FLOATING (FIXED)

LOS 30.a: Demonstrate how an interest rate swap can be used to convert a floating-rate (fixed-rate) loan to a fixed-rate (floating-rate) loan.

CFA® Program Curriculum, Volume 5, page 359

The most common interest rate swap is the *plain vanilla* interest rate swap. In this swap, Company X agrees to pay Company Y a periodic fixed rate on a notional principal over the tenor of the swap. In return, Company Y agrees to pay Company X a periodic floating rate on the same notional principal. Payments are in the same currency, so only the net payment is exchanged.

Most interest rate swaps use the London Interbank Offered Rate (LIBOR) as the reference rate for the floating leg of the swap. Finally, because the payments are based in the same currency, there is no need for the exchange of principal at the inception of the swap. This is why it is called *notional* principal.

> **Example: Converting fixed to floating and floating to fixed**
>
> Company X has a $100 million, 2 year, 5% fixed rate semi-annual pay debt. Payments are actual day count over a 360-day year. The company expects interest rates to fall and would prefer to have a floating rate debt.
>
> Company Y has a $100 million, two-year, floating rate semiannual pay debt at LIBOR plus 100 basis points. Payments are actual day count over a 360-day year. The company expects interest rates to rise and would like to use a swap to convert the debt to fixed rate.
>
> A $100 million, two-year, 5.5% semiannual pay swap versus LIBOR plus 125 basis points is available to both X and Y.

©2017 Kaplan, Inc.

Figure 1: Converting Fixed-Rate Debt to Floating for Company X

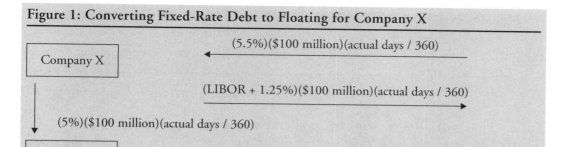

The net result is Company X is now paying a synthetic floating rate of LIBOR plus 75 basis points.

- Pay 5% on fixed rate debt.
- Pay LIBOR plus 1.25% on swap.
- Receive 5.5% on swap.

Company X has effectively removed its fixed-rate liability exposure and converted it to LIBOR exposure. Its fixed-rate debt would have had a higher duration and now its debt has the lower duration of a floating rate liability. Company X is effectively speculating LIBOR will fall.

Figure 2: Converting Floating-Rate Debt to Fixed-Rate Debt for Company Y

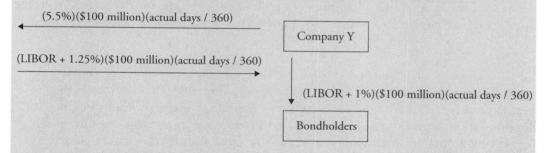

The net result is Company Y is now paying a synthetic fixed rate of 5.25%.

- Pay LIBOR plus 1% on floating rate debt.
- Receive LIBOR plus 1.25% on swap.
- Pay 5.5% on swap.

Company Y has effectively removed its floating rate liability exposure and converted it to fixed rate exposure. Its floating rate debt would have had a lower duration and now its debt has the higher duration of a fixed rate liability. Company Y is effectively speculating LIBOR will rise.

DURATION OF AN INTEREST RATE SWAP

LOS 30.b: Calculate and interpret the duration of an interest rate swap.

CFA® Program Curriculum, Volume 5, page 361

The duration properties of swaps are another reason for their popularity. Each counterparty in a swap is essentially either of the following:

- Long a fixed cash flow and short a floating cash flow.
- Short a fixed cash flow and long a floating cash flow.

You should recall that duration is the sensitivity of an asset's price to changes in a relevant interest rate. Here are two important points with respect to fixed and floating-rate instruments:

1. For fixed-rate instruments, duration will be higher because the change in interest rates will change the present value of the fixed cash flows.

2. For floating-rate instruments, duration is close to zero because the future cash flows vary with interest rates, and the present value is fairly stable with respect to changes in interest rates.

A *floating-rate* instrument can have a non-zero duration if its next cash flow has been set, which is the case with swaps. The convention is to treat the duration of the floating rate side of the swap as being half the reset period. For example, for a 6-month reset, the duration would be taken to be 0.25, for a quarterly reset it would be taken to be 0.125, etc.

Because we know that the duration of a zero-coupon bond is its maturity, the duration of the floating payments where the next payment is known will be the time to the next payment. At inception or just after a settlement for a *quarterly* reset swap, the duration of the floating payments is 0.25; for a *semiannual* reset swap, the duration is 0.5; et cetera. Just before the payment is due, however, the duration is 0.0. Hence, the *average* duration of a floating instrument over the reset period is one-half the length of its settlement periods.

For a pay-floating counterparty in a swap, the duration can be expressed as:

$$D_{\text{pay floating}} = D_{\text{fixed}} - D_{\text{floating}} > 0$$

Because the floating-rate payor receives fixed cash flows, taking the receive-fixed/pay-floating position in a swap increases the dollar duration of a fixed-income portfolio. The modified duration of the portfolio will move an amount determined by (1) the relative values of the notional principal of the swap and the portfolio's value and (2) relative values of the modified duration of the swap and that of the portfolio.

©2017 Kaplan, Inc.

Professor's Note: Calculating swap duration is simple; it is the difference in the durations of the two sides of the swap. The swap diagram is an easy way to remember how to calculate swap duration. The arrow coming in represents an asset; add the duration of what is received on the swap. The arrow going out represents a liability; subtract the duration of what is paid on the swap. The result is the swap duration.

Example: Pay-floating swap duration

At the inception of a 2-year swap, the duration of the fixed payments is 1.1, and the duration of the floating payments is 0.25. What is the duration of the swap to the pay-floating party to the swap?

Answer:

The duration of the swap is 1.1 – 0.25 = 0.85.

This is +0.85 to the receive fixed and pay floating counterparty.

MARKET VALUE RISK AND CASH FLOW RISK

LOS 30.c: Explain the effect of an interest rate swap on an entity's cash flow risk.

CFA® Program Curriculum, Volume 5, page 362

It is common to refer to converting a floating-rate liability to fixed-rate as a hedge. In the sense that it reduces cash flow risk, it is a hedge. However, it is essentially converting highly visible cash flow risk into less visible market value risk.

Cash flow risk is reduced by entering the swap because the uncertain future floating-rate payments on the liability are essentially converted to fixed payments that can be more easily planned for and budgeted, resulting in a reduction in cash flow risk. However, the low duration of the floating-rate liability is now converted to the higher duration of a fixed-rate liability. The liability market value will now fluctuate more as interest rates change. For example, if interest rates fall, the liability will rise in market value, creating a corresponding decline in the firm's theoretical market value of equity.

Some argue that these changes in market value are unrealized, which is true. They are nonetheless real, and financial theory would clearly suggest they should affect the market value of the firm and of the equity. The swap reduces cash flow risk but increases market value risk.

USING SWAPS TO CHANGE DURATION

LOS 30.d: Determine the notional principal value needed on an interest rate swap to achieve a desired level of duration in a fixed-income portfolio.

CFA® Program Curriculum, Volume 5, page 363

The duration of the portfolio plus a swap position (i.e., the target duration) is calculated as:

$$V_p(MD_T) = V_p(MD_p) + NP(MD_{swap})$$

where:
V_p = original value of the portfolio
MD_i = modified duration i (i = swap, target, portfolio without swap)
NP = notional principal of the swap

Usually, the portfolio manager selects a swap of a certain maturity which determines the modified duration of the swap, MD_{swap}. He then selects the NP that will achieve the desired MD_T. Rearranging, we can solve for the amount of notional principal necessary to achieve the target duration:

$$NP = \left(V_p\right)\left(\frac{MD_T - MD_p}{MD_{swap}}\right)$$

 Professor's Note: This is just a variation of the basic bond hedging formula but set up to calculate notional principal rather than the number of contracts.

Example: Determining the notional principal

A manager of a $60 million fixed-income portfolio with a duration of 5.2 wants to lower the duration to 4.0. The manager chooses a swap with a net duration of 3.1. What NP should the manager choose for the swap to achieve the target duration?

Answer:

From the given information, we have:

$$V_p = \$60,000,000$$
$$MD_p = 5.2$$
$$MD_{swap} = 3.1$$
$$MD_T = 4.0$$

$$NP = (V_p)\left(\frac{MD_T - MD_p}{MD_{swap}}\right)$$

$$NP = \$60,000,000\left(\frac{4.0 - 5.2}{-3.1}\right) = \$23,225,806$$

Because the manager wants to *reduce* the duration of his portfolio, he should take a receive-floating/pay-fixed position in the swap with that notional principal. Remember that a receive-floating swap has a negative duration, so we enter −3.1 in the equation.

For the Exam: Be sure to enter the net duration of the swap correctly in the denominator of the equation (i.e., negative if pay-fixed; positive if receive-fixed). You can tell if you have entered it correctly because the sign on the notional principal should always be positive.

WARM-UP: CURRENCY SWAPS

A *currency swap* is different from an interest rate swap in two very important ways:

1. There are two notional principals, one in each currency, and the counterparties generally exchange the principals on the effective date and return them at the maturity date.

2. Because the cash flows in a currency swap are denominated in different currencies, the periodic interest payments are not usually settled on a net basis, so each counterparty makes a payment to the other in the appropriate currency.

A *plain vanilla currency swap* is one in which the floating-rate cash flows (usually based on LIBOR) are in dollars, while the other cash flows (in another currency, like euros) are based on a fixed rate. However, because swaps are OTC instruments, the counterparties can design them any way they choose (e.g., floating for floating, dollar floating and foreign fixed, fixed for fixed).

One of the more common reasons for a firm to engage in a currency swap is to gain access to loanable funds in a foreign currency that might be too costly to obtain from a bank, the reason being that the firm does not have close relationships with banks in the country of the desired currency.

A firm may also have issued a foreign-currency bond earlier, and now the firm wishes to *convert* it into a domestic obligation. A swap can help with that, too. If a U.S. company has a fixed-rate note denominated in euros and wishes to make it a synthetic dollar loan, the U.S. firm can enter into a receive-euro/pay-dollar swap. Because the plain vanilla currency swap exchanges fixed foreign currency for floating dollars, the U.S. firm's synthetic position will now be a floating-rate dollar obligation.

The following demonstration illustrates the mechanics of the swap in combination with the loans on both sides of the swap. Also, for added measure, we put the dealer in the mix, too! Dealers are involved in most transactions, and you may see them as part of an exam question.

Example: Currency swap

A U.S. company has a liability of €10 million in fixed-rate bonds outstanding at 6%. A German company has a $15 million FRN outstanding at LIBOR. The exchange rate is $1.5/€. The U.S. company enters into a plain vanilla currency swap with the swap dealer in which it pays LIBOR on $15 million and receives the swap rate of 6.0% on €10 million. The German company also enters into a plain vanilla currency swap with the same dealer, in which it pays a swap rate of 6.1% on €10 million and receives LIBOR on $15 million. One-year LIBOR is currently 5.2%.

Calculate each party's net borrowing cost, the principal cash flows at the initiation and maturity of the contract, and first-year cash flows (assume annual settlement).

Answer:

The cash flow for each settlement date for this plain vanilla currency swap is illustrated in the figure below.

Cash Flows for a Plain Vanilla Currency Swap

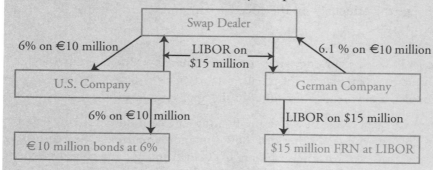

The U.S. company's net borrowing cost: LIBOR on $15 million

(6% on €10 million) + (LIBOR on $15 million – 6% on €10 million)

The German company's net borrowing cost: 6.1% on €10 million

(LIBOR on $15 million) + (6.1% on €10 million – LIBOR on $15 million)

©2017 Kaplan, Inc.

The swap dealer's spread: 0.1% on €10 million = €10,000

(LIBOR on $15 million – 6% on €10 million) + (6.1% on €10 million – LIBOR on $15 million)

Not only are the firms paying in different currencies, but they get access to the funds because they exchange notional principals at the beginning of the swap.

The cash flows of the notional principals at the initiation of the swap are shown in the figure below.

Exchange of Notional Principals

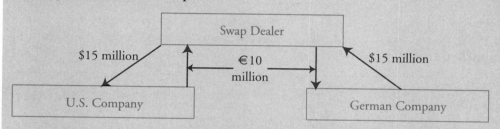

The U.S. Company

At the end of the first year, the U.S. company pays interest on its euro borrowing. It pays LIBOR and receives euros under the swap (the negative sign means outflow):

interest on euro borrowing	= −€600,000	= €10,000,000 × 0.060
euros received under swap	= €600,000	= €10,000,000 × 0.060
U.S. dollars paid under swap	= −$780,000	= $15,000,000 × 0.052
net cash flow	= −$780,000	

At the beginning of the period, the U.S. company gets a dollar principal and will pay dollars on the amount that was once a euro loan.

The German Company

The German company gets euros and will pay interest on its U.S. dollar borrowing. It receives LIBOR and pays euros under the swap:

interest on U.S. dollar borrowing	= −$780,000	= $15,000,000 × 0.052
euros paid under swap	= −€610,000	= €10,000,000 × 0.061
U.S. dollars received under swap	= $780,000	= $15,000,000 × 0.052
net cash flow	= −€610,000	

The Swap Dealer

The net cash flow to the swap dealer is:

euros received from German firm	= €610,000	= €10,000,000 × 0.061
euros paid to U.S. firm	= €600,000	= €10,000,000 × 0.060
net cash flow	= €10,000	= €10,000,000 × 0.001

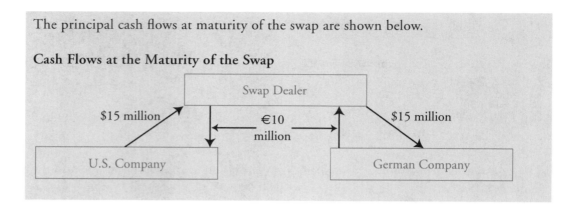

LOS 30.e: Explain how a company can generate savings by issuing a loan or bond in its own currency and using a currency swap to convert the obligation into another currency.

CFA® Program Curriculum, Volume 5, page 370

As mentioned earlier, a counterparty may use a currency swap to gain access to a foreign currency at a lower cost. Borrowing in a foreign country via a foreign bank may be difficult, and the interest rates may be high. A U.S. firm that wishes to initiate a project in a foreign country, say Korea, might not have the contacts necessary to borrow Korean currency (the won) cheaply. It may have to pay a high interest rate, such as 9%. A Korean counterparty may exist that would like to borrow dollars to invest in the United States but finds that banks in the United States charge 7.2% because they are unfamiliar with the Korean firm.

The U.S. firm can borrow at 6% in the United States because it has established relationships with those banks. It swaps the principal (borrowed dollars) with the Korean counterparty for the won, which the Korean firm borrowed at 7% in Korea. The U.S. firm uses its proceeds from its new business to pay the won interest to the Korean counterparty, who in turn pays won interest on its bank loan to the Korean bank. The Korean firm pays the dollar interest to the U.S. firm, who in turn pays dollar interest on its loan to the U.S. bank.

Here are the important points to this exchange:

- The U.S. firm is now paying 7% on a won loan on which it would have had to pay 9% if it had borrowed from a Korean bank.
- The Korean firm is now paying 6% on a dollar loan on which it would have had to pay 7.2% if it had borrowed from a U.S. bank.

©2017 Kaplan, Inc.

An easier way to understand the analysis is to draw the swap diagram:

Figure 3: Effect of Currency Swap Cash Flows on Interest Payments

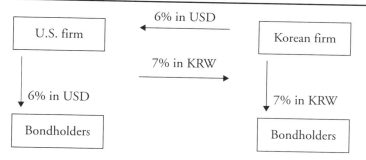

A dealer might have increased the swap interest rates 10 basis points for each counterparty with the dealer earning the spread. But the resulting 7.1% for the U.S. firm is still less than 9%, and the resulting 6.1% is still less than 7.2% for the Korean firm.

Converting Foreign Cash Receipts

LOS 30.f: Demonstrate how a firm can use a currency swap to convert a series of foreign cash receipts into domestic cash receipts.

CFA® Program Curriculum, Volume 5, page 375

Dealers will contract with a firm in a currency swap that does not require an exchange of notional principals. This essentially becomes a series of exchange-rate purchases in the future at a fixed exchange rate. The amounts exchanged are a function of both the current exchange rate and interest rates (swap rates) in the countries involved.

As an example, let's consider a U.S. firm that wishes to convert its quarterly cash flows of €6 million each to dollars upon receipt. The exchange rate is currently €0.8/$, and the swap rates in the United States and Europe are 4.8% and 5%, respectively. To obtain the swapped dollar cash flow, we first back out the notional principal in euros, translate this to a dollar notional principal, and then calculate the interest in dollars:

$$NP\left(^{0.05}/_4\right) = 6,000,000$$

$$NP = \frac{6,000,000}{^{0.05}/_4} = 480,000,000$$

The corresponding dollar amount is €480,000,000 / (€0.8/$) = $600,000,000. The quarterly interest payments on this amount would be $600,000,000(0.048 / 4) = $7,200,000.

The swap would then allow the firm to exchange its €6,000,000 quarterly inflow for $7,200,000 per period. The maturity of the swap would be negotiated to meet the needs of the firm. You should note that no exchange of principals was required.

For the Exam: Follow these steps in determining the appropriate swap:

1. Divide the foreign cash flow received by the foreign interest rate to determine the corresponding foreign-denominated notional principal (NP).

   a. This is the foreign NP that would have produced the foreign cash flow at the given foreign interest rate.

2. Using the current exchange rate, convert the foreign NP into the corresponding domestic NP.

3. Enter a swap with this NP.

   a. Pay the foreign cash flows received on the assets and receive the equivalent domestic amount.

   b. The amount of each domestic cash flow is determined by multiplying the domestic interest rate by the domestic NP.

Example: Currency swap without a notional principal exchange

A firm will be receiving a semiannual cash flow of €10 million. The swap rates in the United States and Europe are 6% and 5%, respectively. The current exchange rate is €0.9/$. **Identify** the appropriate swap needed to convert the periodic euro cash flows to dollars.

Answer:

For the euros, the NP = €10,000,000 / (0.05 / 2) = €400,000,000. The corresponding dollar amount is €400,000,000 / 0.9 = $444,444,444. Using these values for the swap, the firm will give the swap dealer €10,000,000 every six months over the maturity of the swap for:

$444,444,444(0.06 / 2) = $13,333,333

EQUITY SWAPS

LOS 30.g: Explain how equity swaps can be used to diversify a concentrated equity portfolio, provide international diversification to a domestic portfolio, and alter portfolio allocations to stocks and bonds.

CFA® Program Curriculum, Volume 5, page 380

An equity swap is a contract where at least one counterparty makes payments based upon an equity position. The other counterparty may make payments based upon another equity position, a bond, or just fixed payments. We will begin with that example.

Example: Equity swap with fixed payments

A firm owns a stock portfolio that is closely correlated with the S&P 500. The firm is concerned that the stock market will fall over the next year. A 1-year, quarterly equity swap is available with a notional principal equal to the value of the portfolio and a fixed rate of 7%. **Diagram** the net quarterly cash flows to a hedge.

Answer:

The net effect for the firm is a fixed-rate return of 7% / 4 = 1.75% per period as shown below.

Quarterly Cash Flows to an Equity Swap

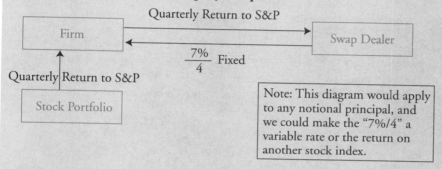

Note: This diagram would apply to any notional principal, and we could make the "7%/4" a variable rate or the return on another stock index.

The swap does create some secondary risks, including:

- Counterparty risk if the swap dealer experiences difficulty and is unable to make the swap payments as expected to the firm.
- Basis risk if the return on the stock portfolio does not exactly match the S&P return payments the firm must make on the swap.
- Some cash flow risk in that the S&P payments to the swap dealer are unlikely to match the fixed payments to the firm. If a net is paid, the firm must have the cash available. Note: if the firm had sold the stock and actually bought fixed rate bonds, there is no cash flow risk as the firm just collects coupons.

Swaps to Create International Diversification

As a variation on the previous example, suppose the firm had a $500 million equity portfolio and swapped $100 million to receive the 7% fixed rate. The firm effectively has 20% fixed rate bond exposure. Now the firm does a second swap for $50 million, paying the S&P return and receiving the return for the MSCI, an international stock index. This would further diversify the portfolio by creating a 10% allocation to international equity.

This second swap will have the same secondary risks as the first swap, but the cash flow risk is potentially even greater because the firm is receiving an index return rather than a known fixed rate. Consider the worst case scenario, where the S&P return paid is very large due to a high return on the S&P but the MSCI return is a large negative. The firm contracted to receive the MSCI return and when that return is negative, that means the firm must pay the MSCI return. The firm could end up making two payments with no receipt in a worst case scenario. Notice paying the MSCI return out when it is negative simply replicates the loss in value that would have occurred if the firm owned the MSCI and it declined. However, the swap requires cash to be paid, while owning the MSCI would only be a decline in market value. Economically they are the same result but the swap creates cash flow issues.

Benefits of using the swap are that transaction costs for the swap are generally lower than actually selling domestic stocks to buy international stocks. The swap can be for a defined period if this is a temporary exposure that is desired. Also the swap can be structured as payment in U.S. dollars to limit the foreign currency exposure from owning foreign denominated assets and any need to hedge the currency exposure. The dealer may consider these factors in pricing the swap, so the firm should consider whether the pricing is still attractive (to the firm).

Example: Diversifying concentrated positions

An investor has an overweighed 30,000 share position in a stock with a current market value of $80 per share and a dividend yield of 2%. The investor wishes to reduce the position by half for a position in the S&P 500. **Demonstrate** how this can be accomplished with a swap.

Answer:

The owner of the stock would probably approach a dealer and swap the returns on $1.2 million = (30,000 × $80) / 2 worth of the stock for the returns on a $1.2 million investment in the S&P 500. Each settlement period (e.g., quarter) the total return on each position is calculated. The net amount is transferred between the parties.

Changing Allocations of Stock and Bonds

Another type of swapping of index returns can occur between, for example, large- and small-cap stocks. A firm with an equity portfolio that is 60% in large-cap stocks, 30% in mid-cap stocks, and 10% small-cap stocks can use a swap to synthetically adjust this position. If the value of the portfolio is $200 million and the firm decides to make the large- and mid-cap exposure equal without touching the small-cap position, then it can become a counterparty in a swap that receives the return of the S&P Mid-Cap 400 Index and pays the return on the Dow Jones Industrial Average Index on a notional principal of 15% of $200 million (i.e., $30 million). Ignoring tracking error, this will synthetically make the portfolio a 45% large-cap, 45% mid-cap, and 10% small-cap stock portfolio over the life of the swap. The small-cap position is unaffected.

This concept can also be applied to the synthetic adjustment of a *bond portfolio*. A firm with a given portfolio of high-grade and low-grade bonds can enter into a swap that pays the return on an index of one type (e.g., the high-grade) and receives the return on the index of another type (e.g., the low-grade). *Do not confuse this with an interest rate swap!* In the swap based on bond returns, there is an interest component and a capital gain component just as there is in an equity swap.

Example: Changing allocations of stocks and bonds

We will consider a manager of a $120 million bond portfolio that consists of $80 million in investment-grade corporate bonds and $40 million in U.S. Treasuries. The manager wants to switch the weights. **Demonstrate** how this can be accomplished with a swap.

Answer:

Once again, the manager approaches a dealer about swapping the returns on indices like the Barclays Capital Long-Term Treasury Bond Index and the Merrill Lynch Corporate Bond Index. The notional principal will be $40 million.

INTEREST RATE SWAPTIONS

LOS 30.h: Demonstrate the use of an interest rate swaption 1) to change the payment pattern of an anticipated future loan and 2) to terminate a swap.

CFA® Program Curriculum, Volume 5, page 389

For the Exam: Be able to explain why and how a manager would use a swaption as well as calculate the payoff or cash flows to the swaption if exercised.

An *interest rate swaption* is an option on a swap where one counterparty (buyer) has paid a premium to the other counterparty (seller) for an option to choose whether the swap will actually go into effect on some future date. The terms of the swap are usually determined at the time of the swaption's inception, prior to the effective date of the swap. Swaptions can be either American or European in the same way as options. European-style swaptions may only be exercised on the expiration date, whereas an American-style swaption may be exercised on any day up to and including the expiration date.

There are two types of swaptions:

1. *Payer swaption:* A payer swaption gives the buyer the right to be the fixed-rate payer (and floating-rate receiver) in a prespecified swap at a prespecified date. The payer swaption is almost like a protective put in that it allows the holder to pay a set fixed rate, even if rates have increased.

2. *Receiver swaption:* A receiver swaption gives the buyer the right to be the fixed-rate receiver (and floating-rate payer) at some future date. The receiver swaption is the reverse of the payer swaption. In this case, the holder must expect rates to fall, and the swap ensures receipt of a higher fixed rate while paying a lower floating rate.

The key point is that the terms of the underlying swap and the swap fixed rate (SFR) are negotiated and set at the purchase of the swaption. The purchaser of the swaption can wait and see if subsequent market moves make that SFR attractive or not and then decide whether to turn on the underlying swap.

Payer Swaption

- If market interest rates move high enough at the expiration of the swaption such that the new SFR is above the swaption SFR, the holder of the payer swaption will exercise the option. Paying the swaption SFR is better than the terms on a new swap. The swaption swap has positive value.
- If interest rates move low enough such that the new SFR is below the swaption SFR, the holder would let the swaption expire worthless and only lose the premium paid. The swaption swap has negative value.

Receiver Swaption

- If interest rates move high enough and the new SFR is above the swaption SFR, the holder of the swaption would let it expire worthless and only lose the premium paid. The SFR that would be received on the swaption SFR is unattractive and the swaption swap has negative value. A better SFR is available on a new swap.
- If market interest rates move low enough and the new SFR is below the swaption SFR, the swaption will be exercised. The swaption swap has positive value with an above market SFR to be received.

Using Swaptions to Hedge a Future Loan Transaction

A corporate manager may wish to purchase a fixed-rate payer swaption to synthetically *lock in* a maximum fixed rate to be paid on an FRN to be issued in the future. If interest rates decline, the manager can always let the option expire worthless and take advantage of lower rates. The time line is illustrated in Figure 4. Today the manager enters into a swaption by paying a premium. The option expires at the time the loan will be taken out. For generality, Figure 4 does not specify a floating- or fixed-rate loan.

- The payer swaption would convert a future floating-rate loan to a fixed-rate loan.
- The receiver swaption would convert a future fixed-rate loan to a floating-rate loan.

Figure 4: Swaption and Future Loan

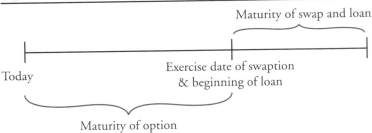

As an example, if a manager is planning to take out a 3-year loan of $10 million at a floating rate, say LIBOR plus 250 basis points, then the manager could hedge the risk of rising interest rates by purchasing a payer swaption with a notional principal of $10 million. (The premium might be $200,000, but the amount is not important for our discussion here. You should just know that an up-front premium is usually required.) The swap would be to receive 90-day LIBOR each quarter, to hedge the loan payments, and pay a fixed rate. The fixed rate might be 3.6% or 0.9% each quarter. At the exercise date of the swaption and the beginning of the loan, one of the following two scenarios will result.

1. The fixed rate on 3-year swaps that pay LIBOR is *greater than* 3.6%. Then the manager will exercise the swaption to pay the contracted 3.6% and receive LIBOR. We will recall our formula for a floating-rate borrower who is a floating-rate receiver in a swap:

$$\text{net payment} = NP[\text{swap rate} + (\text{loan spread})](D_t / 360)$$

In this case, the floating-rate loan plus swap will become a synthetic fixed-rate loan with the following quarterly payments (assuming 90-day settlement periods):

$$\text{net payment} = \$10,000,000(0.036 + 0.025)(90 / 360) = \$152,500$$

2. The fixed rate on 3-year swaps that pay LIBOR is *less than* 3.6%, say 3.2%. Then the manager will let the swaption expire, which means there was no realized benefit for the $200,000 premium paid. The manager *may* contract, at a zero cost, to enter into a 3-year swap with a fixed rate of 3.2%. In this case, the floating-rate loan plus swap will become a synthetic fixed-rate loan with quarterly payments (assuming 90-day settlement periods):

$$\$142,500 = \$10,000,000 \times (0.032 + 0.025) \times (90 / 360)$$

Scenario 2, the no-swaption exercise, could have had the manager not engage in any swap, even at the lower strike rate of 3.2%. That would be up to the manager. The concept is fairly simple. If exercised, the swap does its job. If not exercised, the manager is free to hedge or not hedge.

Using Swaptions to Potentially Terminate an Existing Swap Early

The actions outlined previously can easily be modified to apply to other situations. A manager who is under contract in an existing swap can enter into a swaption with the exact characteristics of the existing swap but take the other counterparty's position. It is possible to match the payments and characteristics because the premium can be adjusted to make the contract worthwhile to the dealer.

Figure 5 has the same general form as Figure 4, but it has been relabeled to depict a *cancellation* of an existing swap with a swaption.

Figure 5: Swaption Cancels Swap

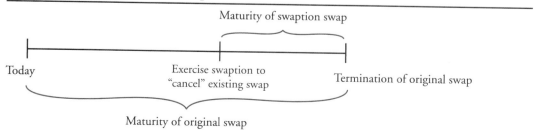

A manager in a pay-floating swap with a given NP and swap fixed rate (SFR) would simply contract to be the receive-floating counterparty in a swaption that has an exercise date in the future. If the NP and SFR are the same for both the swaption and the swap, then upon exercise the swaption's cash flows will effectively *cancel* the cash flows of the existing swap. If the manager buys the swaption from the same dealer with whom the original swap was contracted, the position would effectively be closed. The purchaser of the swaption can then wait until expiration of the swaption and decide if market conditions make it attractive to turn on the swaption swap and effectively cancel the existing swap.

Synthetically Adding or Removing a Call Feature on Existing Debt

 Professor's Note: There is no direct Learning Outcome Statement for the section on bond calls but it is in the assigned text. It would be an unlikely question.

A company has a 10-year, non-callable bond liability and wishes it were callable in three years. The company would buy a 3-year swaption on a 7-year swap to pay floating and receive fixed. Now assume three years have passed:

- If interest rates are low enough, the company can exercise the swaption and enter the 7-year swap (the remaining term of the bond issue) to receive fixed and pay floating. The fixed receipts on the swap cover the fixed coupon payments on the bond and effectively convert it to floating (at now-low rates). This replicates the economic benefit the company would have received if the bond could have been called. If desired the company could even enter a new additional swap to receive floating (covering the floating payments the company must make on the executed swaption) and pay fixed. Interest rates are down and this new swap SFR will be low. It is as if the company called its debt and refinanced at new lower interest rates.
- If interest rates are high enough that the company would not have wanted to call the bond, the company does nothing and lets the swaption expire worthless.

Another company has a 5-year bond issue outstanding that is callable in 1 year. Further suppose the company does not expect rates to be low enough to make calling the bond worthwhile, or alternatively, the company needs cash today. The company could sell a 1-year swaption on a 4-year swap to pay fixed. Now assume one year has passed:

- If rates are high enough to make the swaption worthless, the purchaser of the swaption (who would receive fixed) will let it expire worthless. With high rates, the company will not call the bond.
- Alternatively if rates fall low enough, the purchaser of the swaption will exercise and receive the swaption's SFR. In addition, the company will call the bonds in the low rate environment. The net is the company benefits from calling the bond but loses when the swaption is exercised and requires the company to pay fixed. The company gains and loses the benefit of calling the bond and economically is in a position as if the bond had not been callable.

©2017 Kaplan, Inc.

KEY CONCEPTS

LOS 30.a

Interest rate swaps are used to change the nature of the cash flows (either fixed or floating) on assets and liabilities. A floating-rate (fixed-rate) payment on a liability can be effectively converted to a fixed-rate (floating-rate) by entering a pay-fixed, receive-floating (pay-floating, receive-fixed) swap. The goal is for the cash flow received on the swap to offset the original payment on the liability, such that the nature of the net payment on the liability is opposite from the original. For a floating- (fixed-) rate asset, the manager will enter a pay-floating, receive-fixed (pay-fixed, receive-floating) swap. The goal is to have the payment on the swap offset the receipt on the asset, such that the net receipt is opposite in nature from the original.

LOS 30.b

$$D_{swap} = D_{asset} - D_{liability}$$

For a pay-floating counterparty in a swap, the duration can be expressed as follows:

$$D_{pay\ floating} = D_{fixed} - D_{floating} > 0$$

For a pay-fixed counterparty, the duration can be expressed as follows:

$$D_{pay\ fixed} = D_{floating} - D_{fixed} < 0$$

LOS 30.c

Cash flow risk, uncertainty regarding the *size* of cash flows, is a concern with floating-rate instruments. Because their cash flows are reset each period according to the prevailing rate at the beginning of the period, however, their market values are subject to only minor changes.

Market value risk is a concern with fixed-rate instruments. A decline in interest rates, for example, increases the value of the liability (or pay-fixed side of a swap), thus increasing the liability of the borrower.

For individual assets and liabilities, the tradeoff is between the market value risk associated with fixed rates and the cash flow risk associated with floating rates.

LOS 30.d

The duration of the portfolio plus a swap position (i.e., the target duration) is calculated as:

$$V_p(MD_T) = V_p(MD_p) + NP(MD_{swap})$$

where:
V_p = original value of the portfolio
MD_i = modified duration i (i = swap, target, portfolio without swap)
NP = notional principal of the swap

Usually, the manager selects a swap of a certain maturity which determines the modified duration of the swap, MD_{swap}. He then selects the *NP* that will achieve the desired MD_T. Rearranging, we can solve for the amount of *NP* necessary to achieve the target duration as:

$$NP = \left(V_p\right)\left(\frac{MD_T - MD_p}{MD_{swap}}\right)$$

LOS 30.e

Borrowing in a foreign country via a foreign bank may be difficult, and the interest rates may be high. A U.S. firm that wishes to initiate a project in a foreign country, say Korea, might not have the contacts necessary to borrow Korean currency (the won) cheaply. A Korean counterparty may exist that would like to borrow dollars to invest in the United States.

The U.S. firm borrows in the United States because it has established relationships with banks in the United States. It swaps the principal (borrowed dollars) with the Korean counterparty for the won, which the Korean firm borrowed in Korea.

LOS 30.f

Follow these steps in determining the appropriate swap:
1. Divide the foreign cash flow received by the foreign interest rate to determine the corresponding foreign-denominated notional principal (NP).

    a. This is the foreign NP that would have produced the foreign cash flow at the given foreign interest rate.

2. Using the current exchange rate, convert the foreign NP into the corresponding domestic NP.

3. Enter a swap with this NP.

    a. Pay the foreign cash flows received on the assets and receive the equivalent domestic amount.

    b. The amount of each domestic cash flow is determined by multiplying the domestic interest rate by the domestic NP.

©2017 Kaplan, Inc.

LOS 30.g

A manager can swap all or part of the return on a portfolio for the return on a domestic equity index, the return on a foreign index, or the return on a fixed-income index. A manager desiring an exposure to foreign equities equivalent to 15% of the existing portfolio, for example, could enter a swap with a foreign NP equivalent to that amount. The manager pays the swap dealer the return on that portion of the portfolio and receives the return on the foreign equity index equivalent to an investment in the amount of the notional principal.

LOS 30.h

An *interest rate swaption* is an option on a swap where one counterparty (buyer) has paid a premium to the other counterparty (seller) for an option to choose whether the swap will actually go into effect on some future date. Swaptions can be either American or European in the same way as options.

1. *Payer swaption:* A payer swaption gives the buyer the right to be the fixed-rate payer (and floating-rate receiver) in a prespecified swap at a prespecified date. The payer swaption is almost like a protective put in that it allows the holder to pay a set fixed rate, even if rates have increased.

2. *Receiver swaption:* A receiver swaption gives the buyer the right to be the fixed-rate receiver (and floating-rate payer) at some future date. The receiver swaption is the reverse of the payer swaption. In this case, the holder must expect rates to fall, and the swap ensures receipt of a higher fixed rate while paying a lower floating rate.

The key point is that the terms of the underlying swap and the swap fixed rate (SFR) are negotiated and set at the purchase of the swaption. The purchaser of the swaption can wait and see if subsequent market moves make that SFR attractive or not and then decide whether to turn on the underlying swap.

CONCEPT CHECKERS

1. Which of the following would best transform a floating-rate liability to a fixed-rate liability? Enter into a contract to:
   A. pay fixed on an interest rate swap.
   B. receive floating on a currency swap.
   C. pay floating on an equity swap.

2. Which of the following statements *most accurately* describes the rights of the counterparties in a swaption structure?
   A. The holder of a receiver swaption has the right to enter a swap agreement as the fixed-rate receiver.
   B. The holder of a payer swaption has the right to enter a swap agreement as the fixed-rate receiver.
   C. The seller of a payer swaption has the right to enter a swap agreement as the fixed-rate payer.

3. A firm has most of its liabilities in the form of floating-rate notes with a maturity of two years and quarterly reset. The firm is not concerned with interest rate movements over the next four quarters but is concerned with potential movements after that. Which of the following strategies will allow the firm to hedge the expected change in interest rates?
   A. Enter into a 2-year, quarterly pay-fixed, receive-floating swap.
   B. Buy a swaption that allows the firm to be the fixed-rate payer upon exercise. In other words, go long a payer swaption with a 1-year maturity.
   C. Buy a swaption that allows the firm to be the floating-rate payer upon exercise. In other words, go short a payer swaption with a 1-year maturity.

4. A firm issues fixed-rate bonds and simultaneously becomes a fixed-rate receiver counterparty in a corresponding plain vanilla interest rate swap. Which of the following *best* describes the subsequent, effective periodic interest payments of the firm? (SFR = swap fixed rate)
   A. Pay fixed rate on debt and SFR, reduced by receiving LIBOR.
   B. Pay LIBOR and SFR, reduced by receiving fixed rate on debt.
   C. Pay LIBOR and fixed rate on debt, reduced by receiving SFR.

5. For a plain vanilla interest rate swap, a decrease in interest rates will *most likely*:
   A. increase the value of the pay-fixed side of the swap.
   B. decrease the value of the pay-fixed side of the swap.
   C. leave the value of the pay-floating side unchanged.

6. A common reason for two potential borrowers in different countries to enter into a currency swap is to:
   A. borrow cheap domestic and swap for foreign to reduce borrowing costs.
   B. borrow cheap foreign and swap for domestic to reduce borrowing costs.
   C. speculate on interest rate moves.

©2017 Kaplan, Inc.

7. A firm has an $8 million portfolio of large-cap stocks. The firm enters into an equity swap to pay a return based on the DJIA and receive a return based on the Russell 2000. To achieve an effective 60/40 mix of large-cap to small-cap exposure, the notional principal of the swap should be:
    A. $6.0 million.
    B. $4.8 million.
    C. $3.2 million.

8. For a pay-floating counterparty, the duration of the swap will generally be:
    A. less than the duration of the fixed-rate payments.
    B. equal to the duration of the fixed-rate payments.
    C. greater than the duration of the fixed-rate payments.

9. A firm will be receiving a semiannual cash flow of €20 million. The swap rates in the United States and Europe are 4.0% and 4.6%, respectively. The current exchange rate is €1.2/$. **Identify** the appropriate swap needed to convert the periodic euro cash flows to dollars.

10. A manager of a $40 million dollar fixed-income portfolio with a duration of 4.6 wants to lower the duration to 3. The manager chooses a swap with a net duration of 2. **Determine** the notional principal that the manager should choose for the swap to achieve the target duration.

11. You are the treasurer of a company with a 4-year, $20 million FRN outstanding at LIBOR. You are concerned about rising interest rates in the short term and would like to refinance at a fixed rate for the next two years. A swap dealer arranges a 2-year plain vanilla interest rate swap with annual payments in which you pay a fixed rate of 8.1% and receive LIBOR. The counterparty receives 7.9% and pays LIBOR. Assume that the counterparty has a $20 million fixed-rate debt outstanding at 8%. One-year LIBOR is currently 7%. **Diagram** and **compute** each party's net borrowing cost and first-year cash flows.

For more questions related to this topic review, log in to your Schweser online account and launch SchweserPro™ QBank; and for video instruction covering each LOS in this topic review, log in to your Schweser online account and launch the OnDemand video lectures, if you have purchased these products.

ANSWERS – CONCEPT CHECKERS

1. **A**   Pay fixed means receive floating. The floating receipt on the interest swap will cover the floating payments on the liability, leaving a net pay fixed position overall. Using a currency swap introduces another currency and is not appropriate, even though receive floating is part of a correct solution. Pay floating is wrong, as is introducing equity returns into the situation.

2. **A**   The holder of a receiver swaption has the right to enter a swap agreement as the fixed-rate receiver.

3. **B**   The firm is paying floating now but may want to lock in a fixed rate of interest if interest rates rise one year from now. Hence, buy a swaption that allows the firm to be the fixed-rate payer upon exercise. In other words, go long a payer swaption with a 1-year maturity.

4. **C**   A swap diagram is a good way to solve this, as well as knowing swap terminology. The question asks for the net payment.

   On the debt the firm is paying:

   > fixed rate on debt

   On the swap the firm is receiving the swap fixed rate,

   > a reduction in payment: −SFR

   > and paying floating: LIBOR

   This is a net payment of:

   > fixed rate on debt − SFR + LIBOR

   Looking at the answer choices, this is equivalent to Pay LIBOR and fixed rate on debt, reduced by receiving SFR.

5. **B**   Choice C is not correct because changes in rates affect both sides of the swap, and choice B best describes the result from a decrease in rates. The pay-fixed side of the swap will be paying an amount greater than the SFRs of newly issued swaps.

6. **A**   A domestic borrower may be able to borrow at, say, 6% and swap the principal for a foreign currency. The domestic borrower will pay the counterparty the interest on the foreign currency received. This will presumably be lower than the rate the domestic borrower would have to pay if he had borrowed directly from a foreign bank. The foreign counterparty pays the interest on the domestic loan, which is presumably lower than that it would pay if it borrowed directly from a domestic bank.

7. **C**   The notional principal should be 40% of the portfolio's value.

8. **A**   Although most of the duration is associated with the fixed payments, the next *floating* payment is predetermined. Therefore, the duration of a quarterly-reset swap might be the duration of the fixed payments minus 0.125 (0.25 / 2 = 0.125).

9.   For the euros, the NP = 20,000,000 / (0.046 / 2) = €869,565,217. The corresponding dollar amount is $724,637,681 = €869,565,217 / 1.2. Using these values for the swap, the firm will give the swap dealer €20,000,000 every six months over the maturity of the swap for $724,637,681(0.04 / 2) = $14,492,754.

10. From the given information, we have:

V = \$40,000,000

MD_V = 4.6

MD_{swap} = 2.0

MD_T = 3.0

NP = \$40,000,000 × [(3.0 – 4.6) / –2] = \$32,000,000

The manager should take a receive-floating/pay-fixed position in the swap with a \$32,000,000 notional principal.

11. The box and arrow diagram is shown below:

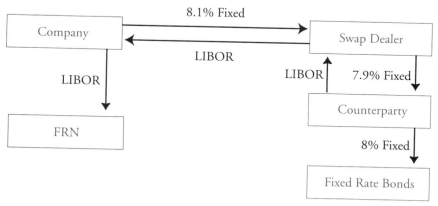

Your net borrowing cost is:

(LIBOR – LIBOR) + 0.081 = 0.081 = 8.1%

The counterparty's net borrowing cost is:

(0.080 – 0.079) + LIBOR = LIBOR + 0.001 = LIBOR + 0.1%

The swap dealer's spread is:

0.002 = 0.20% = 20 basis points = (0.081 – 0.079) + (LIBOR – LIBOR)

At the end of the first year, assuming LIBOR is 7%, your fixed-rate payment under the swap is:

fixed-rate payment = (0.081 – 0.07)(\$20,000,000) = \$220,000

Your total interest costs equal the LIBOR-based interest payments plus the swap payment:

\$20,000,000(0.07) + \$220,000 = \$1,620,000

At the end of the first year, the counterparty's fixed-rate receipt under the swap is:

(fixed-rate receipt) = (0.079 – 0.07)(\$20,000,000) = \$180,000

The counterparty's total interest costs equal the 8% interest payment on their outstanding fixed-rate debt minus the swap payment:

\$20,000,000(0.08) – \$180,000 = \$1,420,000

The cash flows to the swap dealer are:

\$220,000 – \$180,000 = (\$20,000,000 × 0.002) = \$40,000

Everybody is happy. You've converted floating-rate debt to fixed-rate debt, your counterparty has converted fixed-rate debt to floating-rate debt, and the swap dealer has made \$40,000 without being exposed to interest rate risk.

SELF-TEST: RISK MANAGEMENT APPLICATIONS OF DERIVATIVES

Use the following information for Questions 1 through 6.

George Kaufman, portfolio manager and CEO of Kaufman Co., is extremely busy. He has a number of important issues that must be dealt with before the end of the week.

The portfolio Kaufman manages consists of $40 million in bonds and $60 million in equities. The modified duration of the bond portfolio is 6.3. The beta of the equity portfolio is 1.25. The holding period for each is one year. Kaufman also has the authority to borrow up to $25 million which may be invested on a short-term basis to earn the spread between the borrowing rate and the investing rate.

Kaufman is afraid that interest rates will raise 25 basis points in the near future and would like to decrease the duration of the bond portion of the portfolio to 5.0 for a short period. He prefers to use futures contracts to do this because it is a temporary change and he does not want to sell bonds in the portfolio. Kaufman is considering using a Treasury bond futures contract that has a modified duration of 4.2, a yield beta of 1.1, and a price (including the multiplier) of $245,000.

Kaufman would like to borrow money three months from today so he can invest at the expected higher interest rates. However, he would like to take advantage of today's lower interest rates for the loan. To do this he is considering using derivatives to hedge against the higher expected future interest rates. A cash settlement will be made based on the actual interest rate three months from now based on the terms of the derivative used. If Kaufman decides on this strategy, he would borrow $20 million at 5% for nine months. The loan date would start three months from today.

The equity portion of the portfolio has performed extremely well over the recent past and Kaufman must decide on one of the following two strategies:

Equity Strategy 1: Kaufman could hold on to his current profits for the next six months which should make the reported annual return rank in the top one percentile of similar portfolios. Again, Kaufman prefers to use futures contracts instead of selling stocks to lock in the profits. The portfolio is composed of the same stocks and sector weightings as the S&P 500. The contract on the index is at 2000 (with a multiplier of 250), and it expires in six months. The risk free rate is 2% and the dividend yield on the index is 3%.

Equity Strategy 2: Kaufman believes there is a chance the market may move significantly over the next six months. To benefit from the expected move in the market, Kaufman could increase the equity portion of the portfolio from its current beta of 1.25 to 1.4 by using equity index futures. The appropriate equity index futures contract that Kaufman is considering using has a beta of 0.90 and a price (including the multiplier) of $335,000.

Finally, Kaufman Co. is expecting a $6 million cash inflow in four months and would like to pre-invest the funds to create the same exposure to the bond and stock market that is found in the original portfolio. The most appropriate stock index futures contract

©2017 Kaplan, Inc.

for accomplishing this has a total price (including the multiplier) of $315,650 and a beta of 1.10. The most appropriate bond index futures contract has a total price of $115,460, a yield beta of 1.05 and an effective duration of 6.2.

1. Assume Kaufman Co. uses derivatives to hedge the loan rate, which of the following options would be *least appropriate* to use?
   A. An interest rate collar.
   B. Buy an interest rate call.
   C. Buy an interest rate put on the price of Treasury futures.

2. If no futures are used to change portfolio duration, the value of the bond portfolio given a 25 basis point increase is *closest* to:
   A. $37,480,000.
   B. $39,370,000.
   C. $39,580,000.

3. The number of Treasury bond futures contracts that Kaufman would need to reduce the duration of the bonds in the portfolio is *closest* to:
   A. sell 51 contracts.
   B. sell 56 contracts.
   C. buy 269 contracts.

4. Kaufman is interested in increasing the beta of the equity portfolio to 1.4 for a brief period of time. Kaufman is expecting a(n):
   A. increase in the market; a long position in approximately 30 contracts will accomplish this target.
   B. increase in the market; a long position in approximately 27 contracts will accomplish this target.
   C. decrease in the market; a short position in approximately 72 contracts will accomplish this target.

5. How many S&P index futures contracts would Kaufman need to buy or sell to create a six-month synthetic cash position?
   A. Buy approximately 121 contracts.
   B. Sell approximately 121 contracts.
   C. Sell approximately 400 contracts.

6. The *most appropriate* strategy to pre-invest the anticipated $6 million inflow would be to:
   A. buy 22 bond futures contracts and buy 13 stock futures contracts.
   B. buy 21 bond futures contracts and buy 35 stock futures contracts.
   C. buy 22 bond futures contracts and sell 13 stock futures contracts.

SELF-TEST ANSWERS: RISK MANAGEMENT APPLICATIONS OF DERIVATIVES

1. **A** Kaufman wants to hedge against increasing interest rates in anticipation of taking out a loan. An interest rate collar can consist of either a long floor and short cap or a long cap and short floor. A long cap and short floor would protect against increasing interest rates but an interest collar consisting of a long floor and short cap would protect against decreasing interest rates, not increasing interest rates, making this an inappropriate option choice and the correct answer. Buying an interest call option would pay off interest rates rose above the strike rate. Likewise, an interest put on the price of Treasuries would also pay off if interest rates rose causing the price of Treasury futures to fall below the strike price of the option.

2. **C** In this case, use the modified duration of the bond portfolio, 6.3, to find the value of the portfolio given a 25 basis point increase in rates:

   New value = $40,000,000 × (1 – (6.3 × 0.0025)) = $39,370,000

3. **B** Contracts = (Yield Beta) $[(MD_{Target} – MD_P) / MD_F][V_P / (P_F(Multiplier))]$

   Contracts = 1.1 × [(5 – 6.3) / 4.2] × ($40,000,000/$245,000) = –55.59

   To reduce the duration of the portfolio, take a short position in the futures contract. Note that we must round the number of contracts up to 56 since partial contracts cannot be traded.

4. **A** Number of Contracts = (Target Beta – Portfolio Beta/Beta on Futures) × (Value of the portfolio/Price of the futures × the multiplier).

   Number of Contracts = [(1.4 – 1.25) / 0.90] × ($60,000,000 / $335,000) = 29.85 contracts.

   The positive sign indicates that we should take a long position in the futures to "leverage up" the position. If that is Kaufman's goal, he must be expecting an increase in the market.

5. **B** [$60,000,000 × $(1.02)^{0.50}$] / (2000 × $250) = 121.19 contracts

   Kaufman would need to sell the contracts to create the synthetic cash (zero equity) position. If he were converting cash to a synthetic equity position, he would of course buy contracts.

6. **A** Take the existing portfolio weights, 40% debt and 60% equity and apply them to the new money that is coming in. Also, "mirror" the duration and beta of the original portfolios.

   Number of bond futures = 1.05 × [(6.3 – 0) / 6.2] × [(6,000,000 × 0.40) / 115,460] = 22.18 contracts

   Number of stock futures = [(1.25 – 0) / 1.10] × [(6,000,000 × 0.60) / 315,650] = 12.96

   Kaufman Co. would take a long position in both the stock index and bond futures contracts because it is synthetically creating an existing portfolio until the actual $6 million is received and can be invested.

©2017 Kaplan, Inc.

FORMULAS

manager's true active return = manager's total return − manager's normal portfolio return

manager's misfit active return = manager's normal portfolio return − investor's benchmark return

$$\text{total active risk} = \sqrt{(\text{true active risk})^2 + (\text{misfit active risk})^2}$$

$$\text{true information ratio} = \frac{\text{true active return}}{\text{true active risk}}$$

information ratio (IR):

$$IR_P = \frac{\text{active return}}{\text{active risk}} = \frac{R_P - R_B}{\sigma_{(R_P - R_B)}} \approx IC\sqrt{IB}$$

utility adjusted return: $U_A = R_A - \lambda_A \sigma_A{}^2$

$$VAR = \left[\hat{R}_P - (z)(\sigma)\right] V_P$$

$$\sigma_{\text{daily}} \cong \frac{\sigma_{\text{annual}}}{\sqrt{250}}; \quad \sigma_{\text{monthly}} \cong \frac{\sigma_{\text{annual}}}{\sqrt{12}}; \quad \sigma_{\text{daily}} \cong \frac{\sigma_{\text{monthly}}}{\sqrt{22}}$$

forward contract credit risk exposure: $value_{\text{manager}} = PV_{\text{inflows}} - PV_{\text{outflows}}$

Sharpe ratio: $S_P = \dfrac{\bar{R}_P - \bar{R}_F}{\sigma_P}$

Sortino ratio: $\text{Sortino} = \dfrac{\bar{R}_P - MAR}{\text{downside deviation}}$

return over maximum drawdown: $\text{RoMAD} = \dfrac{\bar{R}_P}{\text{maximum drawdown}}$

$$R_{DC} = (1 + R_{FC})(1 + R_{FX}) - 1 = R_{FC} + R_{FX} + (R_{FC})(R_{FX})$$

$$R_{DC} = \sum_{i=1}^{n} w_i (R_{DC,i})$$

$$\sigma^2(R_{DC}) \approx \sigma^2(R_{FC}) + \sigma^2(R_{FX}) + 2\sigma(R_{FC})\sigma(R_{FX})\rho(R_{FC},R_{FX})$$

$$\sigma(R_{DC}) = \sigma(R_{FX})(1 + R_{FC})$$

where:

R_{FC} = the return on a foreign currency denominated risk-free asset

$$\beta_i = \frac{Cov(i,m)}{\sigma_m^2}$$

$$\text{number of contracts} = \left(\frac{\beta_T - \beta_P}{\beta_f}\right)\left(\frac{V_p}{P_f(\text{multiplier})}\right)$$

$$\text{number of contracts} = (\text{yield beta})\left(\frac{MD_T - MD_P}{MD_F}\right)\left(\frac{V_p}{P_f(\text{multiplier})}\right)$$

Note that for synthetic positions, V_p must be a future value amount. If the desired change in beta or duration is the contract's beta or duration, they have no effect on the calculation of number of contracts.

$$\text{interest rate call payoff} = (NP)[\max(0, LIBOR - \text{strike rate})](D / 360)$$

$$\text{interest rate put payoff} = (NP)[\max(0, \text{strike rate} - LIBOR)(D / 360)]$$

$$\Delta_{call} = \frac{C_1 - C_0}{S_1 - S_0} = \frac{\Delta C}{\Delta S}$$

$$\text{gamma} = (\text{change in delta}) / (\text{change in S})$$

$$D_{\text{pay floating}} = D_{fixed} - D_{floating} > 0$$

$$D_{\text{pay-fixed}} = D_{floating} - D_{fixed} < 0$$

$$NP = (V_p)\left(\frac{MD_T - MD_P}{MD_{swap}}\right)$$

©2017 Kaplan, Inc.

CUMULATIVE Z-TABLE

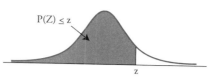

$P(Z \leq z) = N(z)$ for $z \geq 0$

$P(Z \leq -z) = 1 - N(z)$

z	0	0.01	0.02	0.03	0.04	0.05	0.06	0.07	0.08	0.09
0	0.5000	0.5040	0.5080	0.5120	0.5160	0.5199	0.5239	0.5279	0.5319	0.5359
0.1	0.5398	0.5438	0.5478	0.5517	0.5557	0.5596	0.5636	0.5675	0.5714	0.5753
0.2	0.5793	0.5832	0.5871	0.5910	0.5948	0.5987	0.6026	0.6064	0.6103	0.6141
0.3	0.6179	0.6217	0.6255	0.6293	0.6331	0.6368	0.6406	0.6443	0.6480	0.6517
0.4	0.6554	0.6591	0.6628	0.6664	0.6700	0.6736	0.6772	0.6808	0.6844	0.6879
0.5	0.6915	0.6950	0.6985	0.7019	0.7054	0.7088	0.7123	0.7157	0.7190	0.7224
0.6	0.7257	0.7291	0.7324	0.7357	0.7389	0.7422	0.7454	0.7486	0.7517	0.7549
0.7	0.7580	0.7611	0.7642	0.7673	0.7704	0.7734	0.7764	0.7794	0.7823	0.7852
0.8	0.7881	0.7910	0.7939	0.7967	0.7995	0.8023	0.8051	0.8078	0.8106	0.8133
0.9	0.8159	0.8186	0.8212	0.8238	0.8264	0.8289	0.8315	0.8340	0.8365	0.8389
1	0.8413	0.8438	0.8461	0.8485	0.8508	0.8531	0.8554	0.8577	0.8599	0.8621
1.1	0.8643	0.8665	0.8686	0.8708	0.8729	0.8749	0.8770	0.8790	0.8810	0.8830
1.2	0.8849	0.8869	0.8888	0.8907	0.8925	0.8944	0.8962	0.8980	0.8997	0.9015
1.3	0.9032	0.9049	0.9066	0.9082	0.9099	0.9115	0.9131	0.9147	0.9162	0.9177
1.4	0.9192	0.9207	0.9222	0.9236	0.9251	0.9265	0.9279	0.9292	0.9306	0.9319
1.5	0.9332	0.9345	0.9357	0.937	0.9382	0.9394	0.9406	0.9418	0.9429	0.9441
1.6	0.9452	0.9463	0.9474	0.9484	0.9495	0.9505	0.9515	0.9525	0.9535	0.9545
1.7	0.9554	0.9564	0.9573	0.9582	0.9591	0.9599	0.9608	0.9616	0.9625	0.9633
1.8	0.9641	0.9649	0.9656	0.9664	0.9671	0.9678	0.9686	0.9693	0.9699	0.9706
1.9	0.9713	0.9719	0.9726	0.9732	0.9738	0.9744	0.9750	0.9756	0.9761	0.9767
2	0.9772	0.9778	0.9783	0.9788	0.9793	0.9798	0.9803	0.9808	0.9812	0.9817
2.1	0.9821	0.9826	0.983	0.9834	0.9838	0.9842	0.9846	0.985	0.9854	0.9857
2.2	0.9861	0.9864	0.9868	0.9871	0.9875	0.9878	0.9881	0.9884	0.9887	0.989
2.3	0.9893	0.9896	0.9898	0.9901	0.9904	0.9906	0.9909	0.9911	0.9913	0.9916
2.4	0.9918	0.9920	0.9922	0.9925	0.9927	0.9929	0.9931	0.9932	0.9934	0.9936
2.5	0.9938	0.994	0.9941	0.9943	0.9945	0.9946	0.9948	0.9949	0.9951	0.9952
2.6	0.9953	0.9955	0.9956	0.9957	0.9959	0.9960	0.9961	0.9962	0.9963	0.9964
2.7	0.9965	0.9966	0.9967	0.9968	0.9969	0.9970	0.9971	0.9972	0.9973	0.9974
2.8	0.9974	0.9975	0.9976	0.9977	0.9977	0.9978	0.9979	0.9979	0.9980	0.9981
2.9	0.9981	0.9982	0.9982	0.9983	0.9984	0.9984	0.9985	0.9985	0.9986	0.9986
3	0.9987	0.9987	0.9987	0.9988	0.9988	0.9989	0.9989	0.9989	0.9990	0.9990

Index

A

absolute-return vehicles 78
active return 28
active risk 28, 101
actual extreme events 109
ad valorem fees 36
alpha and beta separation approach 34
analytical VAR 103
angel investors 72
assets-under-management (AUM) fee 77

B

backfill or inclusion bias 65
back office 99
back-tested 107
basket 7
bear spread 177
bid-ask spread 100
bottom-up approach 37
box spread 185
breakeven price 167
buffering 19
bull spread 175
butterfly spread 178
butterfly spread with calls 178
butterfly spread with puts 181
buyout funds 57, 72
buy-side analyst 37

C

call options 165
call premium 166
cap rate 193
cap strike 193
cash flow at risk (CFAR) 107
cash flow risk 217, 231
centralized 98
changing allocations of stock and bonds 226
closeout netting 117
collar 183
collateral 117
commingled real estate funds (CREFs) 56
commodity 57
commodity markets 62
Commodity Pool Operators 80
commodity trading advisors 80
compensation structure 77
completeness fund 31

conventions 79
convertible arbitrage 75
converting foreign cash receipts 223
convert loans from fixed (floating) to floating (fixed) 214
core-satellite approach 29
corporate venturing 72
covered call 170
credit default swap 117
credit derivatives 117
credit risk 100, 110
credit spread forward 118
credit spread option 118
credit VAR 108, 110
cross-default-provisions 110
currency swaps 219
current credit risk 110

D

decentralized 98
deleveraging 79
delta hedging 199, 201
delta-normal method 104
direct commodity investment 74
direct equity real estate investing 71
discretionary trading strategy 81
distressed debt arbitrage 82
distressed securities 59, 63, 76, 81
domestic risk-free rate 155
downside deviation 79
duration of an interest rate swap 216

E

effective beta 140
emerging market 76
enhanced derivatives products companies (EDPCs) 117
enhanced indexing 26
enterprise risk management (ERM) system 98
equal-weighted index 5
equitizing 24
equity futures 7
equity market neutral 76
equity swaps 224
ESG (environmental, social, governance) risk 101
event risk 82
exchange-traded funds (ETF) 6

©2017 Kaplan, Inc.

F

factor push analysis 109
financial risks 99
fixed-income arbitrage 76
floor rate 193
floor strike 193
foreign risk-free rate 155
forward contract 111
free float-adjusted market capitalization index 5
front office 99
full replication 8
fund-of-funds 76, 78

G

global macro strategies 76
growth investing 11

H

hedged equity strategies (a.k.a. equity long-short) 76
hedge funds 58, 75
Herstatt risk 100
high water mark (HWM) 77
historical simulation 105
historical VAR 105
holdings-based style analysis 16
hypothetical events 109

I

incentive fee 72, 73
incremental VAR 107
index mutual funds 6
indirect commodity investment 74
information coefficient 27
information ratio 3, 27
interest rate caps 193
interest rate collar 196
interest rate options 187
interest rate put 191
interest rate swaptions 227
investment policy statement (IPS) 3
investor breadth 27

J

J factor risk 82
jump-to-default risk 110

L

large-cap investors 12
leverage 79
leverage limits 116
limited liability companies (LLCs) 73

limited partnerships 73
limiting exposure 116
liquidity 114
liquidity limits 116
liquidity risk 100
lock-up period 77
long-only value investing 81
long/short 24

M

managed futures 58, 63
management fee 73
market capitalization-weighted index 4
market liquidity risk 82
market neutral 24
market neutral strategy 21
market-oriented investing 11
market risk 82, 99
market value risk 231
marking to market 116
maximum loss optimization 109
merger arbitrage 76
micro-cap investors 12
mid-cap investors 12
minimum acceptable return (MAR) 119
minimum credit standards 117
misfit active return 32
model risk 100
Monte Carlo VAR 105

N

non-financial risks 99

O

operations risk 100
optimization 9
option spread strategies 175

P

pairs trading 24
pair trade 21
payer swaption 228
payment netting 117
performance-based fee 36
performance netting risk 101
performance stopout 116
plain vanilla currency swap 219
plain vanilla interest rate swap 214
political risk 101
popularity bias 65
portable alpha 24
portfolio 7
portfolio insurance 172

position limits 116
potential credit risk 110
price-weighted index 4
private equity 56, 62, 82
private equity fund 57
program trades 7
protective put 172
put options 167

R

real estate 56, 61
real estate investment trusts (REITs) 56
receiver swaption 228
regulatory risk 101
relevance of past data 65
return on VAR 115
return over maximum drawdown (RoMAD) 118
return(s) 79
returns-based style analysis 12
risk-adjusted return on invested capital (RAROC) 118
risk budgeting 107, 115
risk factor limits 116
risk governance 98
risk management process 97
risk reduction 97

S

scenario analysis 108
scenario analysis limits 116
sell-side analysts 37
semivariance 79
settlement netting risk 101
settlement risk 100
Sharpe ratio 79, 118
short extension 24
short extension strategies 23
small-cap investors 11
socially responsible investing (SRI) 20
Sortino ratio 119
sovereign risk 100

special purpose vehicles (SPVs) 117
stages 72
stale price bias 65
straddle 181
stratified sampling 9
stress testing 108, 109, 120
style analysis 12
style drift 20, 78
stylized scenarios 108
survivorship bias 65
systematic trading strategies 80

T

tail value at risk (TVAR) 108
tax, accounting, and legal/contract risk 101
time line 73
top-down approach 37
total active risk 32
total return swap 8, 118
tracking risk 101
transportable alpha 24
true active return 32
true information ratio 32
typical trading volume 100

U

using swaps to change duration 218

V

value at risk (VAR) 102, 119
value investing 10
variance-covariance method 103
venture capital 70, 71
venture capital funds or trusts 71
venture capitalists 71

W

worst-case scenario 109

Z

zero-cost collar 183, 197

 ©2017 Kaplan, Inc.